WALKING TOGETHER

The Future of Indigenous Child Welfare on the Prairies

Voices from the Prairies

Previous publications in the Voices from the Prairies series:

Putting a Human Face on Child Welfare (2007)

Passion for Action in Child and Family Services (2009)

Awakening the Spirit: Moving Forward in Child Welfare (2012)

Reinvesting in Families: Strengthening Child Welfare Practice for a Brighter Future (2014)

Transforming Child Welfare: Interdisciplinary Practices, Field Education, and Research (2016)

Imagining Child Welfare in the Spirit of Reconciliation (2018)

WALKING TOGETHER

The Future of Indigenous Child Welfare on the Prairies

Voices from the Prairies

edited by

Jason Albert, Dorothy Badry, Don Fuchs, Peter Choate, Marlyn Bennett, and H. Monty Montgomery

Suggested Citation: Albert, J., Badry, D., Fuchs, D., Choate, P., Bennett, M., & Montgomery, H., (Eds.). (2022). *Walking Together: The future of Indigenous child welfare on the Prairies*. Regina, SK: University of Regina Press.

Cover Design: Duncan Campbell, University of Regina Press
Text Design: John van der Woude, JVDW Designs
Copy Editor: Alison Jacques
Proofreader: Patricia Furdek
Indexer: Patricia Furdek
Cover Art: "Children Silhouettes" by Sylwia Nowik / Adobe Stock

Library and Archives Canada Cataloguing in Publication

Title: Walking together : the future of Indigenous child welfare on the Prairies / edited by Jason Albert, Dorothy Badry, Don Fuchs, Peter Choate, Marlyn Bennett, and H. Monty Montgomery.
Other titles: Walking together (2022)
Names: Albert, Jason, editor. | Badry, Dorothy Eleanor, 1958- editor. | Fuchs, Don, 1948- editor. | Choate, Peter, editor. | Bennett, Marlyn, 1963- editor. | Montgomery, H. Monty, 1962- editor.
Description: Series statement: Voices from the Prairies ; 7 | Includes bibliographical references and index.
Identifiers: Canadiana (print) 20220272425 | Canadiana (ebook) 20220272735 | ISBN 9780889778931 (hardcover) | ISBN 9780889778900 (softcover) | ISBN 9780889778917 (PDF) | ISBN 9780889778924 (EPUB)
Subjects: LCSH: Indigenous children—Services for—Prairie Provinces. | LCSH: Indigenous children—Prairie Provinces—Social conditions. | LCSH: Child welfare—Prairie Provinces.
Classification: LCC HV745.P7 W35 2022 | DDC 362.7/78970712—dc23

10 9 8 7 6 5 4 3 2 1

U OF R PRESS

University of Regina Press, University of Regina
Regina, Saskatchewan, Canada, S4S 0A2
TEL: (306) 585-4758 FAX: (306) 585-4699
WEB: www.uofrpress.ca

We acknowledge the support of the Canada Council for the Arts for our publishing program. We acknowledge the financial support of the Government of Canada. / Nous reconnaissons l'appui financier du gouvernement du Canada. This publication was made possible through Creative Saskatchewan's Creative Industries Production Grant Program.

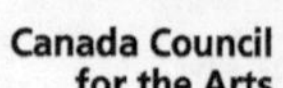

Conseil des Arts
du Canada
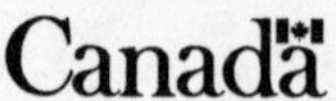

This book is dedicated to all Indigenous children—First Nations, Métis, and Inuit—who never came home and to the families who have experienced such profound loss and grief. So many lives were irrevocably changed through the colonial practices of government including the residential school system and oppressive child welfare policies. We acknowledge you, your children, and the disrupted bloodlines that have become part of the life journey of Indigenous people in Canada.

This book is also dedicated to all the children and families now living with the continuing, unfolding legacy of the residential school system, the Sixties Scoop, and the Millennium Scoop. The time for change is now.

We dedicate this book to all of you who have lived these experiences and who continue to demonstrate resiliency and hope for the future for children, families, communities, and Nations.

Contents

ix Invocation
xi Foreword · *Jason Albert*
xv From the Editors
xix Acknowledgements
xxi Introduction · *Dorothy Badry and Don Fuchs*

Part I: Policy

3 CHAPTER 1: Canada's "Old Mindset" and the Struggle to Fully Honour Jordan's Principle · *Brittany Mathews, Jennifer King, and Cindy Blackstock*

25 CHAPTER 2: Bill C-92: The Restoration of Indigenous Jurisdiction and Right Relations in Canada · *Hadley Friedland and Koren Lightning-Earle*

47 CHAPTER 3: Colonial Threads of Fetal Alcohol Spectrum Disorder in Canada and Australia: Parallel Stories · *Robyn Williams, Dorothy Badry, Don Fuchs, Yahya El-Lahib, Michael Doyle, Bernadette Iahtail, and Peter Choate*

Part II: Practice

73 CHAPTER 4: Indigenous Social Work: Colonial Systems Can't Change What They Don't See as Wrong · *Gabrielle Lindstrom, Tsapinaki, and Peter Choate*

93 CHAPTER 5: Making Connections for Our Children: Indigenous Youth Transitioning out of Care · *Kelly Provost—Miah'nistik'anah'soyii (Sparks in a Fire) and Christina Tortorelli*

113 CHAPTER 6: Child Advocacy Work in Alberta: The Importance of Children's Voices on Critical Issues · *Del Graff and Arlene Eaton-Erickson*

135 CHAPTER 7: Grassroots of Child Welfare Advocacy for Indigenous Children in Alberta: The Creating Hope Society · *Bernadette Iahtail*

Part III: Research

151 CHAPTER 8: Walking Courageously: The Voices of Indigenous Child Welfare Workers in Manitoba · *Eveline Milliken and Linda Dano-Chartrand*

Part IV: Education

175 CHAPTER 9: The Heart of Allyship: Examining the Pursuit of Ally Relationships with Indigenous Peoples in Child Welfare and Social Work Education · *Jennifer Hedges, Eveline Milliken, and Elder Mae Louise Campbell*

197 CHAPTER 10: Post-Secondary Indigenous Education as It Relates to Indigenous Child Welfare · *Jason Albert and Susannah Walker*

219 Epilogue · Peter Choate

225 Abstracts
231 Contributors
241 Subject Index
2xx Author Index

Invocation

Blackfoot Prayer...(aah tsee moosh gaan)

Hi Yo iss tsee baah daah bee yoop (in humbleness I call on you the Source of Life)...nooh gooh doo git (hear my Prayer). Aah mooh is bik sin aak sin neet sin nape noohk tsee gim mooh gin naan (the spirit and intent that this book is written, help us [First Nations people] to move forward in the best possible way to a Holistic, Healthy way of life). Naah gooh geeh doo tsee ksik guys bin naan gaah naah Soo gaah bee (give us the trail to walk upon into a healthy prosperous life).

Naah bee yoo sin (request for a long life of healthy living)

Gaah mooh daahn (salvation for all)

—Elder Leonard Bastien—Weasel Traveller

Foreword

Jason Albert

ASSOCIATE PROFESSOR, SCHOOL OF INDIGENOUS SOCIAL WORK, FIRST NATIONS UNIVERSITY OF CANADA

I must begin by acknowledging the Treaty 6 territory on which my family and ancestors have lived for many generations. Treaty 6 is the location of my campus of the School of Indigenous Social Work at First Nations University of Canada, Saskatoon, Saskatchewan. I am the son of Marilyn Morrissette of Muskeg Lake Cree Nation (maskêko-sâkahikanihk) and Ron Albert of Sweetgrass First Nation (nakîwacîhk) in the Treaty 6 area of Saskatchewan. My father was a product of the residential school system. He knew first-hand the hardships that Indigenous people faced because of these schools. He was a strong believer in gaining the tools, knowledge, and experience in areas necessary to provide and support your people: "nîkânastamâkêwin (leadership) is the ultimate way to serve your people and provides an avenue for change so that Indigenous people are able to survive and continue to live the life that has served them for many generations" (R. Albert, personal communication, January 4, 2001). While he had a negative experience in his education, he always stressed that his children receive an education so we can help and give back to our people. I followed in my mother's social work footsteps and embarked on a journey in the social work profession.

When I was a young person, my parents emphasized the *nehiyaw pimatisiwin* (Cree Way of Life) and would tell me to establish relationships with people who will show me guidance, respect, and knowledge because these types of relationships will last a lifetime. Relationships are important in Indigenous society and are seen as never ending. As an Indigenous person from Sweetgrass First Nation and Muskeg Lake Cree Nation, I am fortunate to have established a wonderful relationship with those involved with this book: Dorothy Badry, University of Calgary; Don Fuchs, University of Manitoba; Peter Choate, Mount Royal College; Monty Montgomery, University of British Colombia; and Marlyn Bennett, University of Manitoba. One of the editors, Don Fuchs, has never hesitated to provide guidance and mentorship through our sixteen years together on the Prairie Child Welfare Consortium (PCWC). He continues to show integrity and respect not only to me but to those who continue to sit on the committee. Another committee member and amazing colleague, Dorothy Badry, has treated me like an equal and provided an insurmountable amount of knowledge. I worked with Monty Montgomery for several years during his time at the University of Regina; he has been nothing but professional, and when I was completing my PhD, he shared his experiences and would often touch base to see how the process was going. This was my first time sitting on committee with Marlyn Bennett and Peter Choate, but during this short experience they have been amazing. They have brilliant minds and have not hesitated to share their knowledge and provide guidance when necessary. Although the editors have an unbelievable amount of experience, they are the most grounded individuals I have met.

This book is a collection of work by accomplished Indigenous and non-Indigenous authors discussing child welfare. It is the seventh book from the PCWC; they are all amazing works, and the PCWC continues to produce great scholarship. We are fortunate that in this book, all chapters have an Indigenous author or co-author. This is an exciting endeavour, as Indigenous writers are given a platform to showcase their perspective, knowledge, wisdom, and experience. The contributors are inspirations to the Indigenous child welfare community. They bring a great deal of experience and knowledge to this area, and I am truly honoured and humbled to be a part of the book.

The PCWC was founded in 1999, and we are proud and honoured to have held the first meeting at First Nations University of Canada (FNUniv) (formerly Saskatchewan Indian Federated College). The visionaries of the PCWC established a tri-provincial response to enhance, promote, and build capacity for child and family well-being in Indigenous communities across the Prairie provinces. At the time, this was a major achievement in child welfare in Saskatchewan, with the Federation of

Sovereign Indigenous Nations (formerly Federation of Saskatchewan Indian Nations) supporting and signing an MOU (memorandum of understanding) with First Nations University of Canada. Having an agreement with schools and agencies in the Prairie provinces meant there was an opportunity for change. The School of Indigenous Social Work at the First Nations University of Canada, for example, recognizes the importance of family and provides an alternative to those who have been victimized by the conventional child welfare system.

My co-author and I wrote a chapter on post-secondary education and child welfare for this collection. Chapter 10 discusses the development of the School of Indigenous Social Work's curriculum on teaching Indigenous child welfare. The approach is based on an Indigenous perspective and, specifically, four Cree principles: nisitohtamowin (understanding), manitowakêýimowin (believing), kiskinwahamâtowin (learning), and kiskêýihtamowin (knowledge). We believe this program and curriculum are a great resource for social work programs across this country. I need to thank my co-author, Susannah Walker, enrolled citizen from Waganakising Odawa (Michigan), for her support, guidance, and reciprocity in co-writing the chapter on post-secondary Indigenous education. She is a gifted academic who will continue to make a difference in this field. We are excited to present this topic in a book that will be used by not only social work students but also social work practitioners.

The topic of Indigenous child welfare is receiving a lot of attention with some Indigenous communities implementing Bill C-92, *An Act respecting First Nations, Inuit and Métis children, youth and families*. It is time to know and understand Bill C-92, and this book does a terrific job in providing a comprehensive understanding of this bill. We are excited about this volume, which includes dynamic authors and interesting topics, all the while respecting an Indigenous perspective and approach to Indigenous child welfare. I am truly honoured to be part of this book as an editor and co-author. Writing this foreword has been a rewarding journey, and I am thankful to have been chosen for this distinguished responsibility. Keep the candle lit and continue work to improve the lives of Indigenous people.

From the Editors

We are pleased to publish this book that continues the thread of Voices from the Prairies. The publication of this book marks volume seven in the scholarly publications of the Prairie Child Welfare Consortium (PCWC). To date the PCWC has hosted eight symposia across the Prairies: in Saskatoon in 2001; Winnipeg, 2003; Edmonton, 2005; Regina, 2007; Winnipeg, 2009; Edmonton, 2012; Saskatoon, 2014; Winnipeg, 2016; and Calgary, 2018, with attendance at our gatherings increasing on a regular basis. In 2018 the PCWC hosted the National Conference on Child Welfare in collaboration with the national table of Provincial and Territorial Directors of Child Welfare. Alex Scheiber, deputy director of Child Welfare in British Columbia and chair of the Provincial and Territorial Directors of Child Welfare Committee, and Dr. Jackie Sieppert, former dean of the Faculty of Social Work, University of Calgary, provided leadership to the conference.

Key partners in the PCWC include the faculties of Social Work from the University of Calgary, University of Regina, University of Manitoba, and the First Nations University of Canada Indigenous School of Social Work. Other partners have included the Saskatchewan Ministry of Social Services, the Federation of Sovereign Indigenous Nations (formerly the Federation of Saskatchewan Indian Nations), Manitoba Family Services and Consumer Affairs, Northwest Territories Department of Health and Social Services, Alberta Ministry of Children's Services, and the Métis Nation of Alberta Children and Family Services. The 2018 National Conference—The Future of Child Welfare in Canada—was sponsored by PolicyWise for Children and Families in Alberta, the Provincial and Territorial Directors of Child Welfare, the PCWC, and the University of Calgary Faculty of Social Work and supported by ConventionALL Management and Raincoast Ventures.

Harold Tarbell served as the master of ceremonies. The Sorrel Rider Drum Group led by Frank Turning Robe welcomed delegates with drum songs.

This was our first national gathering, and the conference was fully subscribed with over 300 participants. This gathering showed us that indeed the need exists for people in Canada to come together and talk about the state of child welfare, particularly for Indigenous children and families. We look forward to seeing the ways in which Bill C-92 unfolds and its impact on the child welfare system in Canada. We look forward to the day that we can gather again and talk about critical issues affecting children and families. We are grateful to those voices who spoke to us in 2018 and who continue to offer leadership in the growing momentum of change in child welfare in Canada today.

Keynote speakers at the National Conference on Child Welfare included the following:

- Senator Murray Sinclair, who reminded everyone "that the monster that was created in the residential schools moved into a new house, and that monster now lives in the child-welfare system." He was referring to the overrepresentation of Indigenous children in care. He stated that the child welfare system as it operates today is hurting Indigenous children and families and called for new ways of engagement between child welfare and communities.

- Dr. Raven Sinclair, whose talk was called "Duty of Care: The Sixties Scoop, Cultural Loss, and the Canadian Legal System."

- Dr. Jeannine Carrière, who gave a talk titled "All My Relations: The Impact of Identity Politics on Métis Children in Care."

- The Honourable Graydon Nicholas, whose talk was titled "Jurisdictional Possibilities for Indigenous Governments on Indigenous Child Welfare."

- Jennifer King, First Nations Child & Family Caring Society of Canada, whose talk was called "Honouring Jordan's Principle: Put Kids First."

- Kenn Richard, founder and director of special projects, Native Child and Family Services of Toronto, who, along with a panel, provided a presentation titled "Four Phases of Reconciliation in Child Welfare."

We remain hopeful that, post-pandemic, the PCWC will be able to have a gathering again on the Prairies that we call home and to host a book launch.

We believe child welfare is currently at a pivotal and historical time of change in Canada and that pressure is mounting for significant change. We want to acknowledge specifically the work of the First Nations Child and Family Caring Society; the leadership of Dr. Cindy Blackstock, a champion for change; and all of the people working at this organization. We deeply appreciate their contribution to this book, calling for a new mindset and new narratives in child welfare in Canada. We echo that call, and we hope that all Indigenous children in Canada will be able to fully access funding that will provide local services and supports for children whose lives intersect with the child welfare system and who have the right to grow up in their community.

> *Reconciliation means working together on what is best for our children.*
>
> —Dr. Chief Robert Joseph

Acknowledgements

The work of this book reflects an interprovincial collaboration among the Prairie Child Welfare Consortium (PCWC) partners including the First Nations University of Canada, the University of Calgary, the University of Manitoba, and the University of Regina. This book would not be possible without the many contributors who have worked with our editorial team for the past year in submitting their chapters. We want to thank all of the contributors, who are educators, researchers, social workers, and leaders.

This book reflects an interprovincial, intersectoral, and international collaboration among the PCWC, the faculties of Social Work at the University of Calgary, University of Manitoba, and University of Regina, and the First Nations University of Canada. We also acknowledge the long-standing relationship the PCWC has had with steering committee members including the partner universities, Manitoba Department of Families, Alberta Children's Services, Saskatchewan Child and Family Services, the Federation of Sovereign Indigenous Nations, and the Métis Nation of Alberta.

This book would not have been possible without the contributions of many people, including the authors, the editorial team, and the reviewers. We also have two contributors from Australia, Dr. Robyn Williams and Dr. Michael Doyle, who have helped to deepen our understanding of the similar threads and parallels of colonization in Canada and Australia.

The peer reviewers gave of their time and talents to support and promote excellence in scholarship. The following people served as reviewers, worked collaboratively with the editorial team, and provided critical feedback and suggestions on chapters: Dr. Jason Albert, Dr. Peter Choate, Dr. Dorothy Badry, Dr. Rick Enns, Dr. Deb Goodman, Dr. Gwen Gosek, Julie Mann Johnson, MSW, RSW, Dr. Daniel Kikulwe, Dr. Gabrielle Lindstrom, Rebecca Martel, Bruce McLaurin, Dr. Denise Milne, Dr. H. Monty Montgomery, Dr.

Jackie Sieppert, Dr. Vicki Russell, Chris Tortorelli, MA, RSW, Dr. Susannah Walker, and Dr. Robyn Williams.

We are deeply appreciative of our long-standing relationship with the University of Regina Press and in particular want to thank senior acquisitions editor Karen May Clark and editorial assistant David McLennan, as well as the entire URP team for supporting the development of the manuscript.

Introduction

Dorothy Badry and Don Fuchs

This is the seventh book emerging from the Prairie Child Welfare Consortium (PCWC), marking a milestone in publishing the Voices from the Prairies series. Some of you may ask, what is the PCWC, where does it call home, and who is involved?

The PCWC has a rich history. It was started in 1999 through a dialogue that began about the state of child welfare in Canada and the challenges faced by Indigenous people in the system. The Prairie provinces in Western Canada—that is, Alberta, Saskatchewan, and Manitoba—reflect a distinct part of the Canadian landscape. From 1867 to 1914, the Canadian West experienced a wave of mass immigration from Europe, with people looking for economic opportunity including the right to acquire land that was the traditional territory of many Indigenous communities. The Prairies were aggressively settled, and the harmful practice of banning Indigenous culture was established. The aggressive appropriation of Indigenous land and the creation of the industrial and residential school system were contributing factors to the intergenerational trauma that continues to deeply impact Indigenous people in Canada today.

It is against this backdrop that the work of the PCWC continues in an effort to bring forward scholarship about contemporary child welfare issues that impact the Indigenous Peoples of Canada. The voices in this book reflect the need to take up the work of child welfare in new ways that reflect contemporary human rights frameworks. A critical need exists to recognize and establish autonomy and local governance in the delivery of child welfare services to First Nations, Inuit, and Métis communities. The delivery of child welfare services needs to be fully resourced, and programs such as Jordan's Principle must be fully available and accessible in rural, remote, and urban communities.

In 2021 the discovery of mass unmarked graves on or around former residential schools offered a grim reminder of the cultural genocide of Indigenous people that marks colonial history in Canada. These discoveries created an echo around the world calling for justice, and it is recognized that many untold stories are yet to emerge. We acknowledge the loss and grief associated with these discoveries and echo the calls for justice, repatriation, and reparation.

This book includes both well-established and new and emerging scholars from across the Prairies. In Chapter 1, Brittany Mathews, Jennifer King, and Cindy Blackstock examine the ways in which Canada's "old mindset" impeded the full implementation of Jordan's Principle in the way it was intended to fully support families. Through an examination of both policy and practice, this chapter offers insight into the struggles and challenges families face in accessing services for their children. Jordan's Principle emerged as a critical response to the short life of Jordan River Anderson, who lived with disabilities and health problems that never allowed him to leave the hospital, as the supports he needed were never available in his home community. The First Nations Child & Family Caring Society of Canada continues to advocate for the rights of children to be supported and served in their home communities and to end "discriminatory underfunding of First Nations child and family services" (Attorney General of Canada Memorandum of Fact and Law—March 12, 2021, Caring Society <https://fncaringsociety.com/sites/default/files/t-1621-19_t-1559-20_-_applicants_memorandum_of_fact_and_law_dated_march_12_2021.pdf> (June 21, 2022).

In Chapter 2, Hadley Friedland and Koren Lightning-Earle provide insight on the impact of Bill C-92—*An Act respecting First Nations, Inuit and Métis children, youth and families*—and its applications in child welfare. It is a well-known fact that First Nations have not had jurisdiction over the delivery of child welfare services and that Indigenous children are highly overrepresented in the child welfare system in Canada. As this book was being prepared, the Cowessess First Nation took the lead in Canada as the first to sign a historical agreement to control its own child and family services. This chapter unpacks the basics of the new Act and identifies core areas where new hopes and possibilities open up in the delivery of child welfare services.

In Chapter 3, Robyn Williams, Dorothy Badry, Don Fuchs, Yahya El-Lahib, Michael Doyle, Bernadette Iahtail, and Peter Choate offer insights into the connection between Fetal Alcohol Spectrum Disorder (FASD) and colonization. This writing team includes Indigenous scholars, disability scholars, and writers from both Canada and Australia who identify the parallels of colonization in both countries. The narrative of Maaja sets the stage and offers a realization of the personal and societal costs of unrecognized FASD. Further, this chapter highlights the need for decolonizing FASD and recognizing the importance of culture as intervention.

In Chapter 4, Gabrielle Lindstrom and Peter Choate identify the concern of the overrepresentation of Indigenous children in care and focus on the ways in which racially based investigations are problematic. The authors argue that real change will not come without recognition of the underlying problems, such as underfunding of prevention and gaps in achieving the social determinants of health in Indigenous communities. They identify ten practices that are impeding progress on these concerns and offer five steps to mitigate these challenges.

In Chapter 5, Kelly Provost and Chris Tortorelli explore key challenges including specific unmet recommendations made by the Truth and Reconciliation Commission of Canada and the Office of the Child and Youth Advocate Alberta (OCYA). They point out that Indigenous ways of knowing—informed by generations of oral stories, rich in connection to the spirit, land, and people—reinforce connection as critical to achieving positive change. They indicate that the path forward for Indigenous youth transitioning from care begins with a sense of belonging—specifically, the opportunity to know their clan, their story, and their traditions and to pass along their proud connections to future generations.

In Chapter 6, Del Graff and Arlene Eaton-Erickson raise a critical concern of the OCYA in Alberta: the overrepresentation of Indigenous children in care and the fact that the majority of children and youth served in advocacy work are Indigenous. The OCYA is concerned about the need to approach work with children and youth from a wholistic perspective and to this end has taken up critical questions around balancing individual and collective rights of children and youth. The authors maintain that the work of the OCYA is child centred and that the rights of children and youth are the primary focus of advocacy work in Alberta.

In Chapter 7, Bernadette Iahtail describes the development and ongoing work of the Creating Hope Society (CHS) in Edmonton, a unique Indigenous-controlled grassroots service organization focused on advocacy for Indigenous children involved in the child welfare system. Iahtail indicates that the CHS is a learning and educational organization that is deeply involved in the community and provides hope and supports to children and families through various cultural events. She points out that the key principles guiding the journey of this organization include building on the resiliency of survivors, remembering the past while moving forward into the future, and learning from and acknowledging the past while continuing to forge ahead.

In Chapter 8, Eveline Milliken and Linda Dano-Chartrand maintain that transforming child welfare depends on supporting Indigenous child welfare workers who work in mandated agencies. Central to this transformation, they argue, is the sense of cultural safety for workers. They put forward five recommendations that contribute to increased cultural safety for Indigenous child welfare workers in Manitoba's mandated child welfare agencies. In addition, they discuss five factors that detract from the workers' sense of cultural safety.

In Chapter 9, Jennifer Hedges, Eveline Milliken, and Elder Mae Louise Campbell maintain that an urgent need exists for transformation in child welfare and that educators and students need resources to help them engage meaningfully with social justice movements. The authors explore the role of allyship in child welfare and discuss the need for transformative education to more effectively prepare social justice workers who, in turn, can contribute to the transformation of the child welfare system.

In Chapter 10, Jason Albert and Susannah Walker demonstrate how the curriculum of Indigenous child welfare is centred around four principles, which are represented in the Cree context: nisitohtamowin (understanding), manitowakêýimowin (believing), kiskinwahamâtowin (learning), and kiskêýihtamowin (knowledge). The chapter also includes a discussion on how Indigenous people are taking their education back to their community, with the intention of making change in Indigenous child welfare and its operation.

This book brings together the voices of Indigenous and non-Indigenous scholars from the Prairie provinces, and each chapter has an Indigenous author. We believe this is a crucial aspect of scholarship about child welfare that is related to the care and well-being of children with Indigenous ancestry. Knowledge about the care and support of children in the child welfare system is embedded in community, and traditional systems of care have been present for thousands of years. This book draws on this embedded knowledge to provide a substantial contribution to the transformation of child welfare practice and the child welfare system.

In conclusion, we draw attention to the critical discourse raised in Chapter 1 by Mathews, King, and Blackstock, who maintain it is only through courageously and critically moving forward in a manner that centres the well-being of children that Canada can truly hope to change its mindset to support First Nations children in meaningful ways. This PCWC book shares an important knowledge contribution for those researchers, teachers, practitioners, and students who are walking together to promote justice and to brighten the future for Indigenous children, families, and communities.

PART I

Policy

CHAPTER 1

Canada's "Old Mindset" and the Struggle to Fully Honour Jordan's Principle

Brittany Mathews, Jennifer King, and Cindy Blackstock

Introduction

The Canadian federal government's colonial "old mindset" exalting settlers as "civilized" while degrading First Nations peoples as "savage" fuelled the residential school system. While the government apologized for its role in the residential school system in 2008, it has failed to reform itself, meaning the "old mindset" that gave rise to the system continues to infuse Canada's relationship with First Nations children, families, and communities. In 2007, Parliament unanimously adopted Jordan's Principle to ensure First Nations children received the services they need when they need them. Named after Jordan River Anderson, Jordan's Principle aimed to end the government's long pattern of denying First Nations children the same services that other children receive. However, while making public commitments, the federal government worked behind the scenes to make Jordan's Principle so narrow and difficult to access that no child ever qualified (2016 CHRT 2).

Suggested Citation: Mathews, B., King, J., & Blackstock, C. (2022). Canada's "old mindset" and the struggle to fully honour Jordan's Principle. In J. Albert, D. Badry, D. Fuchs, P. Choate, M. Bennett, & H. Montgomery (Eds.), *Walking together: The future of Indigenous child welfare on the prairies* (pp. 3–24). Regina, SK: University of Regina Press.

Canada's failure to implement Jordan's Principle as intended led the First Nations Child & Family Caring Society of Canada (Caring Society) and the Assembly of First Nations to file a human rights complaint against Canada alleging that its approach to Jordan's Principle was discriminatory. The complaint also alleged discrimination in Canada's funding of First Nations child welfare. Canada tried for years to get the case tossed out on jurisdictional grounds while at the same time denying Jordan's Principle requests from First Nations families for essential things like feeding tubes, mobility devices, learning assessments, mental health services, and respiratory equipment (Blackstock, 2011). The federal government even had a spreadsheet that would classify Jordan's Principle requests as "resolved" if the child died or grew into adulthood waiting to receive services. In 2011, Indian Affairs Deputy Minister Michael Wernick gave the public servants who discriminated against these children a public service award, citing how they had withstood the critiques of First Nations, professionals, and litigation (Caring Society, 2021a).

In 2016, the Canadian Human Rights Tribunal (the Tribunal) found that Canada's flawed implementation of Jordan's Principle and failure to properly fund First Nations child welfare amounted to racial discrimination and ordered it to stop (2016 CHRT 2). Indeed, the Tribunal found that "similar to the Residential Schools era, today, the fate and future of many First Nations children is still being determined by the government" (2016 CHRT 2). Much like their response to the passing of Jordan's Principle in the House of Commons, federal politicians welcomed the ruling and the fact that equity in child welfare and Jordan's Principle were among the top calls to action announced by the Truth and Reconciliation Commission of Canada (TRC) a year earlier (TRC 2015c). However, that "welcome" proved to be political theatre, given that the government did not comply. Instead, Canada chose to actively fight several of the twenty subsequent non-compliance and procedural orders issued against the government, even as it conceded that its non-compliance had contributed to unnecessary family separations and the deaths of at least three children (2017 CHRT 7). The Tribunal has often cited the continuation of Canada's "old mindset" as contributing to the non-compliance, culminating in a 2019 order describing the federal government's discrimination as "wilful and reckless" in a "worst-case scenario" (2019 CHRT 39).

This chapter delves into how Canada's old mindset—that is, ways of thinking and doing that have been found to be discriminatory—continues to inform Canada's practices and behaviours concerning Jordan's Principle. It focuses on the systemic nature of the federal government's "old mindset" approach to Jordan's Principle since the 2016 Tribunal order, showing how the federal government's colonial approach has placed children's well-being and lives at risk. While the old mindset systematically affects the federal government's relationships with First Nations, Métis, and Inuit peoples across the board, this chapter focuses on its operation with respect to Jordan's Principle specifically and suggests ways to improve the situation that may be applicable to other contexts. Indeed, the discriminatory "old mindset" was not dulled by Prime Minister Justin Trudeau's political commitments expressed in a 2019 mandate letter to Indigenous Services Minister Marc Miller: "there remains no more important relationship to me and to Canada than the one with Indigenous Peoples" (Office of the Prime Minister, 2019).

Days after the Tk'emlúps te Secwépemc Nation announced the finding of 215 children in unmarked graves on the site of the Kamloops Residential School, Trudeau told Parliament that Canada is not fighting First Nations kids in court and reiterated the government's commitment to "work hand-in-hand toward reconciliation" (Kennedy, 2021). However, the following week, the government was in federal court arguing that First Nations children off-reserve should not get help under Jordan's Principle and the government should not pay any compensation to victims of its discrimination (Caring Society, 2021d).

What Is Jordan's Principle?

Jordan's Principle, created in loving memory of Jordan River Anderson, is a child-first legal rule intended to ensure that First Nations children get the services they need when they need them. Jordan, who was from Norway House Cree Nation in northern Manitoba, was born in a Winnipeg hospital in 1999 with complex medical needs. When Jordan was two, his doctors approved a discharge plan that meant he could leave the hospital to live in the care of a specialized medical foster home in Winnipeg. Jordan's medical needs required that he stay close to the hospital to access the sort of medical care and facilities not available in his home community. The hope was that once Jordan's condition stabilized, he could live with his family in Norway House (Caring Society, n.d.).

Unfortunately, Jordan's discharge plan was interrupted because the governments of Manitoba and Canada could not agree on which government should pay for his in-home care. Instead, the two governments left Jordan in the hospital, at a much higher cost, both financially and in terms of Jordan's well-being. The Government of Canada refused to pay for Jordan's in-home supports, arguing that health care was the province's responsibility. The province of Manitoba took the position that the Government of Canada ought to pay, arguing that services for First Nations were the federal government's responsibility. The resulting dispute over who should pay meant that Jordan languished in the hospital for two more years until he passed away at the age of five. If Jordan were a non-Indigenous child, he would have been discharged when doctors said he was ready, and his care would have been paid for as a matter of course.

Sadly, the discrimination Jordan and his family experienced in trying to access services was not uncommon. Systemic and widespread jurisdictional wrangling between the federal and provincial/territorial governments over payment for services has meant First Nations children routinely experienced delays or denials in services simply because they were First Nations. A 2015 case study of children served by just twelve of the over 105 First Nations child and family service agencies identified 393 jurisdictional disputes in which children were given less or denied a service altogether because they were First Nations (Loxley et al., 2005).

After Jordan passed away, his family wanted to ensure that no other child experienced similar discrimination; they gifted Jordan's name to create a child-first principle to resolving jurisdictional disputes. On December 12, 2007, Jordan's Principle was passed unanimously in the House of Commons, where it was stated "that, in the opinion of the House, the government should immediately adopt a child first principle, based on Jordan's Principle, to resolve jurisdictional disputes involving the care of First Nations children" (Private Member's Motion M-296).

Despite this unanimous show of support, the federal government went on to intentionally corrupt Jordan's Principle to the point where it no longer resembled the family's original intent or served to safeguard children against discrimination. Canada limited its interpretation of Jordan's Principle to First Nations children living on-reserve with multiple, professionally assessed disabilities requiring supports from multiple service providers (2016 CHRT 2). In addition, there was no process to actually receive Jordan's Principle cases, and those that did come to Canada's attention were denied because, as a government official later testified, the government was in a mindset of dispute avoidance (Baggley, 2014).

As a result of Canada's choice to not properly implement Jordan's Principle, the Caring Society and the Assembly of First Nations filed a legal complaint in 2007 at the Canadian Human Rights Tribunal. The complaint alleged that Canada was racially discriminating against First Nations children by underfunding child welfare services on-reserve and failing to implement Jordan's Principle in a manner consistent with the House of Commons motion.

Although Canada tried multiple times to have the complaint dismissed on legal technicalities, the hearings finally started in 2013 before being interrupted when it was discovered that Canada had consciously withheld over 90,000 documents that it ought to have disclosed (2019 CHRT 1). Many of the documents were highly prejudicial to Canada, and the Tribunal called Canada's failure to disclose records "far from irreproachable" (2013 CHRT 16). Hearings resumed months later, and in 2016 the Tribunal issued its landmark decision, substantiating the complaint.

The Tribunal ordered Canada to cease applying its narrow definition of Jordan's Principle and to take measures to immediately implement the full meaning and scope of Jordan's Principle (2016 CHRT 2). Canada chose not to comply. It took twenty non-compliance and procedural orders from the Tribunal to get to a point where First Nations children have received close to a million services since 2016 (ISC, 2021). Of course, Canada takes credit for Jordan's Principle, even though it continues to fight it (see, for example, Trudeau, 2021).

Decisions made by the Canadian Human Rights Tribunal are legally binding. Canada is legally obligated to implement Jordan's Principle as ordered by the Tribunal; this includes ceasing to perpetuate any definition of Jordan's Principle that is not in compliance with the landmark ruling and any subsequent non-compliance orders (2017 CHRT 35). The Tribunal ordered that Canada's implementation of Jordan's Principle must be based on the principles of substantive equality and the best interests of the child, must be needs based, and must account for distinct community circumstances. Sadly, even as Canada takes credit, we submit that the federal government would not have implemented Jordan's Principle as intended had it not been legally ordered to do so. The evidence suggests that Indigenous Services Canada (ISC) has yet to undergo the transformation needed to treat First Nations children fairly without independent and binding oversight.

Canada's "Old Mindset"

In seventeen of the twenty non-compliance and procedural orders issued since 2016, the Tribunal refers to Canada's problematic "old mindset," describing it as "the same type of statements and reasoning that it has seen from the organization in the past" (Caring Society, 2021a; 2016 CHRT 16). Use of the term "old mindset" refers to evidence that government departments are still informed by and operating according to information, policies, reasoning, and justifications that were found to be discriminatory.

Canada's "old mindset" is rooted in colonialism. Today's ISC traces its origins to the Department of Indian Affairs, the federal department that created the residential school system, the reserve system, and numerous other policies and practices of colonialism. These policies and practices were intended to eradicate First Nations, Métis, and Inuit peoples and assimilate them into mainstream white Canadian society—something the TRC found amounted to cultural genocide (2015b). As a result, contemporary bureaucratic structures and the "public service network" are still "grounded in colonial history and ideology" (Vives & Sinha, 2019). In turn, these bureaucratic structures serve to disperse individual responsibility for discrimination; no one is accountable because the "system" is to blame (see, for example, Arendt, 1969).

In the Tribunal's non-compliance orders, the manifestations of Canada's old mindset regarding Jordan's Principle are identified as follows:

- deferring decision-making on key items to a later, often unspecified date;
- replicating policies and practices that have been found to be discriminatory under a different name or umbrella;
- structuring policies and procedures, such as timelines, in ways that are not in the best interest of families or communities but rather in the best interest of government;

- delaying decisions based on invalid ISC claims that further engagement is needed in some cases while making unilateral decisions to maintain the status quo in others, "even when the needs of specific communities or groups have been clearly identified and expressed" (2018 CHRT 4, para. 55);
- failing to prioritize the best interest of the child, to apply a substantive equality approach, and to base decisions on actual needs despite clear and repeated orders by the Tribunal to do so in all instances. This included establishing or proceeding with funding models that divide services into separate programs without proper coordination or funding, thereby replicating the very situation that Jordan's Principle is intended to address, and allowing bureaucrats without expertise to question and override professional treatment plans; and
- failing to act or make changes to known harms.

The most recent example of Canada's old mindset at work relates to capital assets that support Jordan's Principle service delivery to children. There is a serious housing and building shortage in many First Nations communities owing to years of government underfunding (Office of the Auditor General, 2011). This means that even when Canada approves new services under Jordan's Principle or through the First Nations child and family services program, there is often no space to actually deliver the programming for health and well-being and to ensure First Nations children can remain safely at home with their families and communities. Canada is aware of this situation. Although the Tribunal encouraged ISC to develop a strategy to address the infrastructure needs in September 2016, ISC made little progress (2016 CHRT 16). Canada indicated that it had to "engage" with various communities, organizations, committees, and governments before deciding on a capital strategy—a delaying practice already identified by the Tribunal as reflecting Canada's old mindset (Caring Society, written submissions, 2021a).

Canada's failure to make a decision to address capital needs meant families and communities experienced difficulties garnering approval for infrastructure modification and ISC continued to outright deny any new builds (Caring Society, 2021c). Although the Tribunal issued a letter-decision in August 2021 ordering Canada to remedy its discrimination in the provision of capital to enable substantively equal child welfare prevention and Jordan's Principle services, Canada's failure to address infrastructure needs placed children's well-being and lives at risk (Letter-Decision, 2021b). For example, ISC denied home modifications to a child with mobility needs arising from a serious accident, instead funding the child to live in a hotel in the midst of the COVID-19 pandemic with no long-term solution in place (Caring Society, 2021c). Clearly, the operation of Canada's old mindset continues to impact First Nations children profoundly. As discussed below, this is particularly evident with respect to Canada's attempts to offload responsibility, its problematic funding approaches, and its failure to prioritize the best interests of the child.

Offloading Responsibility: Communities as the Face of Canada's Non-compliance

Canada's old mindset remains apparent in some aspects of the service coordination model, particularly with respect to authority and control. Service coordinators are community-based individuals who assist families in submitting Jordan's Principle requests. Positions are staffed by First Nations communities and other First Nations non-governmental organizations and funded by Canada. On paper, the service coordination model responds to a need identified by First Nations leaders, namely that First Nations know what is best for their children and are in the best position to provide quality and culturally relevant support to families. Unfortunately, Canada's failure to adhere to the legal orders on Jordan's Principle has placed First Nations service coordinators in the uncomfortable position of being the face of Canada's non-compliance. Inconsistencies in decision-making by Canada, changes to ISC policy, and the fall-out from Canada's legal challenges to the Tribunal's orders on Jordan's Principle are felt by service coordinators and others working at the community level, not by Canada. In short, Canada has structured service coordination in ways that reflect the best interests of the government and not the best interests of children, families, or communities.

Since 2016, Canada has tasked service coordinators with building relations with communities and service providers, in addition to assisting families, while the government maintains ultimate control over decision-making. While the role of service coordinators is to support families in placing a request to Jordan's Principle, the power and authority to approve the request lies with ISC. Requests are sent to ISC (to a regional public servant called a "focal point," a regional manager, or headquarters in Ottawa, depending on the nature of the request) for decision.[1] Not surprisingly, families do not always understand this distinction. As a First Nations policy advisor explained to the Caring Society, "Families do not always understand that it is not Service Coordinators making the decisions about requests and can get upset with Service Coordinators when services are denied or delayed" (Nova Scotia Jordan's Principle advisor, personal communication, January 27, 2021).

An evaluation of service coordination in Alberta by the First Nations Health Consortium (FNHC) also raised concerns about how community-based service coordinators and other workers are forced to "mediate" between families and the federal government regarding Jordan's Principle requests (Sangster et al., 2019). The FNHC is responsible for developing and implementing an enhanced service coordination model to support families, yet Canada remains in control of Jordan's Principle administration, policies, determinations, and funding distribution. According to the evaluation, FNHC staffers reported that a number of difficulties with focal points arose from this situation, including lack of clarity on supporting documentation, discrepancies in decision-making, and delays in communication and funding dispersal (Sangster et al., 2019).

Efforts by service coordinators to navigate government bureaucracy are exacerbated by inconsistent decision-making on the part of the government. The Caring Society has observed inconsistent decision-making across provinces and territories, evidenced by Jordan's Principle denial data. For example, a breakdown of 2019–20 denial rates shows a significant discrepancy among provinces and territories. The percentage of individual requests denied ranges from 3.4 per cent in Manitoba to a staggering 26.3 per cent in British Columbia (Iamsees, 2020). Even within ISC regional offices, inconsistent decision-making continues. Conversations with

1 In some cases, Canada has entered into an agreement with a First Nation or First Nation organization so that the community or organization can approve requests without having to seek determination from ISC. Nishnawbe Aski Nation's Choose Life initiative (https://www.nan.ca/resources/jordans-principle) is one example.

Atlantic service coordinators between November 2020 and February 2021 found inconsistent decision-making between focal points within the same province and between decision-makers at the national level (Caring Society, 2021c). Service coordinators have described instances where Canada has denied requests that were previously approved for other children or, indeed, for the same child even though their needs have not changed.

Inconsistencies are compounded by the absence of clear information in ISC denial letters to families about why the request was refused (Caring Society, 2021b, 2021c). Specific details in denial letters are important so that families know what information they can provide when seeking a successful appeal or a judicial review of an ISC decision. Denial letters can also be submitted to the Tribunal to push for further compliance. It seems that Canada's vague denial letters are an effort to thwart accountability. Inconsistencies and poor communication place community-based service coordinators in an untenable position of having to relay decisions by ISC to families while not being able to explain why the support has been denied or what information families can provide to appeal successfully. Needless to say, this can seriously erode trust between service coordinators and families. The old mindset is evident when ISC, as the ultimate authority, tasks service coordinators with delivering bad news alongside unclear information.

Canada's need for control and authority is directly linked to the colonial and paternalistic mindset that still underpins many of its policy decisions. Canada's control over decision-making and authority can also be seen in the high threshold of information that ISC requires in order to determine Jordan's Principle requests. Although the Tribunal has ruled that families need only provide information and documentation that is "reasonably necessary" to determine a case, Canada continues to set a high documentation threshold and offloads the responsibility to meet its ever-changing threshold to families and service coordinators (2017 CHRT 35; Caring Society, 2021c). This contributes to delays in decision-making and service provision, creating needless barriers for First Nations families accessing Jordan's Principle. The Caring Society has heard from service coordinators in multiple Atlantic regions about confusion over the information required by Canada to approve requests, including the need to "map out" the process for each request, an ongoing process that they continue to spend a lot of time on (Nova Scotia Jordan's Principle advisor, personal communication, January 27, 2021). The FNHC evaluation also highlighted the delays and frustration resulting "from the unclear, inconsistent and burdensome federal expectations regarding the information that must be provided in order for a Jordan's Principle request to be submitted" (Sangster et al., 2019, p. xxi).

Implicit in the high level of documentation required is an unwillingness to recognize the capacity and jurisdiction of First Nations families to determine what is in the best interests of their children or what their children need in terms of supports and services. The amount of documentation required by ISC often leaves families with the feeling that they must "prove" the needs of their children to Canada (Caring Society, 2021c). The FNHC found that Canada's shifting responsibility to First Nations families to "prove" that substantive equality applies in their case is time consuming, is traumatizing for some families, and proves to be a barrier. Indeed, the FNHC found that "the process itself violates the principle of substantive equality, because First Nations people must spend additional time and resources advocating for the government to address heightened needs created by the government's discriminatory treatment" (Sangster et al., 2019, p. 13).

Another example of Canada requiring unnecessarily detailed documentation relates to eligibility. When the Tribunal confirmed the eligibility of First Nations children without *Indian Act* status who are recognized by their communities for the purposes of Jordan's Principle (2020 CHRT 36), service coordinators were told by ISC that they were required to obtain a letter from the Chief and Council each time a child without status placed a Jordan's Principle request. It was only later that the service coordinators learned that an email or fax would be sufficient and, importantly, that no such documentation is required for urgent cases. This distinction may seem minor, but service coordinators have high workloads and competing demands, and the additional administrative burden of obtaining an official letter is significant. False messaging by ISC has a significant impact on families who have no choice but to weather the delays in decision-making and service provision resulting from unnecessary administrative burdens (Caring Society, 2021b). In its evaluation, the FNHC also found that the lack of clear federal directives on Jordan's Principle eligibility contributed to delays in decision-making in the regional office (Sangster et al., 2019).

As the situation stands, community-facing service coordinators navigate a complex and ever-changing bureaucratic environment, while Canada continues to maintain its authority over funding and decision-making. The service coordinator model allows Canada to avoid accountability for its non-compliance while placing service coordinators in the uncomfortable position of being the face of Canada's non-compliance. The continuation of Canada's old mindset is apparent in its attempts to justify its failure to fulfill the Tribunal orders, particularly those regarding eligibility, by offloading responsibility to community-based service coordinators.

Funding Approaches

Canada's approach to funding is another issue the Tribunal referenced in its discussion of Canada's old mindset. Specifically, the Tribunal found that "The gaps and adverse effects [suffered by First Nations children and families] are a result of a colonial system that elected to base its model on a financial funding model and authorities dividing services into separate programs without proper coordination or *funding and was not based on First Nations children and families' real needs and substantive equality* [emphasis added]" (2019 CHRT 39, para. 13).

Canada's offloading of responsibility to service coordinators while retaining authority and failing to take a consistent approach to Jordan's Principle is exacerbated by its failure to properly resource and fund its service coordination model. For example, in one Atlantic region, as of February 2021, four service coordinators were responsible for 660 Jordan's Principle files (Caring Society, 2021b). The organization manages by sharing the work with other positions, such as family support workers; they would never turn families away, but at a certain point the need becomes unmanageable with the resources provided (Caring Society, 2021b). Canada initially told the organization they qualified for only one service coordinator because funding was based on population (a per capita approach). The Tribunal has been clear in its assessment that population size should not be taken as a proxy for community need. Given that service coordinators are tasked with supporting families in requesting supports through Jordan's Principle, it is children and families who bear the brunt of Canada's failure to properly fund these positions. Families may be (rightly) frustrated if service coordinators are stretched thin because of a lack of capacity, yet this anger is likely to be directed at the First Nations agency or organization tasked with providing assistance and not at the federal government or its funding models.

Canada's old mindset continues to prioritize what is easiest for government over the needs and circumstances of children, especially when it comes to funding. This is evidenced by ISC's insistence on funding services based on its own fiscal calendar. For example, ISC may require families to have their child reassessed for services to continue across ISC fiscal years even when there is no professional reason for the child to be reassessed. This means that families are required to submit their child for unnecessary assessments in order to "re-apply" for previously approved supports or services, despite nothing changing in the child's context or needs (Caring Society, 2021c). This practice disproportionately impacts children with disabilities and special needs who require ongoing support and places an unnecessary burden on families. Indeed, the Tribunal was forced to order ISC to stop using its interpretation of the *Financial Administration Act* (FAA) as a reason for denying services to children or refusing to implement other Tribunal orders. The Tribunal ruled that its orders and the FAA should be used together, not against each other. If there is a conflict between a Tribunal order and the FAA, the orders of the Tribunal have primacy over the FAA (Letter-Decision, 2021b).

ISC's preoccupation with government-determined fiscal cycles over the lived realities of children also has an exasperating impact on the in-school supports many children require. School boards have raised concerns about the funding structure of Jordan's Principle approvals, which are based on the fiscal year and inconsistent with the school calendar. If a child needs an educational assistant or special education teacher, for example, Canada's funding agreements will cover the cost of staffing only until March 31, yet school staff are hired based on the school calendar. As explained by service coordinators, "Canada may make verbal commitments regarding an extension, but without a funding agreement in place, monies are not truly guaranteed, and schools still see hiring with Jordan's Principle funds as a risk" (Caring Society, 2021b, p. 38).

Refusal to provide secure, long-term funding is yet another aspect of Canada's old mindset, evidenced by the government's unwillingness to relinquish control of and authority over short-term funding arrangements. Canada's insistence on short-term funding arrangements is inconsistent with the best interests of First Nations families and communities and, in many cases, amounts to Canada overriding professional assessments (Caring Society, 2021c). Short-term funding creates a sense of uncertainty and risk for service providers, families, and communities alike. Many First Nations communities place group requests through Jordan's Principle for community-based programs meant to target gaps in service provision.[2] The establishment of programs and services with short-term funding is a precarious endeavour. Service providers have raised concerns about the potential of short-term funding to result in discontinued or disrupted services and the impact this would have on families; it leads families to internalize the message that "they don't matter, their children don't matter" (Vives & Sinha, 2019, p. 17). Even the FNHC in Alberta, which has provided enhanced service coordination to over 1,100 individuals, indicated that in 2019 its funding was approved on a yearly basis with the "potential" to renew for an additional two years (Sangster et al., 2019).

Overall, while greater community control is the goal (Assembly of First Nations, 2018, 2021; Bill C-15, 2021), Canada is legally responsible for the proper implementation of Jordan's Principle and is therefore responsible for making sure that communities have the resources to do the work properly. The ongoing underfunding of services for First Nations in other areas raises concerns as to whether Canada will attempt to offload responsibility for Jordan's Principle in the same manner that it has with the administration of other services. Indeed, since the 1980s Canada has been offloading responsibility for services like policing, health care, and social services to communities, which lack the funds or ultimate authority to make decisions (Chambers & Burnett, 2017).

Despite the compliance issues outlined above, the number of Jordan's Principle requests from families and communities continues to grow (Iamsees, 2020). We submit that the number of requests is directly related both to Canada's failure to acknowledge and address discrimination in other services for First Nations children and to the persistence of the old mindset across government departments. Whereas Canada is legally required to fund Jordan's Principle and First Nations child welfare according to the principles ordered by the Tribunal (substantive equality, best interests of the child, needs based, funding that accounts for distinct community circumstances), Canada has not applied these standards to other

2 Group requests are requests made to Jordan's Principle for services to address the needs of a large number of children (2017 CHRT 35). Individual requests address the needs of a single child or children within a family.

federal departments and has made no indication that it intends to do so. Indeed, it has taken twenty non-compliance and procedural orders at the Tribunal to force Canada to honour these principles in just those two areas of federal responsibility. Other federal programs appear to be carrying on in a manner fully reflective of the old mindset.

As one example, Vives and Sinha (2019) compared the list of programs and services that Canada could fund for children on-reserve in Manitoba with the services that were actually available in the community of Pinaymootang First Nation. They found that the federal funds allowed for the full implementation of only two of the fourteen services for children that *could* be provided on-reserve through the federal government. Indeed, "local, regional, and provincial service providers indicated that they did not believe there to be a single First Nations community in the province where all the services...were available" (p. 15). When asked about the discrepancy, Canada responded that "the federal government simply transferred the funds in the amount specified...[and] it was the responsibility of the Band and local service providers to decide which of the possible programs they would provide" (pp. 14–15). This is the same discredited reasoning that Canada used to try to get the human rights complaint dismissed at the outset: that Canada is "just" the funder and that it is up to communities to deliver the actual service. The Tribunal found this reasoning to be both false and discriminatory, yet it appears that this same mindset is still being used to govern Canada's approach in other service areas (2016 CHRT 2).

Privileging Government Interests over the Best Interests of Children

Canada continues to privilege its own government interests, especially financial considerations and maintenance of government bureaucracy, over the best interests of children. Indeed, the central tenet of Canada's old mindset is failure to act on solutions to known harms to First Nations children in favour of maintaining its own interests. This privileging of government interests underpins Canada's actions and has resulted in serious harms against First Nations children for generations. In 1907, as chief medical inspector for the federal Department of Indian Affairs, Dr. Peter Henderson Bryce found that children in residential schools were dying at alarming rates as a result of profoundly unequal healthcare funding coupled with poor healthcare practices such as terrible sanitation, overcrowding, and poor ventilation. He issued a report to Duncan Campbell Scott, the chief bureaucrat on the residential school file for the Department of Indian Affairs. Instead of fixing the problems, which would have saved the lives of countless children, Scott cut funding to Bryce's research, indicating that the department did not intend to act upon the recommendations issued because they were incongruent with the government's interest in maintaining the system of partnership between the government and the churches (Hay et al., 2020; TRC, 2015a). Bryce, not deterred by Scott's stonewalling, wrote directly to Prime Minister Wilfrid Laurier; sadly, the prime minister also chose not to save the children's lives (Bryce, 1905). One hundred years later, Canada's conduct toward Bryce, who raised the alarm about the links between unequal health care and the deaths of children in residential schools, was consistent with the federal government's refusal to fund the home supports that Jordan River Anderson needed, including improvements to make the home accessible to small items like a thirty-dollar shower head (Obomsawin, 2019). As in the residential school era, Canada knew First Nations children were suffering as a result of jurisdictional disputes and knew what was needed to address the problem, yet chose to do nothing.

Unfortunately, many First Nations families and communities have come to expect that Canada will privilege government interests over those of children. Canada's colonial history and years of legal battles against First Nations, on issues from land rights to the case for First Nations kids at the Tribunal, have eroded trust in Canada's word and intentions. For example, on learning in 2013 that Canada was appealing the federal court decision that upheld Jordan's Principle and ordered the government to pay for her son Jeremy's care, Maurina Beadle—a courageous leader for Jordan's Principle—said she "was not surprised one bit. They say one thing and mean another. That's why I didn't let my guard down. I didn't celebrate too much" (Chambers & Burnett, 2017, p. 113).

Five years after the Tribunal's finding of discrimination against Canada, legal orders continue to be needed to direct Canada to put the needs and best interests of children before those of government. In 2018, the Caring Society was notified of an eighteen-month-old infant diagnosed with a rare, potentially life-threatening medical condition. "S. J." required a scan to determine the level of medical intervention needed to provide proper care. The scan was only available in Edmonton, so S. J.'s family submitted a request to Jordan's Principle for coverage of travel costs from Toronto to the Alberta city. The request was denied because S. J. was not eligible for *Indian Act* status (2019 CHRT 7). At this point, Canada's policy was to limit eligibility for Jordan's Principle to children with *Indian Act* status or who lived on-reserve, despite this practice being "rooted in a deeply colonial ideology and practice, consistent with the 'old mindset'" (2019 CHRT 7, para. 63). Indeed, the Tribunal found that Canada had failed to respond to S. J.'s needs and best interests and failed to undertake a substantive equality analysis. Rather, Canada chose to maintain its bureaucratic approach that the Tribunal has repeatedly identified as problematic.

Another example relates to Canada's position on post-majority care. Canada's conduct suggests an unwillingness to go beyond the bare minimum required by the Tribunal's orders. In this case, the Caring Society was told about a young person set to "age out" of Jordan's Principle care at the height of the COVID-19 pandemic (Cape Breton service coordinators, personal communication, January 25, 2021). Service coordinators were aware that ISC had established a provision regarding child welfare care to extend support beyond the age of majority so that youth set to age out would not lose support during the pandemic. They asked ISC to extend the child and family services (CFS) policy to Jordan's Principle. ISC refused, offered no transition plan, and was fully prepared to see the youth evicted at the height of the pandemic. Thankfully the province stepped in and agreed to fund the youth at the same level. Again, these examples highlight the continuation of the old mindset within ISC, in that the best interests of the child are not at the forefront of government decision-making.

Cultural Change Is Needed

Why does Canada keep violating legal orders and harming First Nations children? We believe the answer lies in the toxic persistence of Canada's old mindset. Canada has not learned from its egregious conduct in regards to the residential school system, the Sixties Scoop, and other harmful practices intended to assimilate First Nations children into the broader Canadian society. Canada has not learned from its discriminatory conduct and has failed to change its behaviour.

Lessons can be drawn from other historical examples of state crimes against humanity, including the Holocaust. Political philosopher Hannah Arendt (1969) noted how bureaucracies serve to disperse accountability for state crimes against humanity, as individual public servants cast off individual accountability to the "system." Given the TRC's finding of cultural genocide, Arendt's work offers important insights into the operation of state harms against First Nations children in Canada: "In a fully developed bureaucracy there is nobody left with whom one can argue, to whom one can present grievances, on whom the pressures of power can be exerted. Bureaucracy is the form of government in which everybody is deprived of political freedom, of the power to act; for the rule by Nobody is not no-rule, and where all are equally powerless, we have a tyranny without a tyrant" (Arendt, 1969, p. 81).

Consistent with Arendt's analysis, the Tribunal notes that eliminating discrimination and preventing it from reoccurring require mindsets to change (2019 CHRT 39). Even though this discrimination and the resulting harms are known, the policies and practices associated with this mindset continue to be "rationalized and normative" (Blackstock, 2009, p. 34). In this case, Canada's "good" intentions, alongside the "good" intentions of its public service, have only served to absolve the government of responsibility and accountability in the face of discrimination. In other words, it will take more than "good people" with good intentions to shift Canada's old mindset and truly address inequities.

The concept of Canada's old mindset implies a culture within ISC (and, by extension, the federal government as a whole) that informs decision-making. Cultural change may begin with policy change but requires a daily challenging of ingrained assumptions and ways of thinking, reacting, and doing. It also requires a reinforced sense of individual accountability for the human impacts of decision-making within the bureaucracy and of valuing dissent as necessary to good government. Unfortunately, as we stated at the outset, the evidence suggests that the mindset and culture of ISC have yet to undergo the sort of transformational change needed to treat First Nations children fairly, based on substantive equality and their best interests and through a lens that understands colonialism, without independent oversight.

The remedy to Canada's old mindset begins with systemic change to address the inequities that First Nations children experience. Addressing the discrimination endemic to colonialism is key to First Nations children having a better opportunity to live a life of dignity and respect (PAHO Commission on Equity and Health Inequalities in the Americas, 2019). The Spirit Bear Plan (Caring Society, 2017) provides a roadmap to end the inequalities against First Nations children, youth, and families and begin to address Canada's old mindset at the levels of both government bureaucracy and individual public servants. Endorsed by First Nations across Canada, the Spirit Bear Plan outlines five steps that Canada can take, immediately, to remedy its discriminatory practices and behaviours. To date, Canada has refused to implement the Spirit Bear Plan yet has also failed to identify or propose an alternative plan to end either the inequalities or its discriminatory practices. Unfortunately, Canada's failure to respond to the Spirit Bear Plan is another example of the old mindset in operation.

Truly achieving full implementation of Jordan's Principle and achieving equity for First Nations children will require more than praising good intentions and vilifying bad intentions. It will take collective action to hold Canada accountable, alongside binding legal orders and an ongoing, daily commitment to redress the old mindset that continues to have deep, lasting impacts on First Nations children. Government reform will take an awakening by the public to send a clear and convincing message to all politicians that if they want to be in power, they need to end the state-based injustices foisted onto First Nations, Métis, and Inuit peoples. It is only by courageously and critically moving forward in a manner that centres on the well-being of First Nations children that Canada can truly hope to change its mindset so that First Nations children may have the opportunities to make for themselves lives of dignity and respect.

Learning Questions

1. What is Jordan's Principle and why is it important?
2. What is meant by Canada's "old mindset"? Where does it come from and how has it influenced Canada's implementation of Jordan's Principle?
3. What parallels exist between the mindset that informed the residential school system and Canada's failure to implement Jordan's Principle?

4. How does bureaucracy work to disperse individual responsibility for government discrimination?
5. What can the public do to counter Canada's old mindset and push for equity for First Nations children and families?

References

Arendt, H. (1969). *On violence*. Harcourt Brace.

Assembly of First Nations. (2018, September 12–13). *Jordan's Principle summit: Sharing, learning and growing: Imagining the future of Jordan's Principle*. Assembly of First Nations.

Assembly of First Nations. (2021, March 9–11). *Virtual gathering on Jordan's Principle: First Nations innovation and determination*. Assembly of First Nations.

Baggley, C. (2014, April 30). *Examination-in-Chief*. Transcript Volume 57, p. 1115–1119. [pending more citation information]

Bill C-15. (2021). *An Act respecting the United Nations Declaration on the Rights of Indigenous Peoples*.

Blackstock, C. (2009). The occasional evil of angels: Learning from the experiences of Aboriginal peoples and social work. *First Peoples Child & Family Review*, *4*(1), 28–37. https://doi.org/10.7202/1069347ar

Blackstock, C. (2011). *Jordan & Shannen: First Nations children demand that the Canadian government stop racially discriminating against them*. Shadow report: Canada's 3rd and 4th periodic review to the UNCRC. First Nations Child and Family Caring Society.

Bryce, P. H. (1905, December 5). [Letter to Sir Wilfred Laurier, Premier of Canada]. Laurier Papers, vol. 391, item 104061-65, Library and Archives of Canada. Copy in possession of Collie Historical Research & Consulting.

Chambers, L., & Burnett, K. (2017). Jordan's Principle: The struggle to access on-reserve health care for high-needs Indigenous children in Canada. *American Indian Quarterly*, *41*(2), 101–124.

First Nations Child and Family Caring Society. (n.d.). *Jordan's Principle* [webpage]. Retrieved March 18, 2022, from https://fncaringsociety.com/jordans-principle

First Nations Child and Family Caring Society. (2017). *The Spirit Bear Plan*.

First Nations Child and Family Caring Society. (2021a, February). *Canadian Human Rights Tribunal: The "old mindset" that led to discrimination* [Information sheet].

First Nations Child and Family Caring Society. (2021b, March). *Jordan's Principle and children with disabilities and special needs: A resource guide and analysis of Canada's implementation*.

First Nations Child and Family Caring Society. (2021c, April). *Concerns with ISC's compliance with CHRT orders on Jordan's Principle*.

First Nations Child and Family Caring Society. (2021d, June). *Canada's Judicial Reviews v First Nations Children Federal Court Hearings: June 14–18, 2021* [Information Sheet].

First Nations Child & Family Caring Society of Canada et al. v Attorney General of Canada, 2013 CHRT 16, T1340/7008.

First Nations Child & Family Caring Society of Canada et al. v Attorney General of Canada, 2016 CHRT 2, T1340/7008.

First Nations Child & Family Caring Society of Canada et al. v Attorney General of Canada, 2016 CHRT 16, T1340/7008.

First Nations Child & Family Caring Society of Canada et al. v Attorney General of Canada, 2017 CHRT 35, T1340/7008.

First Nations Child & Family Caring Society of Canada et al. v Attorney General of Canada, 2017 CHRT 7, T1340/7008.

First Nations Child & Family Caring Society of Canada et al. v Attorney General of Canada, 2019 CHRT 1, T1340/7008.

First Nations Child & Family Caring Society of Canada et al. v Attorney General of Canada, 2019 CHRT 7, T1340/7008.

First Nations Child & Family Caring Society of Canada et al. v Attorney General of Canada, (2019, February 4) First Nations Child and Family Caring Society written submissions re retention of jurisdiction, major capital, reallocation policy, funding agreements, and timelines for consultation committee deliberations, T1340/7008.

First Nations Child & Family Caring Society of Canada et al. v Attorney General of Canada, 2019 CHRT 39, T1340/7008.

First Nations Child & Family Caring Society of Canada et al. v Attorney General of Canada, (2021a, May 12) Memorandum of fact and law of the respondent First Nations Child & Family Caring Society of Canada, T-1621-19, T-1559-20

First Nations Child & Family Caring Society of Canada et al. v Attorney General of Canada, (2021b, August 26) Letter-Decision, T1340/7008.

Hay, T., Blackstock, C., & Kirlew, M. (2020, March 2). Dr. Peter Bryce (1853–1932): Whistleblower on residential schools. *CMAJ*, *192*(9).

Iamsees, C. (2020). *Jordan's Principle 5 years later: A band-aid for government neglect?* Yellowhead Institute.

Indigenous Services Canada. (2021, July 20). *Helping First Nations kids* [webpage]. https://www.sac-isc.gc.ca/eng/1568396042341/1568396159824

Kennedy, B. (2021, June 14). This fight over compensation for First Nations kids has been raging for 14 years. On Monday, it's back in court. *Toronto Star*. https://www.thestar.com/news/canada/2021/06/14/this-fight-over-compensation-for-first-nation-kids-has-been-raging-for-14-years-on-monday-its-back-in-court-amid-calls-for-canada-to-just-do-the-right-thing.html

Loxley, J., DeRiviere, L., Prakash, T., Blackstock, C., Wien, F., & Prokop, S. T. (2005). *Wen:De The journey continues: The national policy review on First Nations child and family services research project—phase three*. First Nations Child & Family Caring Society of Canada.

Obomsawin, A., prod. and dir. (2019). *Jordan River Anderson, the messenger* [Film]. National Film Board.

Office of the Auditor General. (2011). *Status report of the Auditor General of Canada to the House of Commons, 2011. Chapter 4: Programs for First Nations on reserves*. Canada.

Office of the Prime Minister. (2019, December 13). *Minister of Indigenous Services Mandate Letter*. https://pm.gc.ca/en/mandate-letters/2019/12/13/minister-indigenous-services-mandate-letter

PAHO Commission on Equity and Health Inequalities in the Americas. (2019). *Just Societies: Health Equity and Dignified Lives. Report of the Commission of the Pan American Health Organization on Equity and Health Inequalities in the Americas*. Washington, DC: Pan American Health Organization.

Private Member's Motion M-296: Support for Jordan's Principle. (2007). Dec. 12, 2007. 39th Parliament, 2nd session. https://www.ourcommons.ca/DocumentViewer/en/39-2/house/sitting-36/journals

Sangster, M., Vives, L., Chadwick, K., Gerlach, A., & Sinha, V. (2019, March 31). *Advancing Jordan's Principle by realizing enhanced service coordination in the Alberta region*. First Nations Health Consortium.

Trudeau, J. (2021, June 21). *Statement by the Prime Minister on National Indigenous Peoples Day*. Prime Minister of Canada.

Truth and Reconciliation Commission of Canada. (2015a). *Canada's residential schools: The history, part 1: Origins to 1939*. McGill-Queen's University Press. https://ehprnh2mwo3.exactdn.com/wp-content/uploads/2021/01/Volume_1_History_Part_1_English_Web.pdf

Truth and Reconciliation Commission of Canada. (2015b). *Honouring the truth, reconciling for the future: Summary of the final report of the Truth and Reconciliation Commission of Canada*. McGill-Queen's University Press. https://publications.gc.ca/collections/collection_2015/trc/IR4-7-2015-eng.pdf

Truth and Reconciliation Commission of Canada. (2015c). *Truth and Reconciliation Commission of Canada: Calls to action*. https://ehprnh2mwo3.exactdn.com/wp-content/uploads/2021/01/Calls_to_Action_English2.pdf

United Nations Declaration on the Rights of Indigenous Peoples Act, SC 2021, c 14.

Vives, L., & Sinha, V. (2019). Discrimination against First Nations children with special healthcare needs in Manitoba: The case of Pinaymootang First Nation. *International Indigenous Policy Journal, 10*(1). doi:10.18584/iipj.2019.10.1.4

CHAPTER 2

Bill C-92: The Restoration of Indigenous Jurisdiction and Right Relations in Canada

Hadley Friedland and Koren Lightning-Earle

On July 7, 2021, a historic and momentous signing ceremony took place in Cowessess First Nation. Chief Cadmus Delorme, Prime Minister Justin Trudeau, and Saskatchewan Premier Scott Moe signed the first coordination agreement under *An Act respecting First Nations, Inuit and Métis children, youth and families* (known as Bill C-92) (Act, 2019), fully recognizing and resourcing, for the first time in Canadian history, a First Nation's jurisdiction over child and family services. The positive and, at times, even lighthearted occasion occurred closely, in both space and time, to the heart-rending recovery of 751 unmarked graves near the old residential school and at a time in history where a staggering 86 per cent of Saskatchewan children in government care are Indigenous (Djuric, 2021).

There is no doubt that law has played, and continues to play, a significant role in the current abysmal status quo for Indigenous children and youth. Can law also create the necessary changes to move beyond it? In this chapter we discuss the purposes, principles, and provisions of Bill C-92, the hopes and possibilities that it opens up, and some of the existing

Suggested Citation: Friedland, H., & Lightning-Earle, K. (2022). Bill C-92: The restoration of Indigenous jurisdiction and right relations in Canada. In J. Albert, D. Badry, D. Fuchs, P. Choate, M. Bennett, & H. Montgomery (Eds.), *Walking together: The future of Indigenous child welfare on the prairies* (pp. 25–45). Regina, SK: University of Regina Press.

and emerging barriers to achieving its goals and aspirations. We start by describing what it intends to achieve and the overarching principles it seeks to uphold, with a particular focus on the significance of the new "best interests of the Indigenous child" analysis it requires. Next, we outline the national standards section, including the requirements for prevention, notice, and representation, and the imperatives for promotion of family and community relationships and for ongoing reassessments for Indigenous children in care. Finally, we turn to the jurisdiction section, under which the *Cowessess First Nation Miyo Pimatisiwin Act* (Cowessess Act, 2021) is now legally recognized as having the force of federal law in Canada, prevailing over provincial laws. We discuss how inherent jurisdiction can and should be recognized through application of the national standards, the process through which Indigenous laws can be recognized as federal law under the Act, and some of the non-legal barriers being encountered. We conclude that the new law creates the possibility for, but also requires restoration of, right relations to positively change the status quo for Indigenous children, families, and communities.

The Purposes, Principles, and Provisions of *An Act Respecting First Nations, Inuit and Métis Children, Youth and Families* (Bill C-92)

An Act respecting First Nations, Inuit and Métis children, youth and families (2019) came into force on January 1, 2020. This Act is the first federal statute directly related to Indigenous child and family services.[3] Its purpose is to affirm and recognize, for the first time in Canadian history, Indigenous peoples' inherent jurisdiction over Indigenous children and families as an Aboriginal (constitutional) right (Act, 2019, s. 8 (a)),[4] to

3 This is the first time the federal government has exercised a power it has always held to legislate in relation to Indigenous children. Social welfare is generally considered the jurisdiction of the province, and Indigenous peoples that of the federal government, resulting in a complex legal terrain for responsibilities relating to Indigenous children. While legally this is almost certainly an area of *overlapping* jurisdiction, both federal and provincial governments have a long history of denying jurisdiction over Indigenous children. See the excellent discussion in Grammond (2018).

4 See also s. 18, which recognizes, as a s. 35 Aboriginal right (note this is worded as an "Aboriginal" right because this term, not "Indigenous," is...

set national standards for child and family services (CFS) delivery relating to Indigenous children and families, as called for by the Truth and Reconciliation Commission of Canada (TRC, 2015), and to contribute to the implementation of the United Nations Declaration on the Rights of Indigenous Peoples (UNDRIP) (UN General Assembly, 2007).

Bill C-92 both recognizes Indigenous jurisdiction over CFS and sets out a formal process whereby Indigenous Nations and groups who wish to exercise this jurisdiction can have their own laws recognized and enforced as federal law anywhere in Canada (Act, 2019, ss. 21–26).[5] In addition, and immediately, the national standards section of the Act, now in force, set minimum standards for all decision-making and service delivery for Indigenous children related to child and family services.[6]

Bill C-92 National Standards Provisions

The national standards section of Bill C-92 has garnered less attention than the jurisdiction section, yet it ought not be underestimated. These provisions now apply to all CFS providers in all provinces and territories (Act, 2019). As a federal statute, Bill C-92 is not a policy or recommendation but rather *law* that must be followed and applied. As a result, CFS providers and provinces must change their practices to align with the national standards. The national standards ensure that Indigenous children across Canada will have equal rights to a minimum standard of services under the law. This is a significant step to address a long history of what Naiomi

...what is used in s. 35 of the *Constitution Act, 1982*, the inherent right to self-government, including "jurisdiction in relation to child and family services," which includes (but is not limited to) legislative authority to draft, administer, and enforce, and develop dispute resolution mechanisms in relation to CFS laws.

5 See ss. 21–26 of the Act (2019) for the powers and limits of the recognition of this as an Aboriginal right, as well as the process in place for enacting and enforcing these laws as federal laws. For more information for First Nations and other Indigenous governing bodies, see Wente & Metallic (2019). For further strategies, see Metallic et al. (2019).

6 For more information for legal professionals tasked with interpreting and implementing the Act, see Friedland (2019). For information aimed at social workers and service providers, see Friedland & Lightning-Earle (2020). See also Turpel-Lafond (2019) and Walkem (2020).

Metallic (2018) describes as "jurisdictional neglect" whereby the federal government fails to legislate in important areas impacting First Nations, resulting in not only a lack of services but also "excessive or inappropriate control" owing to the "absence of normal checks and balances that come with properly regulated government services established through legislation" (p. 16).[7] It is hopeful that the national standards can start to fill this legal vacuum. Provincial laws relating to child and family services all remain in force where there is no conflict. Where provincial laws differ or conflict, Bill C-92 prevails. Where Indigenous laws recognized through the process set out in Bill C-92 are enacted and differ from provincial statutes, Indigenous laws likewise prevail.

Guiding Principles

The first part of the national standards section sets out principles for interpreting and applying decisions under it. The paramount consideration in the national standards section of the Act (2019) remains the best interests of the child (s. 10.1). However, the primary consideration in a "best interests of the Indigenous child" analysis is now a child's physical, psychological, and emotional safety, security, and well-being *and* their need for ongoing relationships with their family and community, as well as the preservation of connections to their culture (s. 10.2). In other words, unlike many statutes that set out a list of best interest factors without prioritizing any, Parliament has now "super-weighted" Indigenous children's relational well-being. This super-weight is important to keep at the forefront of all decisions because without it, where there is merely a list of factors, decision-makers may just focus on the ones they see as most important themselves, and it is then assumed they conducted a proper analysis. Now, relationships with family, community, language, and territory must be prioritized as core aspects of the best interests of Indigenous children.

The factors to be considered under the best interests of the Indigenous child (Act, 2019, s. 10.3(a–h)) include the importance of maintaining an Indigenous child's relationships to their parents, family members,

7 For more on the Caring Society case that Metallic discusses, see *First Nation Child and Family Caring Society et al. v Attorney General of Canada, 2016 CHRT 2.*

community, language, culture, and territory (s. 10.3(c)). Additional factors include consideration of the "nature and strength" of an Indigenous child's relationships with family members beyond just Eurocentric models of the nuclear family (s. 10.3(c)) and "any plans for the child's care including care in accordance with the customs and traditions of the Indigenous group" (s. 10.3(f)). Best interests are required to be interpreted, to the extent possible, in accordance with the Indigenous laws of the child's own people (s. 10.4).

Bill C-92 also requires cases to be interpreted in light of the principles of substantive equality (Act, 2019, s. 9.3) and cultural continuity (s. 9.2), recognizing that cultural continuity is essential to Indigenous children, family, and community well-being (s. 9.2(a)). It stresses that CFS delivery must not contribute to assimilation or cultural destruction (s. 9.2(d)). Bill C-92 stresses that the *effect* of CFS delivery must be evaluated, not just the intent (s. 11). This logically requires ongoing evaluation.

When we offer presentations about the new "best interests" analysis, there is a stark difference in reception between Indigenous CFS workers, who typically either are already doing this or are relieved they now have the authority to do so, and non-Indigenous CFS workers, who often ask us to explain why these factors have been super-weighted. Research that addresses this "why" is increasingly available.[8] Yet the "how" is equally important: the legislation's references to "ongoing" and "relationship" create a deeper meaning and offer tangible milestones. To build relationships, you must have a connection. A child has to know where they are from, and they must know their relatives, see and touch the land, and listen to—and, ideally, speak—the language. This will look different for every child, as it will be unique to their Indigenous identity and circumstances. As a result, CFS workers will have to build relationships with the Indigenous communities where children are from in order to facilitate and maintain relationships and connections. Cultural connections will have to be meaningful and authentic. Gone are the days where a CFS worker can check off the cultural plan box by taking a child to a powwow. Imagine a

8 See, for example, Chapter 6 ("Best Interests of the Indigenous Child") and Chapter 7 ("Protecting a Child's Indigenous Identity, Culture and Heritage") in Walkem (2020). See also Choate et al. (2019); NICWA (2017); Bennett (2015); and Blackstock (2011).

system where children can receive their traditional name, learn the meaning behind the name, and say it in their traditional language, and where they have a connection with their territory because that is where they spend time learning about traditional medicines.

Indigenous children's relationship with their territory and land is recognized as an important part of well-being in the best interests analysis of Bill C-92 (Act, 2019, s. 10.3(d)). This is congruent with many Indigenous teachings and practices for child well-being. For example,

> *The Cree have a practice of making a special ritual of disposing of the newborn's belly button. Rather than throwing it away, they will make a special effort to, for example, bury it in a special place. The belief is that where the belly button is placed helps to define the path the child will take in the world. Burying it helps to keep the child grounded, so that his or her spirit has a home.* (Pazderka et al., 2014, p. 59)

Every child should have the opportunity to participate in their traditional milestones regardless of their in-care status.

Prevention as Priority

The next part of the national standards contains several provisions that address the importance of preventative measures, instead of apprehension, whenever possible. This requires CFS providers to prioritize prevention over other services (Act, 2019, s. 14.1), to provide preventive prenatal care (s. 14.1), to not apprehend any Indigenous child on the basis of socioeconomic conditions alone (s. 15), and to demonstrate "reasonable efforts" to maintain placement with parents or family members (s. 15.1). Now, CFS workers have to make "reasonable efforts" and provide evidence of actions they took to keep the child in the home of parents or family members. "Reasonable efforts" can include providing beds, food, in-home support, or even just rent payment for a month. One could imagine even building additional bedrooms or making minor home repairs to ensure the safety of the current home. Judges and lawyers can (and should) now ask CFS workers in court for documentation of their reasonable efforts for prevention. There is further guidance for compliance from the United

States, where the *Indian Child Welfare Act*, which has been in force for forty years, requires "active efforts" (NICWA, 2018).[9]

Some have asked if the preventative prenatal care provision will end "birth alerts." There is no directive to do so in the Act, but directing preventative prenatal care does allow for other options when there are concerns during pregnancy about the potential safety and well-being of the child at birth. Under Bill C-92, CFS workers have the authority to work with pregnant parents on preventative prenatal care, which includes offering any services likely to be in the best interests of the child at birth. This includes creating plans with the pregnant parent, family members, and the Indigenous governing body for prevention and support for expectant mothers, from basic food and shelter to medical care, and mental and cultural supports, as well as plans for preventative services or even placements upon birth (Felske-Durksen & Friedland, 2020). Realistically, preventative funding for prenatal care will need to increase to achieve this intended purpose.

Notice, Representation, and Placement Priorities in Intervention

Following the prevention provisions, the Act addresses the minimum standards that must be adhered to when apprehension and placement outside of family are considered. The Act requires that notice be given to parents, care providers, and Indigenous governing bodies "*before* any significant measure" is taken regarding an Indigenous child (Act, 2019, s. 12) and it gives party standing to parents and care providers, as well as representation rights to Indigenous governing bodies, in any court proceedings (s. 13). It sets out placement priorities, which start with parents, then family members, members of the same community, any other Indigenous person, and finally, if none of these are possible, any other adult (s. 16.1). Placement with or near siblings (with an expanded definition beyond only biological children of the same parents) or according to customary care plans within the child's community must be considered (s. 16.2).

The Act does not define "significant measures," so there is an opportunity for communities to do so. Significant measures must mean more than

9 For example, active efforts may go beyond making a referral to counselling to actually driving a parent to and from that counselling. For a discussion of what active efforts entail, see NICWA (2018) and Walkem (2020, pp. 60–63).

legal proceedings; otherwise, the Act could have simply said "changes in legal status." The definition we propose at the Wahkohtowin Law and Governance Lodge is "not just legal changes but changes in placements, service provider awareness or responses to issues such as suicidal ideation or behaviour, sexual identity, etc.—anything that could significantly change the day-to-day life of the child, parent and/or care provider, or can impact the likelihood or timeline of apprehension, permanency or reunification" (Act, 2019, s. 16.3).[10] Communities have an opportunity to interpret this broadly and according to what the community defines to be in the best interest of their children. The purpose of informing families and communities of significant measures is to provide opportunities for them to consider measures that affect care. In addition to a natural opportunity for reassessment and promoting family and community relationships (see below), families and communities may offer cultural practices and relational support that can support a child through changes in the child's life.

Reassessment and Promoting Attachments in Out-of-Family Care

Finally, the Act sets out minimum standards for when an Indigenous child is placed in out-of-family care, if there is no other choice, despite following the Act's placement priorities. Bill C-92 stresses the importance of promoting the child's attachments and emotional ties with family members (Act, 2019, s. 16.3) and makes it mandatory to reassess the possibility of placement with family on an ongoing basis (s. 17). How these provisions will be interpreted and operationalized remains an open question at this time. However, this is one of the most essential aspects of the national standards, as it directly addresses a major issue with the previous best interests analysis. On the one hand, CFS providers and judges continue to follow and apply the reasoning from *Racine v Woods* (1983 at para. 187), a case that is over thirty years old and that was decided when the last residential schools were still in operation (TRC, 2015). This decision claimed that the importance of an Indigenous child's cultural connections, described as "the racial element," actually "fades with time" (see also Choate et al., 2019). Much more recently, *Brown v Canada* (2017),

10 For more information about the Wahkohtowin Law and Governance Lodge, see https://www.ualberta.ca/wahkohtowin/index.html.

the so-called Sixties Scoop case, found "uncontroverted evidence" from across Canada that adoptions of Indigenous children into non-Indigenous homes caused "great harm" (para. 4) to these individual children and that the loss of their Indigenous identity "left the children fundamentally disoriented, with a reduced ability to lead healthy and fulfilling lives...[and] resulted in psychiatric disorders, substance abuse, unemployment, violence and numerous suicides." Some researchers argue that the Sixties Scoop was even "more harmful than the residential schools" (*Brown v Canada*, para. 7).[11]

The uncontroverted expert evidence in *Brown v Canada* directly contradicted the ratio in *Racine v Woods*. Indigenous children continue to need family, community, and cultural connections throughout their lifetime, and Bill C-92 (Act, 2019) recognizes that this core need requires ongoing protection.

We argue that maintenance of attachments and emotional ties, as well as the reassessment provisions, suggests that while adoptions are not ruled out completely, erase-and-replace models of permanency, such as adoptions, should be avoided. Given the research that suggests 85 per cent to 95 per cent breakdown rates of Indigenous to non-Indigenous adoptions (Sinclair, 2007), it would be unconscionable for any court to find that an adoption or other permanency order means an Indigenous child, youth, family, or governing body is no longer able to access the Act's rights and protections. To better protect Indigenous children's safety, security, and well-being in the long run, permanence for Indigenous children must include "cultural permanence" (Bennett, 2015). The "addition" model of adoption, accepted as "customary adoption" in some Canadian jurisdictions (Friedland, 2021), or permanent guardianship without legally severing the original parental relationship, along with enforceable access orders for Indigenous parents, family members, or even other community members such as Elders or relatives when necessary and willing, better achieves the purposes of the Act.

Any permanency order where an Indigenous child is placed in the care of non-family members should only be made with evidence of a

11 Citing S. Fournier & E. Crey. (1997). *Stolen from our embrace: The abduction of First Nations children and the restoration of Aboriginal communities*, as cited in Chambers, L., *A Legal history of adoption in Ontario*, (2016) at 120.

collaboratively developed, enforceable, and robust cultural connection plan or cultural safety agreement, which sets out a "circle of caring" (Bennett, 2015) around the child to promote relationships with family and community, as well as cultural continuity and safety. All permanency orders should include regular review dates and an access order, so the child's right to relationship and cultural continuity are legally enforceable.[12]

Bill C-92 Jurisdiction Provisions: Acknowledgement and Recognition of Jurisdiction

The jurisdiction provisions of Bill C-92 begin with a clear acknowledgement and recognition of Indigenous jurisdiction, which echo the provisions regarding the purpose of the Act (Bennett, 2015). It is important to keep this in mind because the Act calls for an immediate practice shift for service providers and decision-makers, not only if or when a particular Indigenous governing body has the capacity and desire to enact a formal written law. Regardless of whether a First Nation or other Indigenous governing body decides to go through the process set out in the Act to enact its own CFS legislation, to administer and enforce its own laws, and/or to establish its own dispute resolution processes, its jurisdiction over its own children and families exists, and is recognized as existing, in Bill C-92. CFS service providers and decision-makers should be reaching out to and consulting with representatives from First Nations and other Indigenous communities in a similar way that they would reach out to and consult with a representative of another province, territory, or country if they discovered a child was originally from another jurisdiction.

Several sections in the national standards create an opportunity, and even an imperative, for service providers and decision-makers to seek

12 Not all provinces currently require cultural connection plans or cultural safety agreements prior to adoption. Those that do, including Alberta and British Columbia, have no mechanisms for enforcement, so the plans are merely a "good faith" agreement. See, for example, Payne (n.d.). Bennett describes Mary Ellen Turpel-Lafond's finding that, in a review of sixty files in 2013, only three had cultural plans (Bennett, 2015, p. 23). On essential elements of this planning, see Bennett, generally, and Carrière (2008). See also Native Counselling Services of Alberta (2015) and South Island Wellness Society (n.d.).

out and defer to Indigenous Nations' authority and knowledge relating to their own children and families regarding CFS. Most fundamentally, fulfilling the Act's purpose of affirming and recognizing Indigenous peoples' inherent CFS jurisdiction (Act, 2019, ss. 8(a) and 18.1). However, in addition, consulting with a representative of an Indigenous governing body seems like the most effective, if not the only, way to achieve the following requirements in the Act:

- requiring adequate information to ensure the transmission of an Indigenous child's "languages, cultures, practices, customs, traditions, ceremonies and knowledge" (s. 9.2(b));
- understanding and explaining the "characteristics and challenges of the region" (s. 9.2(e));
- understanding and explaining how services can be provided in a manner that does not "contribute to the assimilation of the Indigenous group, community or people to which the child belongs or to the destruction of the culture of that Indigenous group, community or people" (s. 9.2(d));
- upholding the Indigenous governing body's right to have the "views and preferences of the Indigenous group, community or people considered in decisions that affect that Indigenous group, community or people" (s. 9.3(d));
- demonstrating that best interests of an Indigenous child are consistent with the Indigenous group's laws or showing why it is not possible to be compliant (s. 10.4); and
- demonstrating compliance with notice requirements, which include giving notice and hearing representations from an Indigenous governing body prior to any CFS-related significant measure in the life of an Indigenous child (s. 12.1).

If every authoritative decision-maker in Canada simply started from this point and demanded that service providers demonstrate how they have upheld Indigenous Nations' inherent jurisdiction on a case-by-case basis—by seeking out and applying Indigenous Nations' views and preferences regarding the best interests of their own children; by taking into account their knowledge of the child's languages, cultures, practices, customs, traditions, and ceremonies as well as the characteristics and challenges of the region; and by acting on the Nation's advice on how to provide services in a manner that does not contribute to assimilation or cultural destruction—they could fulfill the purpose of the Act relating to the recognition and affirmation of Indigenous jurisdiction, even if the majority of Indigenous Nations do not enact their own legislation. In other words, respecting Indigenous jurisdiction can and should be occurring right now through a purposive application of Bill C-92's national minimum standards, as well as Indigenous laws as applicable.

Processes for Law-Making, Service Administration, and Dispute Resolution

The jurisdiction provisions of Bill C-92 set out a process through which an Indigenous governing body can—as one possible way of exercising its existing, inherent jurisdiction—create formal written CFS laws that will be recognized as having the force of federal law. As mentioned above, this may include drafting legislation, administering services, and developing dispute resolution mechanisms (Act, 2019, ss. 18.1 and 18.2). The provisions include a process that requires giving notice of intent (s. 20.1), agreeing to having the notice of intent and the legislation published on a public federal website (s. 25), and making reasonable attempts to negotiate a coordination agreement with the federal and applicable provincial or territorial governments (s. 20.2). If reasonable efforts to negotiate a coordination agreement have been made for a year but fail to result in a coordination agreement, the Indigenous CFS law will still have the force of federal law and prevail over provincial CFS statutes (s. 20.3).

Many people see these jurisdiction provisions as an all-or-nothing proposition. One of the most common questions we are asked when presenting information about this new law is, what about Indigenous communities that are too small or do not have the capacity to take over the full administration of CFS? While some communities are addressing practical issues of scale by working together through central organizations such as tribal councils or political organizations,[13] this is not the only approach.

13 For example, the Anishinabek Nation wrote a draft law that twenty-two of its thirty-nine-member First Nations have chosen to enact in their own communities thus far. See the Anishinabek Nation Draft Child Well-Being...

On a plain language reading of the Act, there is no requirement for an Indigenous governing body to, for example, take on full administration of services if it drafts its own CFS legislation. Legally, with legislative authority, an Indigenous community could decide to draft legislation that consists only of its own minimum standards that all service providers must adhere to when interacting with its children, wherever they may reside. After all, if the federal government can do so, as with the national standards, without taking on direct administration of services, why can't an Indigenous government?

Another community may decide to exercise its jurisdiction by only developing and implementing its own CFS decision-making or dispute resolution process, wisely recognizing that who is interpreting any law and how they are choosing to use their discretion to apply it have a profound impact on the day-to-day realities for children and families. Yet another community may want to develop legislation, administer all services, and create its own dispute resolution process—as the Cowessess First Nation has done. Indigenous Nations do not have to create the same CFS boxes as the provinces. They can craft their own system that works for them. We are only limited by our ability to imagine what is possible. It is an opportunity for Indigenous Nations to revitalize their principles and values regarding children in care and to draft legislation that reflects those values.

Regardless of what an Indigenous government decides, it costs money to develop and implement laws and legal processes. In addition, if they want their law or legal procedures recognized as having the force of federal law under the Act, they must give notice and make reasonable efforts to negotiate a coordination agreement with the federal and relevant provincial and territorial governments, which also takes time and money and is the only path toward funding in the Act.[14] The issue many communities are facing at this point is that the federal government's written requirements for capacity funding and publicly available

---

...Law online at https://www.anishinabek.ca/wp-content/uploads/2020/04/an-Child-Wellbeing-Law.April-2020.pdf.

14 The only substantive reference to fiscal arrangements relating to an Indigenous governing body's exercise of legislative authority relating to the provision of child and family services in the Act is in s. 20(2)(c), which states this *may* be an aspect of a coordination agreement.

information about the Act lean toward the all-or-nothing view, which has no basis in the law itself.

For instance, a requirement for capacity development funding is that the Indigenous governing body be ready to take over delivery of services within five years.[15] Anecdotally, we hear many communities report being told they must create a delegated agency under the province prior to law-making under Bill C-92. Yet this is not a legal requirement in Bill C-92. If First Nations follow this advice, they will "voluntarily" bind themselves to the legal limits of provincially delegated authority. The provincial director would set the terms for their delegation and have the discretion to revoke their delegation at any time, maintaining the current power dynamics for delegated First Nations agencies (DFNAs). Again, anecdotally, we hear that when this is pushed back against, ISC quickly concedes it is not a requirement after all. There is the possibility under an Indigenous governing body's law that it could be the Nation that delegates that authority and that it is not derived from the province; therefore, the Nation would not be bound by the provincial director's decisions.

The Cowessess First Nation Coordination Agreement, the first publicly available example, narrows the national standards by defining "significant measures" as only court related and limits Cowessess's jurisdiction by setting out differences between on-reserve children (service delivery) and off-reserve children (consultation), despite the clear legislative intention that Bill C-92 apply to both on-reserve and off-reserve children.[16] These limitations may represent compromises in order to reach agreement (Cowessess Agreement, 2021).[17] The province still holds ultimate authority over Cowessess First

---

15 See "Selection Criteria" in ISC (2022).

16 See the testimony of then deputy minister Jean-François Tremblay, Indigenous Services Canada, in response to a question regarding application of jurisdiction to off-reserve children by Senator Coyle, where Tremblay states, "It's not an on- versus off-reserve legislation. It's for First Nations, Inuit and Metis, wherever they live in this country. It is legislation that says that they have the jurisdiction. There's nothing that stops them from exercising this jurisdiction across the country, because they are protected by a federal law" (Canada, Parliament, Standing Senate Committee on Aboriginal Peoples., 2019).

17 The Cowessess First Nation's law came into force April 1, 2021, and the coordination agreement was entered into July 6, 2021 (ISC, n.d.). The concern about such compromises is, as one anonymous reviewer helpfully pointed out, they may lead to agreements that go against the spirit of the Act.

Nation children in care off-reserve though they state they will consult with the Nation (Cowessess, July 2021). Cowessess will not have final say over the guardianship of those children, and it is unclear how the province will be held accountable to ensure the wishes of Cowessess are honoured in those consultations. This lack of accountability creates the possibility of inequality in the provision of in-care services and supports between children on- and off-reserve. Notably, while the premier of Saskatchewan appeared at the signing ceremony and spoke in glowing terms about the co-operation and communication between all three levels of government, nothing in the coordination agreement binds Saskatchewan beyond its existing legal obligations under the national standards part of Bill C-92.

Equitable and reliable funding for Indigenous CFS laws and service administration remains a huge concern. Dr. Cindy Blackstock, still in court with the federal government after fifteen years—most recently regarding the government's judicial review of the Canadian Human Rights Tribunal orders regarding discriminatory funding of CFS on-reserve and Jordan's Principle[18]—is deeply concerned that no firm commitments or transparent mechanisms exist for funding the implementation of Indigenous CFS laws (see First Nations Child and Family Caring Society, 2021). The fear and risk here is that this will become just another route toward devolving responsibilities without providing for sufficient and equitable funding and that the optics of the inevitable failures, in light of unequal funding, will reinforce racist stereotypes about Indigenous governments and maintain the status quo as the best of several bad options.[19]

Conclusion

The acknowledgement and recognition of Indigenous jurisdiction over CFS is not only long overdue but a historic and positive step forward. National

18 For a detailed timeline of the proceedings relating to this case, from February 2007, when the original complaint was first filed, to the present (as of the writing of this chapter in February 2022), see First Nations Child and Family Caring Society, n.d.

19 For an excellent discussion on common biases that must be overcome by decision-makers relating to Indigenous governments, parents, and parenting, see Chapter 8 ("Addressing Biases against Indigenous Parents and Parenting") in Walkem (2020).

standards for CFS delivery relating to Indigenous children were included in the calls to action in the final report of Canada's Truth and Reconciliation Commission and reflect decades of research and Indigenous advocacy. The national standards establish a floor that is a good starting point for restoring right relations, including Indigenous jurisdiction in this crucial area. Bill C-92 sets out an array of options for Indigenous governments to exercise their inherent jurisdiction, including through the national standards. It also empowers all CFS workers and decision-makers to act on the acknowledgement of this jurisdiction immediately, through the standards. Building strong relationships of respect and deference will be required to uphold Indigenous legislation, as more and more Indigenous governing bodies exercise their legislative authority.

It is clear that rebuilding respectful relations is necessary to achieve the intent of Bill C-92 and to reach the outcomes that Indigenous children, families, and communities deserve. While the most explicit law-making jurisdiction provisions offer hope, non-legal obstructionist barriers remain and are actively being put in place by federal and provincial governments, that may force compromises to jurisdictional powers and stymie the Act's promise and effectiveness. Indigenous governments are wise to resist non-legal requirements proposed by federal or provincial governments when possible and to proceed with care and caution. With the national standards in force, Bill C-92 is already being interpreted in the courts. We must pay close attention to court decisions and the Act's interpretation. CFS providers have enormous discretion. Interpretations by the courts and the application of the national standards, along with Indigenous CFS statutes and decisions, will create precedents, so the outcome of individual cases can affect all Indigenous children in care and set future directions. If courts do not enforce the national standards and rely instead on past cases, they will inadvertently maintain the status quo.

Minimally, courts should always demand evidence from CFS providers that they have made reasonable efforts to maintain family placements and genuine and actual attempts to follow the placement priorities in every case. The onus must be on service providers to show how they have complied with the Act, not on Indigenous children, youth, families, and communities to have to advocate for their rights to be respected after the fact. In addition, whether through affidavit evidence, representations, statutory materials, or a combination of these sources, there should be no more cases where the courts do not have access to all crucial information about an Indigenous child's family and the community's views on what is in an Indigenous child's best interests. These views reflect lived experiences, local knowledge, and implicit or explicit Indigenous legal principles and are arguably necessary to fulfill the purposes of the Act. They should be given great weight. Courts and CFS providers must be cautious to avoid merely replacing the Indigenous governing body's analysis of an Indigenous child's best interests with their own or with that of a non-Indigenous government or care provider.

Often, CFS decision-makers face a choice between several bad options, and the unknowns are voluminous. Prior to Bill C-92, CFS or the provincial directors were seen as having the final authority. There is now a shift to respecting the authority of Indigenous governing bodies over children in care. Under the Act, they are now properly recognized as the experts on the needs of their children. There is nobody more invested in and affected by the long-term outcomes for Indigenous children than their own families and communities. There is no one who knows the relevant local circumstances and people better. Who better to determine what is in the best interest of the Indigenous child?

When we talk about the essence of Bill C-92, we often say, "It's about relationships, relationships, relationships." The residential schools were explicitly designed to destroy children's original relationships with their families, communities, and cultural "habits and modes of thought."[20] While these schools were still operating, the *Racine v Wood* decision dismissed the value of these key relationships, ostensibly for Indigenous children's "best interests," paving the way for CFS decision-makers to

20 Prime Minister Sir John A. Macdonald stated to the House of Commons in 1883, "When the school is on the reserve the child lives with its parents, who are savages; he is surrounded by savages, and though he may learn to read and write his habits, and training and mode of thought are Indian. He is simply a savage who can read and write. It has been strongly pressed on myself, as the head of the Department, that Indian children should be withdrawn as much as possible from the parental influence, and the only way to do that would be to put them in central training industrial schools where they will acquire the habits and modes of thought of white men" (in TRC, 2015, p. 2).

continue to leave so many "radically isolated"[21] and "fundamentally disoriented" (*Brown v Canada*, 2017) as adults. Relationships are lifelines. Bill C-92 is remedial; it requires the restoration of relationships at all levels. The national standards legislate the recognition and protection of Indigenous children's key relationships—with family members, community, language, and territory—as essential to their present and future well-being. Indigenous children's well-being is always in relation to the well-being of their families and communities, and vice versa. And relationships between non-Indigenous governments and Indigenous governments, on the one hand, and laws, on the other, have profound impacts on all of these relationships, creating conditions where relational well-being can either wither or flourish. Bill C-92 creates ample opportunities for restoring right relations, yet restoring right relations is an essential precondition for actualizing these opportunities.

Learning Questions

1. What are some actions that can assist non-Indigenous service providers and CFS agencies to build relationships with Indigenous communities?
2. How are you attached to your immediate family and extended family? How could those attachments work if you were in care?
3. What programs or services are in your area that could support pregnant mothers?
4. What are things you could do differently in your work or life to support Bill C-92?
5. What is your biggest takeaway from this chapter that you would share with others?

---

21 Walkem (2020) uses this term in her discussion about the outcomes of CFS time limits on Indigenous children in care: "From a long-term perspective, when an Indigenous child is put into care and their ties to their birth family and culture are severed, these children often age out of care with no replacement connections and with significant adverse consequences. They are left, at the end of a process meant to protect them, radically isolated" (p. 85).

References

An Act respecting First Nations, Inuit and Métis children, youth and families, SC 2019, c 24. https://laws.justice.gc.ca/eng/acts/F-11.73/page-1.html

Bennett, K. V. (2015). Cultural permanence for Indigenous children and youth: Reflections from a delegated Aboriginal agency in British Columbia. *First Peoples Child & Family Review*, *10*(1), 99-115.

Blackstock, C. (2011). The emergence of the breath of life theory. *Journal of Social Work Values and Ethics* *8*(1).

Brown v Canada (Attorney General), 2017 ONSC 251.

Canada, Parliament, Standing Senate Committee on Aboriginal Peoples, *Proceedings*, 42nd Parl, 1st Sess (2 May 2019). https://sencanada.ca/en/Content/SEN/Committee/421/appa/53ev-54748-e

Carrière, J. (2008). Maintaining identities: The soul work of adoption and Aboriginal children. *Pimatisiwin: A Journal of Aboriginal and Indigenous Community Health*, *6*(1), 75–78.

Chambers, L. (2016). *A legal history of adoption in Ontario, 1925–2015*. University of Toronto Press.

Choate, P. W., Kohler, T., Cloete, F., CrazyBull, B., Lindstrom, D., & Tatoulis, P. (2019). Rethinking Racine v Woods from a decolonizing perspective: Challenging the applicability of attachment theory to Indigenous families involved with child protection. *Canadian Journal of Law and Society/La Revue Canadienne Droit et Société*, *34*(1), 55–78.

Cowessess First Nation Miyo Pimatisowin Act. (2021, April 1). https://www.cowessessfn.com/wp-content/uploads/2021/04/Cowessess-First-Nation-Miyo-Pimatisowin-Act-Enacted-April-1-2021.pdf

Cowessess First Nation Coordination Agreement. (2021, July 6). [on file with authors]

Djuric, M. (2021, July 9). How Cowessess First Nation's historic child welfare agreement with Canada and Saskatchewan works. *CBC News*. https://www.cbc.ca/news/canada/saskatchewan/how-cowessess-first-nation-child-welfare-agreement-works-1.6095470

Felske-Durksen, C., & Friedland, H. (2020). *Bill C-92: Prenatal provision guide for health care professionals*. Wahkohtowin Law and Governance Lodge. https://www.ualberta.ca/wahkohtowin/media-library/data-lists-pdfs/bill-c-92-prenatal-health-care-guide.pdf

First Nations Child and Family Caring Society. (n.d.). *I am a witness: Tribunal timeline and documents*. Retrieved January 27, 2022, from https://fncaringsociety.com/i-am-witness-tribunal-timeline-and-documents

First Nations Child and Family Caring Society. (2021, July 20). *Looking for clarity in Canada's funding positions on C-92: Part I—The Caring Society position*. https://fncaringsociety.com/sites/default/files/c-92_info_sheet_july_20_final_part_1_v4.pdf

First Nation Child and Family Caring Society et al. v Attorney General of Canada, 2016 CHRT 2.

Fournier, S., & Crey, E. (1997). *Stolen from our embrace: The abduction of First Nations children and the restoration of Aboriginal communities*. Douglas & McIntyre.

Friedland, H. (2019). *Bill C-92: National standards guide for legal professionals*. Wahkohtowin Law and Governance Lodge. https://www.ualberta.ca/wahkohtowin/media-library/data-lists-pdfs/bill-c-92-national-standards-brief-for-legal.pdf

Friedland, H. (2021). Reference re Racine v Woods. In *Judicial tales retold: Reimagining Indigenous rights jurisprudence* (pp. 155–189). Canadian Native Law Reporter.

Friedland, H., & Lightning-Earle, K. (2020). *Bill C-92: Compliance guide for social workers and service providers*. Wahkohtowin Law and Governance Lodge. https://www.ualberta.ca/wahkohtowin/media-library/data-lists-pdfs/bill-c-92-compliance-guide-for-social-workers-and-service-providers.pdf

Grammond, S. (2018). Federal legislation on Indigenous child welfare in Canada. *Journal of Law and Social Policy*, 28(1), 132–151. https://digitalcommons.osgoode.yorku.ca/jlsp/vol28/iss1/7

Indigenous Services Canada. (n.d.). *Notices and requests related to An Act respecting First Nations, Inuit and Métis children, youth and families*. Retrieved March 9, 2022, from https://www.sac-isc.gc.ca/eng/1608565826510/1608565862367

Indigenous Services Canada. (2022). *Capacity-building funding for An Act Respecting First Nations, Inuit and Metis Children, Youth and Families for fiscal year 2021 to 2022*. https://www.sac-isc.gc.ca/eng/1612285531713/1612285570871

Metallic, N. (2018). A human right to self-government over First Nation child and family services and beyond: Implications of the Caring Society case. *Journal of Law and Social Policy, 28*(2), 4–41. https://digitalcommons.osgoode.yorku.ca/jlsp/vol28/iss2/2/

Metallic, N., Friedland, H., & Morales, S. (2019, July 4). *Bill C-92 implementation strategies*. Yellowhead Institute. https://yellowheadinstitute.org/wp-content/uploads/2019/07/post-c-92-community-implementation-strategies-factsheet.pdf

National Indian Child Welfare Association. (2017). *Attachment and Bonding in Indian Child Welfare: Summary of Research*. [NICWA summary of research]. https://www.nicwa.org/wp-content/uploads/2017/09/Attachment-and-bonding-NICWA-final-breif-092817.pdf

National Indian Child Welfare Association. (2018). *A guide to compliance with the Indian Child Welfare Act*. https://www.nicwa.org/wp-content/uploads/2018/01/Guide-to-ICWA-Compliance-2018.pdf

Native Counselling Services of Alberta. (n.d.). *My child's cultural connection plan notes*. https://d10k7k7mywg42z.cloudfront.net/assets/55e0d9f3c0d6714aa5015d08/CCP___Notes.pdf

Native Counselling Services of Alberta. (2015, August 28). *Raising the spirit of children in care*. http://ncsa.ca/blog/archives/2015/08/28/the-bears-den-raising-the-spirit-of-children-in-care/

Payne, R. (n.d.). *The power of cultural connection*. Adoptive Families Association of BC. Retrieved January 27, 2022, from https://www.bcadoption.com/resources/articles/power-cultural-connection

Pazderka, H., Desjarlais, B., Makokis, L., MacArthur, C., Steinhauer, S., Hapchyn, C. A., Hanson, T., Van Kuppeveld, N., & Bodor, R. (2014). Nitsiyihkâson: The brain science behind Cree teachings of early childhood attachment. *First Peoples Child & Family Review*, *9*(1), 53–65.

Racine v Woods, [1983] 2 SCR 173.

Sinclair, R. (2007). Identity lost and found: Lessons from the sixties scoop. *First Peoples Child & Family Review*, *3*(1), 65–82.

Smith, A. (2009). Aboriginal adoptions in Saskatchewan and British Columbia: An evolution to save or lose our children. *Canadian Journal of Family Law*, *25*, 297–367.

South Island Wellness Society. (n.d.). *Cultural connection planning*. Retrieved January 27, 2022, from http://www.siws.ca/siws-services-cultural-connections.html

Truth and Reconciliation Commission of Canada. (2015). *Canada's residential schools: Reconciliation. The final report of the Truth and Reconciliation Commission of Canada* (Vol. 6). McGill-Queen's University Press.

Turpel-Lafond, M. E. (2019). *Primer on practice shifts required by Canada's Act respecting First Nations, Inuit and Métis Children, Youth and Families Act*. Assembly of First Nations. http://irshdc.sites.olt.ubc.ca/files/2019/12/Policy_Primer_Report_ENG.pdf

United Nations General Assembly. 2007. United Nations declaration on the rights of Indigenous Peoples. A/RES/61/295. https://www.un.org/development/desa/indigenouspeoples/declaration-on-the-rights-of-indigenous-peoples.html

Walkem, A. (2020). *Wrapping our ways around them: Indigenous communities and child welfare guidebook* (2nd ed.). Law Foundation of British Columbia.

Wente, M., & Metallic, N. (2019). *What to do with C-92: Day 1: A guide for First Nations and other Indigenous governing bodies*. Wahkohtowin Law and Governance Lodge. https://www.ualberta.ca/wahkohtowin/media-library/data-lists-pdfs/what-to-do-with-c-92--day-1.pdf

CHAPTER 3

Colonial Threads of Fetal Alcohol Spectrum Disorder in Canada and Australia: Parallel Stories

Robyn Williams, Dorothy Badry, Don Fuchs, Yahya El-Lahib, Michael Doyle, Bernadette Iahtail, and Peter Choate

Introduction

Children with Fetal Alcohol Spectrum Disorder (FASD) are disproportionately represented in the child welfare and youth justice system in both Canada and Australia. Canada has a fairly well-evolved system that varies across provinces and territories in responding to FASD through screening assessment, diagnosis, and case planning. By contrast, in Australia there is limited awareness of and training in FASD in systems such as child welfare and justice, and "most children in care were not likely to be assessed for FASD and, as a consequence, receive no access to early interventions to improve their quality of life" (Williams & Badry, 2020, p. 113). We raise discourse on FASD as a disability that remains unrecognized and often forgotten in the child welfare population. FASD

Suggested Citation: Williams, R., Badry, D., Fuchs, D., El-Lahib, Y., Doyle, M., Iahtail, B., & Choate, P. (2022). Colonial threads of Fetal Alcohol Spectrum Disorder in Canada and Australia: Parallel stories. In J. Albert, D. Badry, D. Fuchs, P. Choate, M. Bennett, & H. Montgomery (Eds.), *Walking together: The future of Indigenous child welfare on the prairies* (pp. 47–69). Regina, SK: University of Regina Press.

is one of the consequences of the colonization of the Indigenous people of Canada—which includes three distinct groups: First Nations, Inuit, and Métis people—and the Aboriginal and Torres Strait Islander peoples of Australia, along with Indigenous Peoples in many other countries with similar colonial histories. In this chapter we focus on Canada and Australia and write as scholars who are deeply concerned about the well-being of children and youth with FASD and the challenges they face in the child welfare system.

The focus of this chapter is on the shared colonial experiences, parallels, and threads related to the impact of colonization on Indigenous people in both countries. We position FASD as one of the outcomes of colonization. There is a strong relationship between colonization and disability in terms of how Indigenous cultures and social structures are disciplined, managed, and controlled in ways that facilitate the operation and maintenance of the "colonial nation-state" (Soldatic, 2015, p. 54).

This control has historically also been extended to cultural and social structures. Grounding this discussion in a critical disability framework and relying on critical approaches to interrogate coloniality, we advance the claim that FASD requires a rightful place in the literature as a way to interrogate how disability and Indigeneity have been exploited to facilitate colonial practices and maintain colonial discourses that typecast disabled Indigenous people. Drawing on contemporary literature in the disability studies field (Chisholm et al., 2017; Grech & Soldatic, 2015; Hollinsworth, 2013; Meekosha, 2011; Soldatic, 2013, 2015), we view FASD as a consequence of a colonial agenda to subdue and coerce Indigenous peoples through the introduction of alcohol in both Canada and Australia. Colonization plays a key role in relation to the "production of impairment and disability" (Tulich et al., 2020, p. 3).

The scientific facts are that alcohol use during pregnancy can lead to significant problems for the developing fetus including the risk of a permanent alcohol-related disability: FASD (Cook et al. 2016). While FASD is a diagnosable disability, it is all too often not diagnosed, especially among Indigenous people. There are limited diagnostic resources in rural and remote locations in both Canada and Australia. Hayes (1998) and Hayes et al. (2014) have explored the complexities of alcohol use at harmful levels and highlight the need to consider "the social, historical and political background and the cultural aspects of drinking in order to begin to introduce prevention and early intervention strategies to address alcohol use and pregnancy" (Hayes et al., 2014, p. 360).

Hartz and McGrath (2017) indicate that in Canada, Australia, and New Zealand, Indigenous mothers are younger and have a higher likelihood of living in remote communities with fewer resources than non-Indigenous mothers. FASD has frequently been excluded from, minimized in, and dismissed from discourse on disability and in child welfare practice, positioning it further to the margins of mainstream disability services (Choate & Badry, 2019; Gilbert et al., 2021). However, FASD is a complex phenomenon because it has a social aspect linked to the experience of trauma that is rarely recognized or talked about. Hayes et al. (2014) highlight the need to consider FASD, alcohol use, and pregnancy within the context of a life cycle and to recognize the role history plays.

The Silence of Undiagnosed FASD and First Nations People

Unrecognized and undiagnosed FASD has tremendous consequences in the life of an individual. In another tragic outcome of colonization, the voices of individuals living with FASD are rarely heard and their stories seldom told. Critically, more important stories must be shared and told of the many who have lived with undiagnosed and unsupported FASD. Using an Indigenous epistemology (Wilson, 2001, 2008; Hart, 2010), it is the telling of stories across generations that provides teachings and protection for members of the community and taps into what Wilson (2001) calls relational accountability.

The stories told, similar to the dreamtime stories, have purpose and provide wisdom and knowledge that are shared from one generation to another. Bennett (2016) affirms that listening to the storyteller involves deep listening and respect. The sharing of stories facilitates a genuine transfer of knowledge that is respectful to Indigenous people (Geia et al., 2013). Williams, a co-author of this chapter and a Noongar woman and researcher, was trusted to record and share the stories of FASD among the Noongar people of Western Australia. Stories are more likely to be shared among Indigenous people, particularly if they are of the same nation. Williams has also experienced FASD in her own family and shares the story of an older cousin/brother who lived his life with undiagnosed FASD and was lovingly called Maaja Man.

Maaja Man

Maaja was an Aboriginal man born in the early 1960s in a rural town in Western Australia and raised by his grandmother until her death in 1968, at which point he was taken into the foster care system. Maaja was the third consecutive generation to be removed. His paternal grandmother was removed around 1910, and Maaja's father was removed around 1945, and then Maaja in 1968. Maaja had four siblings, who were also removed. One of his brothers became a father around 1992 and Baby D was born with severe FASD*, microcephaly, and small kidneys, which would tragically claim Baby D's life at the age of three. The baby's father likely also had* FASD *that went unrecognized. Maaja had the physical facial features of* FASD *and microcephaly but there would be no recognition or identification of his disability as he went through life. And even in death, Maaja, age fifty-one, and Baby D at age three, their alcohol-related disabilities stayed unrecognized. The only protection Maaja ever experienced came from his extended Aboriginal family and community. He struggled with alcohol addiction and his behaviour, which was quite immature and characteristic of his disability, got him into problems. He experienced numerous serious assaults throughout his life owing to the vulnerability of his unrecognized disability. One cold winter night in Perth, Maaja was drinking on the streets and passed out, only to wake up and find himself in the morgue at the hospital. He found his way to his Aunty's home and, although quite angry at having been put in the morgue, would not make a formal complaint. Maaja got in trouble with the law and his time in prison exposed him, and he came out of prison* HIV *positive. His strengths were multiple and his love of caring for his younger family members was one of the most important parts of his life. He would clean and cook for his family. Maaja struggled with alcoholism and drugs, and no therapeutic program could assist with his disability. His close family never quite understood Maaja but lovingly accepted his quirks, and he spent his life largely itinerant. In the final years of his life, his family were slowly made aware of* FASD *and the light bulb was turned on for this Aboriginal family. His family deeply regretted that they had not known about his disability, and in his later years he was diagnosed* *with mental health problems that saw him, for the first time in his life, in his own home. He would boast that he lived like a king, eating fresh kangaroo meat and fish that he caught down by the jetty. Maaja was a brilliant and talented artist but poverty, homelessness, and his disability prevented him from reaching his creative potential. With awareness of FASD, his family would have strongly and consistently advocated for him and seen that his itinerant lifestyle was not his choice but a consequence of his unsupported and unrecognized disability. His sister/cousin Robyn dedicated her thesis to Maaja's memory in 2018* (Williams, 2018).

Why Talk about FASD?

It is time to talk about FASD and to recognize it as a complex disability that is rooted in colonialism, which sets the stage for the experiences of Indigenous people in both Canada and Australia. In this chapter, we suggest that colonialism was a framework for historical and genocidal colonial practices that targeted Indigenous communities with the aim to take control of Indigenous Peoples and their lands (Wolfe, 2006). We argue that colonization in both Canada and Australia used various forms of disabling effects to maintain control of Indigenous Peoples and their lands (Morgensen, 2013). Indeed, the colonial backdrop is that children were forcibly removed and stolen from their families in both countries, which has had and continues to have dire social and economic consequences. One of the critical challenges in both understanding and preventing FASD is the prevailing discourse of historical trauma and its consequences. The consequences of colonization have played a critical role in the narrative about FASD that cannot be dismissed. We offer some case examples of FASD in both Canada and Australia to help demonstrate the contemporary ways that colonial practices continue to shape everyday realities of disabled Indigenous children and youth.

Case Examples

These brief case examples have been shared with us anecdotally or emerged from reports of the Office of the Child and Youth Advocate in Alberta, Canada. They highlight the risks and vulnerabilities of children and youth living with prenatal alcohol exposure. FASD is a disability that requires screening, assessment, diagnosis, and intervention over the life course. These young people were all involved with the child welfare system.

Australia

A young Aboriginal boy in Australia with a diagnosis of FASD died after being attacked by a crocodile in a remote area. He had been attempting to run away from foster care and return to his family.

A fifteen-year-old teenager with undiagnosed FASD was visiting his infant son and fourteen-year-old girlfriend at the hospital in Bunbury. During this visit the infant suffered a fractured skull and died. The youth's lawyer advocated for a referral for an FASD assessment and the teenage boy was subsequently diagnosed, which was a mitigating factor in his sentencing (Freckelton, 2017).

Canada

Darian was in child welfare care, and he died from injuries he sustained in a car accident in a stolen vehicle. He had been diagnosed with FASD at age twelve, and it was identified in the report of the Child Advocate of Alberta that he was at high risk of involvement with the justice system (OCYA Mandatory Reviews into Child Deaths, 2019).

The examples of the boys in Australia and Canada identify the concern that children with FASD are at risk. Working with children and youth with FASD requires specialized knowledge that includes information about safeguarding in the community.

The case of Darian was shared by a community agency director and advocate working for Indigenous youth. In a meeting held at a child welfare office, it was mentioned about "43 times" in front of this fourteen-year-old Indigenous youth's mother that he has FASD. Iahtail, acting as an advocate for the child and the mother, said, "*Stop! Stop telling me he has FASD. That does not tell me anything about who this young man is or what he can do. Tell me, what can he do? I don't want to hear about what he can't do because he has FASD.*"

In a report on child deaths in the province of Alberta, the story of Sophia is shared. Sophia was three months old when she passed away. At that time, she was receiving child intervention services through a custody agreement and placed in a foster home. She was found unresponsive in her crib. The Office of the Child and Youth Advocate (2019) found that "Sophia had additional needs because she was affected by her mother's substance use during her pregnancy. Infants, like Sophia, require additional supports to have their needs met" (p. 7). Further, the Child and Youth Advocate made a single recommendation: "Child Intervention Services should review and revise their policies so that the additional needs of substance-affected infants are identified and appropriate resources are provided" (p. 7).

Debriefing the Case Examples: Contextualizing the Disability

What is evident in the case examples and the narrative of Maaja is the risks associated with FASD, particularly when the diagnosis is not recognized and not supported. The stigma and lack of empathy experienced by families of children with FASD are often accompanied by a general lack of understanding about the effects of FASD, which is often not a visible disability. This lack of understanding can lead to exclusion from community and peers and result in social isolation for children and parents. Interventions need to happen early in life, but those can only unfold in a system that recognizes and values the need for screening and diagnosis of disabilities and is aware of the harms associated with prenatal alcohol exposure. Protocols that evaluate for FASD should be part of standard practice in child welfare, disability, and justice services, particularly when we see the consequences of undiagnosed and unsupported children with FASD.

These narratives of risk can be transformed into narratives of resiliency when supports are put in place to wrap community around individuals through the provision of FASD-informed care. Many children and youth benefit from FASD diagnosis where this is available, as it is critical in the design and delivery of services for that individual. We must strive to have similar access to FASD screening, assessment, and diagnosis across all service systems in both Canada and Australia and to create pathways for access to services that can make a difference between life and death.

The Unfolding Legacy of Colonization

The legacy of colonization in Canada and Australia continues to wreak havoc. It is sustained by racism and, more specifically, by unprecedented numbers of Indigenous children in the care of the state. "The unfolding legacy of colonization continues to be mirrored in high rates of incarceration, suicide, substance use disorders, and child welfare involvement in the Indigenous population in Australia" (Williams & Badry, 2020, p. 112). The need exists to decolonize FASD and to recognize its connection to inherited disparity, a significant aspect of the colonial agenda in both countries. We will draw out the parallels between Canada and Australia, through an examination of existing literature, and offer insight into the complexities of FASD. Our goal is to examine the colonial threads of FASD informed by an Indigenous lens.

What do we mean by "colonial threads"? We are referring to threads that have been interwoven throughout the history of the relationship between colonial forces and the original peoples of the land. For the purposes of this chapter, we have identified what we consider five threads of colonialism in child welfare: child removal; Western approaches to child protection; paternalism; racism; and the dispossession of children from their parents and their communities, which is strongly tied to the dispossession of land experienced by the Indigenous peoples of Canada and Aboriginal peoples of Australia.

Fortier and Wong (2019) clearly state that the historical role of the Indian agent was replaced by social workers who played a critical role in the colonial agenda of child removal, particularly in the Sixties Scoop in Canada, which continued to unfold for decades. This position is affirmed by Blackstock (2009). Neu and Graham (2006) identify that a critical result of the colonial agenda in the period from 1860 to 1900 in Canada was the "disabling of indigenous agency" (p. 73), primarily through government control of financial and economic affairs. A similar history of dispossession of land exists in Canada, Australia, the United States, and New Zealand as a result of massive European migration (Buhr, 2011) and the sudden decline in the Indigenous population caused by introduced diseases and direct acts of genocide (Sherwood & Geia, 2014; Tatz, 2001; Australia, National Inquiry into the Separation of Aboriginal and Torres Strait Islander Children from Their Families, 1997).

A small body of literature has emerged on colonial accounting practices and how these positioned Indigenous people for poverty (Buhr, 2011; Gallhofer & Chew, 2000; Greer, 2009; Neu & Graham, 2006). These processes, which remain influential today, have played a key role in the ways that Indigenous people in both Canada and Australia have been economically and socially disadvantaged and their lives managed and controlled by states and social discourses (Lee & Ferrer, 2014; Wolfe, 2006).

In both Canada and Australia, Indigenous children and youth are overrepresented in child welfare and in the youth justice system and continue to be impacted by traumatizing historical events such as the residential schools and the Stolen Generations. It is in the space of the residential schools in Canada and the Stolen Generations of Australia, under the guise of education and labour force development, where childhood became colonized. Alexander (2016) points out that historical accounts of the lives of children are rare in Canadian history, which contributes to a broad "social forgetting" (p. 398) regarding the experiences of Indigenous people in Canada. Jacobs (2014) identifies the common histories of child removal post–World War II by the child welfare system experienced by Indigenous Peoples in Canada, the United States, and Australia. Gatwiri et al. (2021) clearly link the assimilation policies of the Australian government to the overrepresentation of Indigenous children in out-of-home care in that country. Regarding First Nations and Aboriginal and Torres Strait Islanders children, Blackstock et al. (2020) indicate that they are overrepresented in out-of-home care in both Canada and Australia and highlight that these children are the "most sacred members of our societies as they represent the perpetuation of Indigenous peoples" (p. 2).

Indigenous children continue to be placed in out-of-home care in record numbers in both countries, and this leads to the identification of colonization and prevailing colonial attitudes in child welfare as the common denominator in this process. The *Family Matters Report* (Family Matters, 2021) on the overrepresentation of Aboriginal and Torres Strait Islander children in the child welfare system identifies the need for self-determination, cultural authority, and connection to culture as critical in stemming child removal. That families have access to supports and targeted services and that Aboriginal people in Australia have "control over decisions that affect their children" (p. 9) are key building blocks. The report recommends that "law, policy and practice in child and family welfare are culturally safe and responsive" and "governments and services are accountable to Aboriginal and Torres Strait Islander people" (p. 10). It also states that a major challenge in Australia regarding out-of-home care is the lack of a "uniform definition of disability" (p. 85), and much work needs to be done to better understand this population in the child welfare system.

Indigenous children with disabilities face many challenges when placed in Indigenous or non-Indigenous foster homes including, centrally, two competing perspectives in understanding the notion of disability. The definition and perception of disability within Indigenous communities is different from that of mainstream Canada. Consequently, it can be difficult to reconcile traditional Indigenous teachings with contemporary political realities. Further, the National Aboriginal Community Controlled Health Organisation (NACCHO, 2021) in Australia offers a broad definition of Aboriginal health that refers not just to the physical well-being of an individual but also to the social, emotional, and cultural well-being of the whole community, in which everyone is able to achieve their full potential as a human being, thereby bringing about the total well-being of their community. It is a whole-of-life view and includes the cyclical concept of life–death–life.

Within traditional Indigenous Cree teachings, disabilities are considered "special gifts or powers that enable people to communicate with the spiritual world" (Dion, 2017, p. 5). Dion points out that the reality for Indigenous children with disabilities who are living on-reserve is often "social, physical, and economic exclusion, discrimination, and racism, nothing that supports a belief about being 'special'" (p. 6). This reflects the challenges faced in providing equitable disability services for Indigenous people living in their home communities.

Non-Indigenous approaches to disability are based on the medical model of disability, which lodges the disability within the child, who is seen as broken, deficient, and in need of fixing (UN General Assembly, 2008). This approach does not take into account the socioeconomic, cultural, and attitudinal barriers that lead to discrimination, exclusion, and oppression of Indigenous children with disabilities identified by Dion (2017). In Canada, the federal First Nations and Inuit Health Branch policy and programs tend to view children and youth with disabilities as having medical conditions; their supports and services—and eligibility for supports and services—are based on narrowly defined medical diagnostic categories.

Jordan's Principle was named after Jordan River Anderson, a child with complex medical problems who was cared for in hospital for his entire, short life of five years (Blackstock, 2016; see also Chapter 1, this volume). The program known as Jordan's Principle, developed in Canada through the work of the First Nations Child and Family Caring Society, provides financial benefits with a goal of minimizing any provincial/territorial/federal jurisdictional disputes over the funding of supports for First Nations, Inuit, and Métis children who are medically fragile, are ill, or have disabilities. These medicalized approaches tend to ignore not only the rights of children with disabilities but also the social determinants of health. They serve to ration supports and services while ignoring cultural and socio-economic conditions that serve to greatly handicap, oppress, and marginalize children with disabilities, greatly impeding their development outcomes (Dion, 2017; McKenzie & Kufeldt, 2011). Moreover, medicalized approaches to FASD and other neuro-developmental disabilities tend to cut off children and youth from their familial, cultural, and community supports, further isolating and stigmatizing children with disabilities.

Key Historical Points of Colonization

Building on the above discussion, we assert that both Canada and Australia have experienced similar pathways in the processes of colonization and child removal. Key historical points in the history of colonization in both Canada and Australia contributed to similar pathways in the experiences of children subject to removal. These include the Royal Proclamation of 1763 by the British Crown, to promote the establishment of treaties and the surrender of lands through eleven treaties in the 1800s in Canada. Also in Canada, the *Indian Act* of 1876 established residential schools, whose primary goal was assimilation; 132 schools were established (operating between 1857 and 1996) and over 150,000 children were required to attend these schools. In Western Australia, the *Industrial Schools Act* of 1874 was the first law allowing the Australian colonial government to legally remove children. Further, the *Aborigines Protection Act* of 1886 "gave wide powers to the Board and Protectors to involve themselves in the lives of all Aboriginal people in Western Australia, including the care, custody and education of Aboriginal children. The Act also empowers Magistrates to apprentice Aboriginal children to work to the age of 21 years" (Find & Connect, n.d.). The *Aborigines Act* of 1905 had the agenda of "protection, control and segregation of Aboriginal people...

under the control of a Chief Protector" (South West Aboriginal Land & Sea Council, n.d.-b), and the *Natives (Citizenship Rights) Act* 1944 gave authority for Aboriginal people in Australia to apply for citizenship, which could just as easily be removed.

The *Indian Act* in Canada prohibited alcohol sales in First Nations from 1884 until 1985. In Australia, Aboriginal people were prohibited from purchasing alcohol between 1886 and 1963 (*Aborigines Act*, 1886), and this prohibition has long influenced social patterns of alcohol consumption. In the 1950s in Australia, the Child Welfare Department became the only authority able to remove children; proof of child neglect or delinquency warranted removal through the courts, which often happened with limited evidence of such concerns (South West Aboriginal Land & Sea Council, n.d.-a). However, the Child Welfare Department and the courts were prone to interpret the different cultural practices of Aboriginal child-rearing as neglect.

In Canada, June 21 was established as National Aboriginal Day (now National Indigenous Peoples Day) in 1996. In Australia, the report of the National Inquiry into the Separation of Aboriginal and Torres Strait Islander Children from Their Families, known as the Bringing them Home Report, was tabled on May 26, 1997; the following year, May 26 was designated as Sorry Day in recognition of the Stolen Generations. A decade later, on February 13, 2008, Australian Prime Minister Kevin Rudd issued a national apology for the policies of forced child removal and assimilation, and on June 11 of the same year, the Government of Canada formally apologized to all survivors of the residential schools and made a commitment to redress the problems through the Truth and Reconciliation Commission, led by Senator Murray Sinclair. The United Nations had adopted its Declaration on the Rights of Indigenous Peoples in 2007.

The dispossession of both land and children were key components of the colonial agenda, and the removal of children meant that their ties to culture were severed. Further, authorities were aggressive in their taking of children, and many families had to go to extremes to not have their children taken. Stories of resistance and finding ways to continue to practice culture are found in narratives in both Canada and Australia. Missions and settlements in Western Australia were established and many children ran away; the iconic 2002 film *Rabbit-Proof Fence*, based on the true stories of two Aboriginal girls, provided one such resistance narrative.

Resistance became a strategy of keeping culture and maintaining connection to the land. In Australia, in some cases, children were not removed from families if their parents were working doing farm labour—working for flour and sugar instead of for pay (Human Rights and Equal Opportunity Commission, 2006). For those who were removed, relationships and roles became complex.

Removal caused ruptures in relationships, and its impact through separation of siblings was difficult, if not impossible, to repair. The disruption of sibling relationships had a profound impact on children who were removed. For example, the primary role of being a big sister did not always have the same meaning, after being removed, among blood relatives in the mission, although if siblings were in the same mission the bonds may remain intact. But new bonds were formed in the missions, and a big sister often took on that role with many younger children in the mission, sometimes displacing her blood relatives. This played out over and over. However, kinship systems play an important role in Aboriginal culture and many children formed strong bonds with others who were also forcefully relocated to these places far from home.

In Canada in 1967, a twelve-year-old Anishinaabe boy named Chanie Wenjack, from the Marten Falls Reserve, was found dead on the Canadian National Railway tracks after he had run away from a residential school he was forced to go to in northern Ontario. Essentially, "he fell victim to Canada's colonization of Indigenous Peoples" (Gord Downie & Chanie Wenjack Fund, n.d.). He had died of exposure. A subsequent inquiry suggested that "the Indian education system causes tremendous emotional and adjustment problems" (Adams, 1967). Chanie's legacy lives on through the Gord Downie & Chanie Wenjack Fund in Ontario, Canada, which supports creating pathways for reconciliation between Indigenous and non-Indigenous people. *Secret Path* is the title of a book, an album, and an animated film documenting Chanie's life, and funds from all these endeavours support the work of the National Centre for Truth and Reconciliation at the University of Manitoba (see https://secretpath.ca).

The removal of children was identified as cultural genocide by the 2015 Truth and Reconciliation Commission (Blackstock, 2019). Blackstock has been a prevailing voice in the advocacy for Indigenous children in Canada and has consistently identified the failure of the Canadian government in the provision of "culturally based responses to address persistent poverty, addictions, and housing issues" (p. 7). Gatwiri et al. (2021) identify the intentional under-resourcing of Aboriginal child welfare programs in Australia. The parallels between Canada and Australia require advocacy to change a child welfare system that has consistently failed the Indigenous people and facilitated the operation of state control of their bodies, cultures, and land in both countries. As such, service providers within helping professions need to interrogate the intersection between colonization and the operation of state control over Indigenous communities, to support Indigenous calls for resistance, and to facilitate a meaningful truth and reconciliation process that accounts for historical and contemporary manifestation of colonial practices (Fortier & Wong, 2019; Lee & Ferrer, 2014).

Alcohol Use

The introduction of alcohol to the Indigenous peoples of Canada and Australia also served the colonial agenda. While alcohol had been available prior to colonization, there was not mass production or storage, and Indigenous home-brewed alcohol was less potent; it was brewed for a specific reason with strict cultural rules for use and supply was limited. The introduction of colonial alcohol, which was produced and stored in mass quantity, served as part of the colonial agenda to control the Indigenous peoples of Canada. Prohibition of alcohol existed in both countries, and this contributed to problems related to alcohol use. The need exists to address a critical health concern: alcohol use and pregnancy. Alcohol use during pregnancy is deeply stigmatized. Reid et al. (2019) highlight the benefits of midwifery care in which midwives are trained on the issue of alcohol use and pregnancy and suggest these relationships are beneficial in FASD prevention. As Soldatic (2015) asserts in her discussion of the connection between disability and Indigeneity in Australia, the use of the notion of "*re*production" (p. 55) facilitates the control of Indigenous and disabled women's fertility. Such state-led control contributes to the marginalization experiences of disabled and Indigenous women. The interconnectedness between FASD and state control over Indigenous and disabled women's bodies is a clear indication of dominant colonial practices that need to be interrogated and challenged.

Going Forward: Return to Community

In the critical report *Revitalizing Culture and Healing: Indigenous Approaches to FASD Prevention: Revitalizing Culture and Healing*, Van Bibber (2019) states, "It has become increasingly urgent that the legacy of colonization demands a wholistic socio-economic cultural and political response based on Indigenous Rights and Title." Also important is a "cultural health framework," she continues, that would necessarily include "Indigenous research, traditional knowledge and healing, bi-directional capacity building, and wraparound programming. Surrounding a mother and child with care and compassion during the beginning of new life is a powerful path toward addressing, in tangible ways, unfulfilled justice for our people" (p. 2). Recognizing the history of colonization and its legacy, Van Bibber highlights the need for trauma-informed responses where the community is central in taking responsibility for supporting the mother and child.

Revitalizing Culture and Healing also identifies a number of core principles for advancing Indigenous wellness and FASD prevention: community-led approaches, culture-driven approaches, social and structural determinants of health, wraparound support, strengths-based approaches, and life course approaches. Other core aspects focusing on the cultural soundness of a program include whether the program welcomes all; reaches out to women most at risk for substance use during pregnancy; integrates ancestors, Elders, Knowledge Keepers, culture, and language; and follows community protocols. This model offers a critical, well-informed approach to addressing FASD prevention and supporting Indigenous women on issues such as alcohol and pregnancy with a focus on strength and resilience.

Moving forward, there is a great and continuous need to develop culturally and community anchored in-care resources for Indigenous children and youth. Indigenous children are greatly overrepresented in the child welfare system and often come into care with multiple disabilities (Dion, 2017). They are at greater risk for coming into care and for further maltreatment while in care because of frequent moves, a lack of trained social workers, and a lack of culturally appropriate resources in addition to the stigma, racism, and discrimination they face in their schools and their communities.

All children with disabilities in care require safe, stable placements on which they can rely for the support necessary to grow and thrive without the fear of being abruptly taken and replaced in less secure settings. Current models of permanency planning are evolving beyond the traditional colonial models. They are beginning to take into account cultural connections and the great need for support and services for foster parents or kinship parents and other forms of open adoption to care for children coming into care with developmental disabilities. Unfortunately, the development and application of new models of permanent foster/kinship care and open adoption of children with disabilities have not kept pace with the rapidly growing number of children in care. Many children with disabilities in care still fall through the cracks in the child welfare system because of the inconsistency of agency policy and practice, high worker turnover, and the limited amount of training for social workers who work with children and families with disabilities (Blackstock, 2012; TRC, 2015; Dion, 2017). In addition, children in care are continually at risk of trauma and mental health issues such as depression and attachment disorders, sometimes because of maltreatment they experience while in care. This can be attributed to inadequate support from social workers, insufficient financial support, and a lack of training of foster parents, which often result in placement breakdowns and frequent moves for these children (Burnside, 2012).

The oppressive colonial standards, policies, and practices of child welfare structures are slowly changing. Innovative, culturally anchored practices are emerging as Indigenous peoples take on more control of child welfare services for the growing numbers of Indigenous children at risk of coming into care. In addition, there is an increasing awareness of the negative impact of taking children away from their families and community and cultural supports and of the trauma resulting from the lack of forever caring family placements (Choate et al., 2021). However, agencies struggle with the growing demand for and underfunding of supports and services to meet the demands of the growing number of Indigenous children in care. Furthermore, Indigenous children continue to face many societal barriers that have a deleterious effect on their developmental outcomes. Issues of poverty, racism, and stigma continue to perpetuate and exacerbate the oppression of Indigenous children and youth in care and contribute significantly to their poor developmental outcomes, cumulative disadvantages, and social exclusion. The need exists to provide services that are located within communities and in places that are accessible to people in need of supports.

A primary example of community-based FASD services from an Indigenous perspective is found in the Alberta Métis Settlements FASD Network, which "exists to enhance the capacity of our Communities to prevent Fetal Alcohol Spectrum Disorder (FASD) and support those impacted by FASD through coordinated planning, collaboration, education, service delivery and advocacy" (Métis Settlements FASD Network, n.d., 12). The work of the Métis community in collaboration with the Alberta FASD Service Networks to create a culturally connected program and offer services in rural and remote communities in the province stands as a sound example of authentic supports that are grounded in the community. The Métis Settlements FASD Network website is vibrant and easily accessible and provides a regular newsletter, links to Facebook pages, and many resources. The network provides services to 115 people in the community and provides prevention and intervention services through mentoring; FASD-related training for the community, parents, and caregivers; and referrals for assessment and diagnosis. The communities involved include Buffalo Lake, Gift Lake, East Prairie, Kikino, Elizabeth, Paddle Prairie, Fishing Lake, and Peavine Métis Settlement.

Services that are grounded in the community support traditional parenting practices and recognize the numerous strengths in Indigenous communities. As Van Bibber (2019) notes, "Guiding principles of respect in community-based approaches reflect Indigenous teachings that: we are one with the land, water, animals, plants, each other, and all parts of the circle of life; that those around a pregnant or mothering woman take responsibility for ensuring their good health; that the gifts of each child must be nurtured to the fullest" (p. 4). Several of the Alberta network programs provide services in rural, remote, and First Nation communities in all corners of the province.

Conclusion

The number of Aboriginal children in child welfare care is one of the most challenging problems in both Australia and Canada reflecting the long-standing colonial history that contributed to the forced removal of children into state care. The legacy of colonialism is still unfolding, and untold generations have suffered, and continue to suffer, from intergenerational trauma associated with the Stolen Generations, the residential schools, and the Sixties Scoop. The narratives of children identified in the case examples from both countries call us to recognize their deep need for supports and services that are FASD informed and to learn from their experiences. The story of Maaja, as shared by Robyn, reflects the untold story of many individuals who were part of the Stolen Generations and whose trauma continues to resonate across the land of Australia. The colonial history of both countries has so deeply impacted the lives of many and necessitates shared responsibility in responding to FASD. It is our responsibility to share the untold stories of generations past and present, to shine a light on human experience, and to expose the discourse of disability that is embedded in colonial threads.

This work is about accountability for future generations, reciprocity, relationship, and recognition that FASD is one consequence of the trauma associated with the history of colonization. The words of Natalie Clark (2018) at the beginning of her doctoral dissertation resonate deeply in our work on decolonizing FASD:

> *accountable to the not-yet-born who are waiting*
> *accountable to dreams accountable to you accountable to Elders*
> *accountable to truth-telling*
> *accountable to the little people*
> *accountable to ancient transformers*
> *accountable to this moment.* (p. v)

Learning Questions

1. What are the common colonial threads that exist in Canada and Australia?
2. What did you learn from the story of Maaja Man? Why is this story important? Why is it critical to decolonize FASD?
3. What can you do to promote prevention of FASD in your community?
4. What creative and holistic ways can you think of to promote healing, health, and prevention in ways that honour the lived experiences of mothers, children, and families?

5. Reflect on the 'accountable' statements above. What do these statements mean to you?

References

The Aborigines Protection Act 1886 (1887–1890). No. DCCCCXII (912). Retrieved March 17, 2022, from http://www5.austlii.edu.au/au/legis/vic/hist_act/tapa1886265/

Adams, I. (1967, February 1). The lonely death of Chanie Wenjack. *Maclean's*. https://www.macleans.ca/society/the-lonely-death-of-chanie-wenjack/

Alexander, K. (2016). Childhood and colonialism in Canadian history. *History Compass*, *14*(9), 397–406.

Australia. National Inquiry into the Separation of Aboriginal and Torres Strait Islander Children from Their Families. (1997). *Bringing them home: Report of the national inquiry into the separation of Aboriginal and Torres Strait Islander children from their families*. Commonwealth of Australia. https://humanrights.gov.au/sites/default/files/content/pdf/social_justice/bringing_them_home_report.pdf

Bennett, M. (2016). *Digital storytelling with First Nations emerging adults in extensions of care and transitioning from care in Manitoba* [Unpublished doctoral dissertation]. University of Manitoba. https://mspace.lib.umanitoba.ca/xmlui/handle/1993/31252?show=full

Blackstock, C. (2009). The occasional evil of angels: Learning from the experiences of Aboriginal peoples and social work. *First Peoples Child & Family Review*, *4*(1), 28–37. https://doi.org/10.7202/1069347ar

Blackstock, C. (2012) Jordan's Principle: Canada's broken promise to First Nations children? *Paediatrics & Child Health*, *17*(7), 368–370. https://doi.org/10.1093/pch/17.7.368

Blackstock, C. (2016). Toward the full and proper implementation of Jordan's Principle: An elusive goal to date. *Paediatrics & Child Health*, *21*(5), 245–246. https://doi.org/10.1093/pch/21.5.245

Blackstock, C. (2019). Indigenous child welfare legislation: A historical change or another paper tiger? *First Peoples Child & Family Review*, *14*(1), 5–8. https://fpcfr.com/index.php/FPCFR/article/view/367

Blackstock, C., Bamblett, M., & Black, C. (2020). Indigenous ontology, international law and the application of the Convention to the over-representation of Indigenous children in out of home care in Canada and Australia. *Child Abuse & Neglect*, *110*, (Pt.1), Article 104587. https://doi.org/10.1016/j.chiabu.2020.104587

Buhr, N. (2011). Indigenous peoples in the accounting literature: Time for a plot change and some Canadian suggestions. *Accounting History*, *16*(2), 139–160. https://doi.org/10.1177%2F1032373210396334

Burnside, L. (2012). *Youth in care with complex needs: Special report for the Office of the Children's Advocate Winnipeg*. Office of the Children's Advocate,

Manitoba. https://youthrex.com/wp-content/uploads/2019/02/Youth-with-Complex-Needs-Report-final-2.pdf

Chisholm, R., Tulich, T., & Blagg, H. (2017). Indigenous young people with foetal alcohol spectrum disorders: The Convention on the Rights of Persons with Disabilities and reform to the law governing fitness to stand trial in Western Australia. *Law in Context, 35*(2), 85–107

Choate, P., & Badry, D. (2019). Stigma as a dominant discourse in fetal alcohol spectrum disorder. *Advances in Dual Diagnosis, 12*(1/2), 36–52. https://doi.org/10.1108/ADD-05-2018-0005

Choate, P., Bear Chief, R., Lindstrom, D., & CrazyBull, B. (2021). Sustaining cultural genocide—A look at Indigenous children in non-Indigenous placement and the place of judicial decision making—A Canadian example. *Laws, 10*(3), 59. https://doi.org/10.3390/laws10030059

Clark, N. (2018). *Cu7 me7 q'wele'wu-kt. "Come on, let's go berry- picking": Revival of Secwepemc wellness approaches for healing Indigenous child and youth experiences of violence* [Unpublished doctoral dissertation]. Simon Fraser University. https://summit.sfu.ca/item/18083

Cook, J. L., Green, C. R., Lilley, C. M., Anderson, S. M., Baldwin, M. E., Chudley, A. E., Conry, J. L., LeBlanc, N., Loock, C. A., Lutke, J., Mallon, B. F., McFarlane, A., Temple, V. K., & Rosales, T. (2016). Fetal alcohol spectrum disorder: A guideline for diagnosis across the lifespan. *Canadian Medical Association Journal, 188*(3), 191–197. https://dx.doi.org/10.1503/cmaj.141593

Dion, J. (2017). *Falling through the cracks: Canadian Indigenous children with disabilities* (International Human Rights Internships Program, Working Paper Series [Vol. 5(12)]). McGill Centre for Human Rights and Legal Pluralism. https://www.mcgill.ca/humanrights/files/humanrights/ihri_wps_v5_n12_dion.pdf

Family Matters. (2021). *The Family Matters report 2021: Measuring trends to turn the tide on the over-representation of Aboriginal and Torres Strait Islander children in out-of-home care in Australia.* SNAICC – National Voice for Our Children.

Find & Connect. (n.d.) *Aborigines Protection Act 1886 (1887–1906): Summary.* Retrieved July 29, 2021, from https://www.findandconnect.gov.au/guide/wa/WE00403.

Fortier, C., & Wong, E. H. (2019). The settler colonialism of social work and the social work of settler colonialism. *Settler Colonial Studies, 9*(4), 437–456. https://doi.org/10.1080/2201473X.2018.1519962

Freckelton, I. (2017). Assessment and evaluation of fetal alcohol spectrum disorder (FASD) and its potential relevance for sentencing: A clarion call from Western Australia. *Psychiatry, Psychology and Law, 24*(4), 485–495. https://doi.org/10.1080/13218719.2017.1350931

Gallhofer, S., & Chew, A. (2000). Introduction: Accounting and Indigenous peoples. *Accounting, Auditing & Accountability Journal, 13*(3), 256–267. https://doi.org/10.1108/09513570010334081

Gatwiri, K., McPherson, L., Parmenter, N., Cameron, N., & Rotumah, D. (2021). Indigenous children and young people in residential care: A systematic scoping review. *Trauma, Violence, & Abuse, 22*(4), 829–842. https://journals.sagepub.com/doi/full/10.1177/1524838019881707

Geia, L. K., Hayes, B., & Usher, K. (2013) Yarning/Aboriginal storytelling: Towards an understanding of an Indigenous perspective and its implications for research practice. *Contemporary Nurse, 46*(1), 13–17. https://doi.org/10.5172/conu.2013.46.1.13

Gilbert, D. J., Mukherjee, R. A., Kassam, N., & Cook, P. A. (2021). Exploring the experiences of social workers in working with children suspected to have fetal alcohol spectrum disorders. *Adoption & Fostering, 45*(2), 155–172. https://doi.org/10.1177/03085759211011735

Gord Downie & Chanie Wenjack Fund. (n.d.). *Our story*. Retrieved July 4, 2021, from https://downiewenjack.ca/our-story/

Grech, S., & Soldatic, K. (2015). Disability and colonialism: (Dis)encounters and anxious intersectionalities. *Social Identities: Journal for the Study of Race, Nation and Culture, 21*(1), 1–5. https://doi.org/10.1080/13504630.2014.995394

Greer, S. (2009). "In the interests of the children": Accounting in the control of Aboriginal family endowment payments. *Accounting History, 14*(1/2), 166–191. https://doi.org/10.1177%2F1032373208098557

Hart, M. A. (2010). Indigenous worldviews, knowledge, and research: The development of an Indigenous research paradigm. *Journal of Indigenous Voices in Social Development, 1*(1), 1–16. http://hdl.handle.net/10125/15117

Hartz, D., & McGrath, L. (2017). Working with Indigenous families. In G. Thomson & V. Schmied (Eds.), *Psychosocial Resilience and Risk in the Perinatal Period: Implications and Guidance for Professionals* (pp. 44–61). Routledge.

Hayes L. (1998). *Children of the grog: Alcohol lifestyle and the relationship to foetal alcohol syndrome and foetal alcohol effects* [Unpublished honours dissertation]. University of Queensland.

Hayes, L., D'Antoine, H., & Carter, M. (2014). Addressing fetal alcohol spectrum disorder in Aboriginal communities. In P. Dudgeon, H. Milroy, & R. Walker (Eds.), *Working together: Aboriginal and Torres Strait Islander Mental Health and Wellbeing Principles and Practice* (2nd ed., pp. 355–372). Commonwealth of Australia. https://www.telethonkids.org.au/globalassets/media/documents/aboriginal-health/working-together-second-edition/wt-part-5-chapt-20-final.pdf

Hollinsworth, D. (2013). Decolonizing Indigenous disability in Australia. *Disability & Society, 28*(5), 601–615. https://doi.org/10.1080/09687599.2012.717879

Human Rights and Equal Opportunity Commission. (2006, August 1). *Submission to the Senate Legal Constitutional References Committee Inquiry into Stolen Wages*. Australian Human Rights Commission. https://humanrights.gov.au/our-work/legal/inquiry-stolen-wages

Jacobs, M. D. (2014). *A generation removed: The fostering and adoption of Indigenous children in the postwar world*. University of Nebraska Press. https://doi.org/10.2307/j.ctt1d9nmm2

Lee, E. O. J., & Ferrer, I. (2014). Examining social work as a Canadian settler colonial project: Colonial continuities of circles of reform, civilization, and in/visibility. *Journal of Critical Anti-oppressive Social Inquiry, 1*(1), 1–20. https://caos.library.ryerson.ca/index.php/caos/article/view/96/100

McKenzie, B., & Kufeldt, K. (2011). Indigenous issues in child welfare: Themes and implications. In K. Kufeldt & B. McKenzie (Eds.), *Child welfare: Connecting research, policy, and practice* (2nd ed., pp. 353–368). Wilfrid Laurier University Press.

Meekosha, H. (2011). Decolonising disability: Thinking and acting globally. *Disability & Society*, *26*(6), 667–682. https://doi.org/10.1080/09687599.2011.602860

Métis Settlements FASD Network. (n.d.). *About us*. Retrieved March 17, 2022, from https://metissettlementsfasd.ca/about-us

Morgensen, S. L. (2013). The biopolitics of settler colonialism: Right here, right now. *Settler Colonial Studies, 1*(1), 52–76. https://doi.org/10.1080/2201473X.2011.10648801

National Aboriginal Community Controlled Health Organisation. (2021). *Annual report, 2020–2021*. Retrieved March 17, 2022, from https://f.hubspotusercontent10.net/hubfs/5328468/NACCHO Annual Report 2020–21 web.pdf

Neu, D., & Graham, C. (2006). The birth of a nation: Accounting and Canada's First Nations, 1860–1900. *Accounting, Organizations and Society*, *31*(1), 47–76. https://doi.org/10.1016/j.aos.2004.10.002

Noyce, P., dir. (2003). *Rabbit-proof fence* [Film]. Australia: Hanway Films.

Office of the Child and Youth Advocate Alberta. (2019). *Mandatory reviews into child deaths: April 1, 2018–September 30, 2018*. https://www.ocya.alberta.ca/adult/news/mandatory-reviews-april-1-september-30-2018/

Reid, N., Gamble, J., Creedy, D. K., & Finlay-Jones, A. (2019). Benefits of caseload midwifery to prevent fetal alcohol spectrum disorder: A discussion paper. *Women and Birth*, *32*(1), 3–5. https://doi.org/10.1016/j.wombi.2018.03.002

Sherwood, J., & Geia, L. (2014). Historical and current perspectives on the health of Aboriginal and Torres Strait Islander people. In O. Best & B. Fredericks (Eds.), *Yatdjuligin: Aboriginal and Torres Strait Islander nursing and midwifery care* (pp, 7–30). Cambridge University Press.

Soldatic, K. (2013). The transnational sphere of justice: disability praxis and the politics of impairment. *Disability & Society*, *28*(6), 744–755. https://doi.org/10.1080/09687599.2013.802218

Soldatic, K. (2015). Postcolonial reproductions: disability, indigeneity and the formation of the white masculine settler state of Australia. *Social Identities*, *21*(1), 53–68. https://doi.org/10.1080/13504630.2014.995352

South West Aboriginal Land & Sea Council. (n.d.-a). *Impacts of law post 1905*. Kaartdijin Noongar—Noongar Knowledge: Sharing Noongar Culture. Retrieved July 4, 2021, from https://www.noongarculture.org.au/impacts-of-law-post-1905/

South West Aboriginal Land & Sea Council. (n.d.-b). *Stolen generations*. Kaartdijin Noongar—Noongar Knowledge: Sharing Noongar Culture. Retrieved July 4, 2021, from https://www.noongarculture.org.au/stolen-generations/

Tatz, C. (2001). Confronting Australian genocide. *Aboriginal History*, *25*, 16-36.

Truth and Reconciliation Commission of Canada. (2015). *Truth and Reconciliation Commission of Canada: Calls to action*. http://www.trc.ca/websites/trcinstitution/File/2015/Findings/Calls_to_Action_English2.pdf

Tulich, T., Blagg, H., Williams, R., Badry, D., Stewart, M., Mutch, R., & May, S. E. (2020). Introduction. In H. Blagg, T. Tulich, R. Williams, R. Mutch, S. E. May, D. Badry & M. Stewart (Eds.), *Decolonising justice for Aboriginal youth with foetal alcohol spectrum disorders* (pp. 1–7). Routledge.

United Nations Declaration on the Rights of Indigenous Peoples (UNDRIP). Retrieved online May 25, 2022 from https://en.unesco.org/indigenous-peoples/undrip

United Nations General Assembly. (2008, May 3). Convention on the rights of persons with disabilities. A/RES/61/106. https://www.un.org/development/desa/disabilities/convention-on-the-rights-of-persons-with-disabilities.html

Van Bibber, M. (2019). It takes a community, revisited. In *Revitalizing culture and healing: Indigenous approaches to FASD prevention* (pp. 2–4). Centre of Excellence for Women's Health. https://canfasd.ca/wp-content/uploads/2019/11/Indigenous-FASD-Booklet-Revitalizing-Culture-and-Healing.pdf

Williams, R. (2018). *Understanding fetal alcohol spectrum disorder (FASD) through the stories of Nyoongar families and how can this inform policy and service delivery*. Curtin University.

Williams R., & Badry, D. (2020). A decolonizing and human rights approach to FASD training, knowledge, and case practice for justice involved youth in correctional contexts. In H. Blagg, T. Tulich, R. Williams, R. Mutch, S. E. May, D. Badry, & M. Stewart. *Decolonising justice for Aboriginal youth with fetal alcohol spectrum disorders* (pp. 111–133). Routledge. https://doi.org/10.4324/9780429325526

Wilson, S. (2001). What is Indigenous research methodology? *Canadian Journal of Native Education*, *25*(2), 175–179.

Wilson, S. (2008). *Research is ceremony: Indigenous research methods*. Fernwood Publishing.

Wolfe, P. (2006). Settler colonialism and the elimination of the Native. *Journal of Genocide Research*, *8*(4), 387–409. https://doi.org/10.1080/14623520601056240

Websites Consulted

Kaartdijin Noongar—Noongar Knowledge: Sharing Noongar Culture. South West Aboriginal Land & Sea Council. Stolen Generations. https://www.noongarculture.org.au/stolen-generations/

Chanie's Path. https://downiewenjack.ca/our-story/chanies-path/
Secret Path. https://secretpath.ca/#Film
A Look at First Nations Prohibition of Alcohol. Peoples Blog. https://www.ictinc.ca/blog/first-nations-prohibition-of-alcohol
Jordan's Principle. https://fncaringsociety.com/jordans-principle
The Métis Settlements FASD Network. https://metissettlementsfasd.ca/about-us
National Aboriginal Community Controlled Health Organisation (NACCHO). https://www.naccho.org.au/

PART II

Practice

CHAPTER 4

Indigenous Social Work: Colonial Systems Can't Change What They Don't See as Wrong

Gabrielle Lindstrom, Tsapinaki, and Peter Choate

Introduction

It is now well established in Canada, as well as in other colonized nations such as Australia and New Zealand, that social service systems are over-involved in the lives of Indigenous peoples (Cunneed & Tauri, 2019; Fortier & Wong, 2018). These systems include criminal justice and health care as well as child protection. In this chapter, we focus on child protection by illuminating practices that both preclude strength-based Indigenous child intervention approaches and prevent non-Indigenous social work practitioners from conceptualizing and appreciating the capacity of Indigenous peoples to successfully care for their own children. We posit that deficit-based approaches arise from the long history of connection between child protection and assimilative genocidal efforts of the Canadian government. The Truth and Reconciliation Commission of Canada (TRC, 2015) has shown that child protection is connected to the cultural genocide of Indigenous peoples. We highlight

---

Suggested Citation: Lindstrom, G., Tsapinaki, & Choate, P. (2022). Indigenous social work: Colonial systems can't change what they don't see as wrong. In J. Albert, D. Badry, D. Fuchs, P. Choate, M. Bennett, & H. Montgomery (Eds.), *Walking together: The future of Indigenous child welfare on the prairies* (pp. 73–91). Regina, SK: University of Regina Press.

eleven avenues that sustain colonial approaches and represent places to focus for change in practice.

Background

Canada's history with Indigenous peoples is one of cultural genocide, as outlined by the TRC (2015). The actual history might better meet the definition of genocide as laid out in the United Nations Convention on the Prevention and Punishment of the Crime of Genocide, in Article II. In the present Convention, genocide means any of the following acts committed with intent to destroy, in whole or in part, a national, ethnical, racial or religious group, as such:

a) killing members of the group;
b) causing serious bodily or mental harm to members of the group;
c) deliberately inflicting on the group conditions of life calculated to bring about its physical destruction in whole or in part;
d) imposing measures intended to prevent births within the group;
e) forcibly transferring children of the group to another group. (UN General Assembly, 1951)

It is not the intention of this chapter to convince readers that Indigenous peoples are experiencing a cultural genocide in Canada; however, we do advance the contention that definitions emerging from a Eurocentric perspective very often serve to absolve Euro-settler society from taking full responsibility for actions that oppress and destroy cultures deemed as inferior (Kendi, 2017, 2019; Lemkin, 2005; Lentin, 2020). According to Lemkin (2005), cultural genocide involves "the destruction of a nation [and], therefore, results in the loss of its future contribution to the world" (p. 91). Colonization has led to the inability of Indigenous Nations to continue to exist as nations.

Legal scholar Kurt Mundorff (2009) states cultural genocide is "any deliberate act committed with the intention of destroying the language, religion or culture of a...group, such as, for example, prohibiting the use of the group's language or its schools or places of worship" (p. 76). Early colonial policies such as the Royal Proclamation of 1763 established the procedure for obtaining Indigenous lands (Bastien, 2004), and the *Indian*

Act of 1876 articulated policies that laid the foundation for the Indian residential schools, prohibition of spiritual practices, definitions of Indigenous identity, outlawing of economic activities, gender discrimination, segregation, erasure of languages, and continued rupturing of families (Battiste, 2013; Bastien, 2004; Hare & Davidson, 2020; Prete, 2019). Taken together, the policies contained in the *Indian Act* were "oppressive and resulted in cultural genocide. In fact, the federal government systematically tried to strip us of our Blackfoot way of life" (Prete, 2019, p. 5).

These major historical policy developments laid the foundation for the current child welfare system in Canada, which relies on a Eurocentric education system that continues to seek the eradication of Indigenous languages, identities, and knowledges while simultaneously working to advance Canadian society because it is constructed from the philosophy, practices, and ideologies rooted in the Eurocentric paradigm. Instead of having the freedom to construct knowledge from their own cultural paradigm, Indigenous peoples have been corralled into a forced dependency through these paternalistic and genocidal policies, and knowledge of the world around them and their relationships to it have been constructed for them.

Moreover, the definition of genocide applies for several reasons starting with Canada's failure to honour the treaties. Early colonial government made no attempt to understand the meaning of the treaties from an Indigenous perspective. For Indigenous peoples, the "first and foremost objective in the treaty-making process was to have the new peoples arriving in their territories recognize and affirm their continuing right to maintain, as peoples, the First Nations relationships with the Creator through the laws given to them by Him" (Cardinal & Hildebrandt, 2000, p. 7). Treaties therefore represent inviolable promises to act in accordance with those laws, values, and principles given to them from the Creator. Sacred laws that underlie treaty are integral to "peace, harmony, and good relations" and function to not only guide relationships but underlie strong, unified Nations (Cardinal & Hildebrandt, 2000, p. 15).

Treaties from a First Nations perspective are fundamentally rooted in agency, although this perspective is significantly ignored in the colonial understanding of treaty, and at the same time, treaty agreements led to the reservation system, which isolated and separated Indigenous peoples. Reserves were under the direct control of Indian agents, whose responsibility included enforcing policies and practices that prohibited Indigenous ways of life. Indeed, colonial Europeans' prior experience of treaty-making was between similar cultures (e.g., England and Spain), which is an interpretation diametrically opposed to First Nations understandings and mobilization of treaty agreements. Colonial powers had no real interest or investment in understanding what treaties stood for in an Indigenous context, and the written information reflected in the treaties is incomplete because it leaves out the contributions and understandings associated with the oral traditions (Asch, 1997).

Educational policy encapsulated in treaties was one of genocide guised as assimilation, which aimed to eliminate difference through the idea that all people could be thought of as Canadians and share a "common Canadianism" (Cairns, 2014, p. 50). To share a common Canadianism, Indigenous Nations needed to be destroyed and individual identities reshaped into a settler-colonial model of a subjugated citizen. Rather than assimilation, the purpose of colonial interpretations was one of eliminating Indigenous Nations so they could not continue to exist as nations. Treaties interpreted and enacted from a Eurocentric perspective ultimately form the basis for carrying out genocide through the destruction of Indigenous identity and nationhood (Lemkin, 2005).

The Indian residential schools (IRS)—constructed to fully destroy the identity of Indigenous children by "taking the Indian out of the child" (attributed to Sir John A. Macdonald) so that they might be readily absorbed into Canadian society—were another mechanism of cultural genocide. The impacts of the IRS reverberate throughout Indigenous communities via the transmission of intergenerational trauma (IGT), a process that continues to this day. Dr. Peter H. Bryce (1922) stated,

> *For each year up to 1914 he [Bryce] wrote an annual report on the health of the Indians, published in the Departmental report, and on the instructions of the minister made in 1907 a special inspection of thirty-five Indian schools in the three prairie provinces. This report was published separately; but the recommendations contained in the report were never published and the public knows nothing of them. It contained a brief history of the origins of the Indian Schools, of the sanitary condition of the schools and statistics of the health of the pupils, during the 15 years of their existence. Regarding the*

> *health of the pupils, the report states that 24 per cent of all the pupils which had been in the schools were known to be dead, while one school on the File Hills reserve, which gave a complete return to date, 75 per cent were dead at the of the 16 years since the school opened.* (pp. 3–4)

The forced sterilization of Indigenous girls and women was a further attempt to limit reproductive capacity (Clarke, 2021), with reports as recent as 2018 (Black et al., 2021). When considered through the lens of genocide, the forced sterilization of Indigenous women and girls is particularly insidious because the possibility of Indigenous nationhood is destroyed even before it can be embodied in the physical realm.

Genocidal efforts in Canada have also led to the chronic failure to provide the social determinants of health needed for Indigenous populations to thrive (Kolahdooz et al., 2015). Crowshoe et al. (2018) identify a relationship between colonization (particularly the legacy of the IRS) and diabetes in the Indigenous population, and another source shows how "colonization, dispossession of land, and loss of traditional practices contribute to a poorer health status" (Earle, 2011, p. 3). When taken together, the above factors overlap with the child intervention system to further perpetuate the destruction of Indigenous families and relationships in order to reshape Indigenous children under the auspices of settler-colonial societal values and practices.

For the purposes of this chapter, the most profound step has been in relation to Article II(e) of the UN Genocide Convention, given above: "Forcibly transferring children of the group to another group" (UN General Assembly, 1951). This practice was seen through not only the IRS but also the Sixties Scoop and Millennium Scoop along with the continuous overrepresentation of Indigenous children in the care of provincial and territorial child welfare authorities. This overrepresentation followed changes to the *Indian Act* in 1951 (s. 88), which gave provinces control over child welfare on reserves (Bennett, n.d.).

The TRC (2015) documented the history of child intervention in Canada. The commission's report is part of a long legacy of inquiries and documents that have shown the over-surveillance of Indigenous families as part of the goal of assimilation (RCAP, 1996; Kimelman, 1985). Multiple reports from child and youth advocates across Canada have identified challenges in how child protection manages Indigenous cases. The report of the National Inquiry into Missing and Murdered Indigenous Women and Girls documented the link between colonization, assimilation, and the deaths related to this investigation (National Inquiry into Missing and Murdered Indigenous Women and Girls, 2019). None of these various reports and inquiries has resulted in a reduction in the number of Indigenous children in care. Indeed, the 2016 Canadian census noted that Indigenous children aged fourteen and under represent 7.7 per cent of the population in that age group but 52.2 per cent of children in care (Turner, 2016).

In 2020, Canada brought into force Bill C-92—*An Act respecting First Nations, Inuit and Métis children, youth and families*—with the explicit aim of ensuring that Indigenous peoples could take control of child protection matters for their own children, regardless of where they are living in Canada. However, several hurdles bar this legislation from having the force that might be hoped for. The first is that the federal government did not provide financial support for implementation of the legislation, nor did it include regulations with the legislation that would typically help courts sort out intent and implementation outlines. Canada also took the opportunity to use Bill C-92 as a way to shift away from a national approach, offering Jordan's Principle services, and toward one where each Indigenous governing body that sets up its own agency will need to negotiate a separate Jordan's Principle agreement with Canada. This serves as something of a "divide and conquer" approach. In January 2022, an agreement in principle was reached between the Government of Canada, the Assembly of First Nations, the First Nations Child and Family Caring Society, the Chiefs of Ontario, and the Nishnawbe Aski Nation, which may lead to an ultimate solution.

A further challenge with Bill C-92 are judicial precedents that must be challenged in the courts. For example, as the Act calls for application of the "best interests of the *Indigenous* [emphasis added] child," it is meant to overturn the notion that attachment and bonding are more important than culture, as seen in the leading case of *Racine v Woods* (1983). The federal legislation (Act, 2019) has not fully met the stated intention of having Indigenous communities take control of child protection. In our view that is not surprising, as Canada has a long history of partialized responses. The First Nations Child and Family Caring Society had proposed a comprehensive legislative draft, but it failed to receive serious consideration by Canada.

Bill C-92 was recently challenged in the Québec Court of Appeal. The court ruled the legislation constitutional except for sections 21 and 22(3), which effectively renders section 23 unconstitutional: "the provision respecting child and family services that is in a law of an Indigenous group, community or people applies in relation to an Indigenous child except if the application of the provision would be contrary to the best interests of the child" (Court of Appeal of Québec, 2022). Thus, the provincial law would stand as superior. This decision is being appealed by both Canada and Québec to the Supreme Court of Canada.

As of February 2022, several First Nations are in the process of establishing their own legislation and agencies under Bill C-92. As well, several Nations in Alberta are entering into bilateral agreements with the province that will lead the Nations' child and family services agencies to take over control of all cases involving their children, whether on or off reserve. The Nunatsiavut Government (2021) has announced it is taking over its child welfare from the Government of Newfoundland and Labrador. These are important steps in addressing the historical dominant society control of Indigenous children.

The Eurocentric Foundation

As the section above demonstrates, the focus of colonization was to establish the Eurocentric understanding of society as the basis upon which functional, moral, cultural, and legal standards would be set (TRC, 2015). In the case of child protection, this meant that how to parent—that is, what constitutes good-enough parenting and appropriate outcomes of raising a child—would be judged by Eurocentric perspectives (Choate et al., 2020; de Leeuw, 2014). These are based on individualistic cultural beliefs, with the nuclear family as the central definition. Collectivistic and communal cultures, such as Indigenous cultures, fall outside of that paradigm. This approach was heavily linked to the Sixties Scoop, which combined a view of assimilation with beliefs that Indigenous parenting was deficient.

Combined with assimilative and colonial views, child protection developed assessment approaches that were rooted in the Eurocentric framing of family, child development, and parenting. These approaches failed to consider the impact of intergenerational trauma that was inflicted upon Indigenous peoples. The TRC (2015) called upon child protection and the courts to take into account the impact of the IRS when considering the best interests of the Indigenous child. This leads us to ask, what must be different? We propose eleven important shifts that will change the conversation about how child protection work is to be done and how the relationship between child protection and Indigenous peoples is to be rebuilt.

As referred to elsewhere in this book (see Chapter 6) a foundational challenge for change is recognizing that the dominant society, through child protection, sustains the power over Indigenous peoples; in contrast, the transference of power would lead to Indigenous peoples having power regarding their children and families. Such a transfer of power would recognize the multiple levels of intervention that are needed to support children being raised within their ways of knowing and being, which draw from their culture.

Ten Avenues for Shifting Colonial Practices: The Fallacy of Cultural Competence

At the time of its introduction to social work, the concept of cultural competency was revolutionary. It was a way to recognize that anti-oppressive social work required social workers to see issues from the perspective of different lived realities and ways of knowing. It has been criticized because it is hard to imagine how a person from one culture can become competent in another. We agree with the criticism. Later authors have suggested cultural humility is more appropriate and rooted in the notion of understanding the self and others. This joins other approaches such as awareness, sensitivity, appropriateness, and safety as ways to think about the self and the cultural position of clients (Danso, 2018). But, we ask, what is the basis of comparison from which the social worker is seeking to gain this understanding? Typically, it is from the dominant perspective of Eurocentric culture. To know a culture is to be of it and within it. We seek to go further by noting that cultural competence in Indigeneity is not possible, as there are 634 First Nations in Canada plus Inuit and Métis peoples. There is not *an Indigenous culture*. Thus, we suggest any claim to cultural competence is based on a fallacy that it can be achieved by those outside of the culture. It also serves to diminish the voice of those who are truly competent—that is, the peoples of specific Indigenous communities.

With that in mind, we suggest the following ten points as ways to reflect upon how information is gathered in assessment and to think about the specific context of the information.

1. **The place of trauma in assessing cases.** The TRC (2015), in its calls to action regarding child welfare, specifically indicated that the impact of the IRS must be taken into account when investigating Indigenous families (p. 319). While some work has been done in developing trauma-informed care approaches that are responsive to the TRC (2015), more must be done in developing practices that consider how Indigenous peoples conceptualize and experience trauma, since this has direct impacts on assessing the capacity of Indigenous parents to care for their children. Western approaches to trauma-informed care in social work practice have been criticized in other Indigenous contexts (Atwool, 2019; Pihama et al., 2017) as being another example of how Western systems universalize and impose definitions on Indigenous families regardless of whether they are relevant to or consistent with Indigenous peoples' experiences. Atwool (2019) provides an overview of the origins of trauma-informed care within child intervention, pointing out its deficiencies in responding to the intergenerational impacts of historical trauma that Indigenous peoples collectively experience in contemporary contexts. She argues, "Members of the dominant White culture often view colonization as an historical event with limited relevance in today's world" (p. 28). Similarly, Pihama et al. (2017) point out that for Indigenous peoples, in this case the Māori, trauma is experienced in "distinct ways that are linked to the experience of colonisation, racism and discrimination, negative stereotyping and subsequent unequal rates of violence, poverty and ill health" (p. 18). Trauma-informed care must be developed in collaboration with Indigenous communities in order to ensure alignment with Indigenous definitions, understandings, and experiences of trauma. To do otherwise is to see trauma as a health problem belonging to the individual as opposed to centring trauma as a social problem that arises from the colonial process aimed at the Indigenous person. Clark (2016) suggests moving beyond

"decolonizing Western models of trauma, and instead attend to the centring of 'wise practices' and specific Indigenous Nations approaches to within a network of relational accountability" (p. 13).

2. **The place of culture in defining parenting.** As we have written elsewhere (Lindstrom et al., 2016; Lindstrom & Choate, 2016), Indigenous culture, practices, and ways of knowing shape parenting, and despite the genocidal aims of the Canadian government to destroy Indigenous nationhood, Indigenous approaches to parenting are still very much alive. Distinct parenting practices rooted in culture, the role of the child in the community, and the relational worldview of Indigenous peoples are realities that require child intervention approaches and kinship placements be reflective of this diversity by both preparing social workers through an accurate educational curriculum and ensuring the formation of collaborative and authentic partnerships with Indigenous communities in order to reinforce the place of Indigenous culture in definitions of good parenting.

3. **Stepping away from past child intervention history as a barrier to kinship.** When we think of the histories of trauma identified above, including the over-surveillance of Indigenous peoples by child protection, a history of involvement in child intervention is common. This has meant that many family members have a history of child intervention, which has typically served as a barrier to child intervention–approved kinship care. The result has been children placed outside of their kinship systems, causing further fracturing of communal, cultural, and caregiving relationships. A reframing is the acceptance of colonialism as a "forced entry" into child intervention, which should lead to a reconsideration of that history as being indicative of caregiving capacity.

4. **Who is to be assessed in determining appropriate care for a child?** We have shown elsewhere that children raised in Indigenous cultures will be raised in communal caregiving systems. To assess the parent(s) only is to disconnect the assessment from the reality of the child-rearing for the child. It is vital to understand

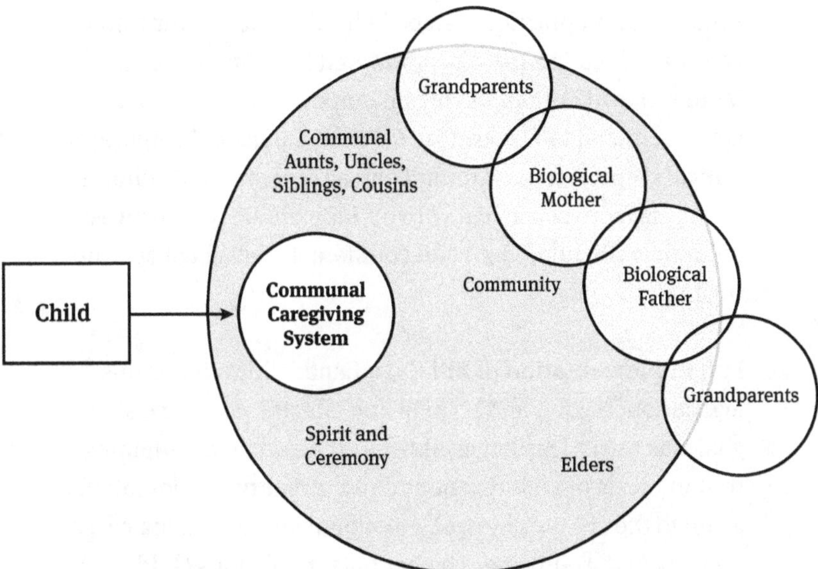

Figure 4.1. Elements that may be considered in assessing a caregiving system as opposed to only a parental system. This is more consistent with Indigenous ways of raising a child.

the totality of the culturally and communally based nature of Indigenous parenting. This would expand assessment to include systems of care such as seen in Figure 4.1. To not do so is to limit the view of the world of the developing Indigenous child.

5. **Challenging the deficit paradigm.** Indigenous culture has been conceptualized by Western society through a series of negations that are reinforced through education as well as socially accepted norms, attitudes, and behaviours. This has led to widespread stereotyping of Indigenous parents, systemic discrimination, and blatant racism. Dismantling the deficit paradigm requires a reframing of definitions, including notions of family and good parenting, that have historically been imposed on Indigenous peoples as well as implementing critical and culturally relevant theoretical frameworks that enable individual social workers to identify and challenge the deficit paradigm in their own thinking. As highlighted by Blackfoot scholar Betty Bastien (2016), Indigenous pedagogical approaches rooted in traditional

principles and practices can be helpful in illuminating how colonial education has disempowered Indigenous families. Moreover, rather than relying on empowerment theory, a Western concept rooted in Eurocentric notions of personal empowerment, critical empowerment grounded in a recognition of cultural agency is more consistent with an Indigenous perspective on autonomy (Bishop, 1998) and counteracts deficit constructions (Bishop, 2003).

6. **Full implementation of Bill C-92.** Canada introduced this legislation in 2019, and it came into effect in 2020. The stated goal was this: "This Act establishes that, when determining the best interests of an Indigenous child, primary consideration is given to the child's physical, emotional and psychological safety, security and well-being. The Act puts Indigenous children first so that they can stay with their families and communities and grow up immersed in their cultures" (ISC, 2019). Full implementation of the law requires not only creating opportunities for Indigenous governing bodies to introduce their own child and family services agency with control over their own children but also ensuring stable funding. The present form of the legislation is insufficient to accomplish reconciliation because it lacks regulations as well as a fulsome structure to ensure Indigenous priorities. Perhaps the largest challenge is how the courts will interpret the law, particularly in matters related to best interest (see Chapter 2, this volume).

7. **Fully implementing Jordan's Principle.**[22] Canada has a long history of fighting against the full implementation of Jordan's Principle, as seen in the ongoing series of legal battles before

22 Jordan's Principle is a child-first principle ensuring First Nations children get the services they need when they need them. Jordan's Principle makes sure all First Nations children living in Canada can access the products, services, and supports they need, when they need them. Funding can help with a wide range of health, social, and educational needs, including the unique needs that First Nations Two-Spirit and LGBTQQIA children and youth and those with disabilities may have.

the Canadian Human Rights Tribunal and the courts. Jordan's Principle is a way for Canada to ensure that children do not suffer further intergenerational harm arising out of colonization, which marginalized children from the supports needed (2017 CHRT 14).

8. **Challenging judicial precedents as currently valid for Indigenous child protection.** Presently, there are several judicial precedents that continue to be applied, including *Racine v Woods* (1983),[23] but that also perpetuate colonial priorities. *Racine* exists at the level of the Supreme Court of Canada, while many decisions upholding Eurocentric understandings of good-enough parenting exist across trial courts, such as those holding the perspective that placing Indigenous children in non-Indigenous homes, which become long-term placements, is preferable to moving a child into Indigenous care. Child intervention across Canada should challenge this, which would also support the placement priories set out in Bill C-92. That law sets priority in the following order: (1) parents, (2) family members, (3) community members, (4) another Indigenous person, and (5) others. A fundamental underpinning of Bill C-92 is recognition that Indigenous peoples are capable of caring for their own children.

9. **Fully engaging First Nations, Métis, and Inuit governing bodies in decision-making regarding Indigenous children.** Too often, consultations with Indigenous governing bodies have been approached in tokenistic ways—a pattern that is paternalistic and rooted in false beliefs about the superiority of the Eurocentric worldview. Indigenous leaders are continuously excluded when it comes to program development, assessment, and child intervention approaches despite the fact that they work closely

23 The 1983 case *Racine v Woods* is the leading child protection case from the Supreme Court of Canada, distinguishing bonding and/or attachment as a more important determinant of best interest for an Indigenous child than cultural connection. Using this case, courts are upholding the permanent placement of Indigenous children in non-Indigenous homes as opposed to placement within their culture (see Choate et al., 2019).

with Indigenous Elders and community members and represent the needs of the community (McMillan, 2021; see also the multiple decisions of the CHRT in respect of Indigenous child welfare). Moreover, Indigenous leaders have a vested interest in ensuring that child-rearing practices and adoption protocols remain culturally defined. At the level of the individual, social workers can begin to develop an openness to Indigenous perspectives by examining their own assumptions and relationship to power. Various theoretical frameworks can facilitate this process (see Cariou, 2020) by providing a lens through which to critique Western values and beliefs, but social workers need adequate support, time, and critical educational resources that can lead to meaningful and sustained changes that are felt within Indigenous communities. As Caldwell and Sinha (2020) challenge, this will be rooted in a reconceptualization of not only the relationship but also the meanings of such things as neglect when applied to Indigenous caregiving.

10. **Seeing cultural connection as embodying culture and not visiting it.** In the context of maintaining cultural connections, part of the care plan for Indigenous children revolves around the notion of providing opportunities for them to visit culture rather than to embody it through regular and sustained connections with their community so they may learn language and cultural protocols as part of their identity. Language is an integral part of Indigenous identity, yet access to Indigenous languages is rarely considered when developing care plans for Indigenous children. Blackfoot scholar Leroy Little Bear (2000) establishes that "language embodies the way a society thinks. Through learning and speaking a particular language, an individual absorbs the collective thought processes of a people" (para. 5). Access to Indigenous culture, community, and kinship systems—and not just an occasional visit to immediate family members—must be regarded as an integral right for Indigenous children.

Conclusion

Colonial constructions of Indigenous peoples endure and are a necessary part of the settler-colonial narrative of Canada. Our current primary, secondary, and post-secondary education systems do not prepare students to learn about Indigenous culture in accurate and authentic ways. Instead, the education system reinforces imperialism and its colonial arm as part of a glorified, Eurocentric nation-building past that brought industry and civilization to Indigenous peoples—a colonial aim that is not lost in social work education. As emerging perspectives in cultural competency and diversity training literature are showing, current training approaches make it difficult for white social workers to conceptualize Eurocentrism as a deeply entrenched system of thought from which racism emerges as not only a system of power but an ideology and individual belief system entangled with settler-colonial definitions of family, good parenting, and the role of the child in society. Confronting and dismantling Eurocentric practices in child intervention requires a reframing of the definitions, theories, and practices that drive apprehensions of Indigenous children.

This chapter has offered an entry point for deeper reflection and critical discussion around the Eurocentric, settler-colonial foundations of nation building, how this process has sought to destroy Indigenous Nations and identity, and the implications this has for Indigenous child intervention approaches. In addition to the eleven avenues identified above, current approaches in diversity and cultural awareness training initiatives must be problematized to make space for other ways of advancing equitable knowledge-delivery formats that align with Indigenous experiences of discrimination and racism in the child welfare system, as opposed to simply conforming to the comfort levels of the Euro-settler peoples. Such an approach is rooted in and consistent with a decolonizing view of social work that is truly anti-oppressive.

Learning Questions

1. If you were to challenge the views of the courts described in this chapter, what types of evidence would you develop?
2. As an individual social worker, where do you see the source of your power? What is an Indigenous family's relationship to power and where does that come from?

3. How would you challenge the deficit paradigm in child welfare? What conversations would you be having with your supervisor and other social workers around you?
4. How would you seek to frame such topics as trauma, family, and parenting using non-colonial paradigms?
5. The authors speak of the challenge white social workers face in trying to conceptualize Eurocentrism as a deeply entrenched system of thought from which racism emerges as a system of power. To what extent do you see this as a problem for non-white, non-Indigenous social workers?

References

An Act respecting First Nations, Inuit and Métis children, youth and families, SC 2019, c 24. https://laws.justice.gc.ca/eng/acts/F-11.73/page-1.html

Asch, M. (1997). *Aboriginal and treaty rights in Canada: Essays on law, equity, and respect for difference*. UBC Press.

Atwool, N. (2019). Challenges of operationalizing trauma-informed practice in child protection services in New Zealand. *Child & Family Social Work, 24*(1), 25–32. https://doi.org/10.1111/cfs.12577

Bastien, B. (2004). *Blackfoot ways of knowing: The worldview of the Siksikaitsitapi*. University of Calgary Press.

Bastien, B. (2016). Indigenous pedagogy: A way out of dependence. In K. Burnett & G. Read (Eds.), *Aboriginal history: A reader* (pp. 14–26). Oxford University Press.

Battiste, M. (2013). *Decolonizing education: Nourishing the learning spirit*. UBC Press.

Bennett, M. (n.d.) *First Nations fact sheet: A general profile on First Nations child welfare in Canada*. First Peoples Child & Family Caring Society. Retrieved June 10, 2021, from https://fncaringsociety.com/sites/default/files/docs/FirstNationsFS1.pdf

Bishop, R. (1998). Freeing ourselves from neo-colonial domination in research: A Maori approach to creating knowledge. *International Journal of Qualitative Studies in Education, 11*(2), 199–219. https://doi.org/10.1080/095183998236674

Bishop, R. (2003). Changing power relations in education: Kaupapa Maori messages for "mainstream" education in Aotearoa/New Zealand. *Comparative Education, 39*(2), 221–238. https://doi.org/10.1080/03050060302555

Black, K. A., Rich, R., & Felske-Durksen, C. (2021). Forced and coerced sterilization of Indigenous peoples: Considerations for health care providers. *Journal of Obstetrics and Gynaecology Canada, 43*(9), 1090–1093. https://doi.org/10.1016/j.jogc.2021.04.006

Bryce, P. H. (1922). *The story of a national crime: Being an appeal for justice to the Indians of Canada*. James Hope & Sons.

Cairns, A. (2001). *Citizens plus: Aboriginal Peoples and the Canadian state.* UBC Press.

Caldwell, J., & Sinha, V. (2020). (Re)Conceptualizing neglect: Considering the overrepresentation of Indigenous children in child welfare systems in Canada. *Child Indicators Research (13)*, 481–512. https://doi.org/10.1007/s12187-019-09676-w

Cardinal, H., & Hildebrandt, W. (2000). *Treaty Elders of Saskatchewan: Our dream is that our peoples will one day be clearly recognized as Nations*. University of Calgary Press.

Cariou, W. (2020). On critical humility. *Studies in American Indian Literature, 32*(3/4), 1–12. https://doi.org/10.1353/ail.2020.0015

Choate, P., CrazyBull, B., Lindstrom, D., & Lindstrom, G. (2020). Where do we go from here? Ongoing colonialism from attachment theory. *Aotearoa New Zealand Social Work, 32*(1), 32–44. https://doi.org/10.11157/anzswj-vol32iss1id702

Choate, P., Kohler, T., Cloete, F., CrazyBull, B., Lindstrom, D., & Tatoulis, P. (2019). Rethinking *Racine v Woods* from a decolonizing perspective: Challenging applicability of attachment theory to Indigenous families involved with child protection. *Canadian Journal of Law and Society/Revue Canadienne Droit et Société, 34*(1), 55–78. https://dx.doi.org/10.1017/cls.2019.8

Clark, N. (2016). Shock and awe: Trauma as the new colonial frontier. *Humanities, 5*, 14. https://doi.org/10.3390/h5010014

Clarke, E. (2021) Indigenous women and the risk of reproductive healthcare: Forced sterilization, genocide, and contemporary population control. *Journal of Human Rights and Social Work, 6*, 144–147. https://doi.org/10.1007/s41134-020-00139-9

Court of Appeal of Québec. (2022, February 10). *Reference to the Court of Appeal of Québec in relation with the Act respecting First Nations, Inuit and Métis children, youth and families*, 2022 QCCA 185. https://courdappelduquebec.ca/en/judgments/details/reference-to-the-court-of-appeal-of-quebec-in-relation-with-the-act-respecting-first-nations-inuit/

Crowshoe, L., Dannenbaum, D., Green, M., Henderson, R., Hayward, M. N., & Toth, E. (2018). Type 2 diabetes and Indigenous peoples. *Canadian Journal of Diabetes, 42*(S1), S296–S306. https://doi.org/10.1016/j.jcjd.2017.10.022

Cunneed, C., & Tauri, J. M. (2019). Indigenous peoples, criminology, and criminal justice. *Annual Review of Criminology, 2*, 359–381. https://doi.org/10.1146/annurev-criminol-011518-024630

Danso, R. (2018). Cultural competence and cultural humility: A critical reflection on key cultural diversity concepts. *Journal of Social Work, 18*(4), 410–430. https://doi.org/10.1177/1468017316654341

de Leeuw, S. (2014). State of care: The ontologies of child welfare in British Columbia. *Cultural Geographies, 21*(1), 59–78. https://www.jstor.org/stable/26168542

Earle, L. (2011). *Understanding chronic disease and the role for traditional approaches in Aboriginal communities*. National Collaborating Centre for

Aboriginal Health. https://doczz.net/doc/7565213/understanding-chronic-disease-and-the-role-for-traditional

First Nations Child & Family Caring Society of Canada et al. v Attorney General of Canada, 2017 CHRT 14.

Fortier, C., & Wong, E. H. (2019). The settler colonialism of social work and the social work of settler colonialism. *Settler Colonial Studies, 9*(4), 437–456. https://doi.org/10.1080/2201473X.2018.1519962

Hare, J., & Davidson, S. F. (2020). Learning from Indigenous knowledge in education. In G. Starblanket, D. Long, & O. P. Dickason (Eds.), *Visions of the heart: Issues involving Indigenous peoples in Canada* (5th ed., pp. 203–219). Oxford University Press.

Indigenous Services Canada. (2019, June 21). *Backgrounder: An Act respecting First Nations, Inuit and Métis children, youth and families: Context.* https://www.canada.ca/en/indigenous-services-canada/news/2019/06/an-act-respecting-first-nations-inuit-and-metis-children-youth-and-families-has-received-royal-assent.html

Kendi, I. X. (2017). *Stamped from the beginning: The definitive history of racist ideas in America*. Hachette Book Group.

Kendi, I. X. (2019). *How to be an antiracist*. Random House.

Kimelman, E. C. (1985). *No quiet place: Review Committee on Indian and Métis adoptions and placements.* Manitoba Community Services.

Kolahdooz, F., Nader, F., Yi, K. J., & Sharma, S. (2015). Understanding the social determinants of health among Indigenous Canadians: Priorities for health promotion policies and actions, *Global Health Action, 8*(1), Article 27968. https://doi.org/10.3402/gha.v8.27968

Lemkin, R. (2005). *Axis rule in occupied Europe: Laws of occupation, analysis of government, proposals for redress* (2nd ed.). Lawbook Exchange.

Lentin, A. (2020). *Why race still matters*. Polity Press.

Lindstrom, G., & Choate, P. (2016). Nistawatsiman: Rethinking assessment of Aboriginal parents for child welfare following the Truth and Reconciliation Commission of Canada. *First Peoples Child & Family Review, 11*(2), 45–59.

Lindstrom, G., Choate, P., Bastien, L., Breaker, K., Breaker, S., Good Striker, E., Good Striker, W., & Weasel Traveller, A., (2016). *Nistawatsimin: Exploring First Nations parenting: A literature review and expert consultation with Blackfoot Elders*. Mount Royal University.

Little Bear, L. (2000). *Jagged worldviews colliding* (Walking together: First Nations, Métis and Inuit perspectives in curriculum). Government of Alberta. https://www.learnalberta.ca/content/aswt/worldviews/documents/jagged_worldviews_colliding.pdf

McMillan, L. J. (2021). Unsettling standards: Indigenous peoples and child welfare. In J. E. Graham, C. Holmes, F. McDonald, & R. Darnell (Eds.), *The social life of standards: Ethnographic methods for local engagement* (pp. 179–198). UBC Press.

Mundorff, K. (2009). Other peoples' children: A textual and contextual interpretation of the genocide convention, article 2 (e). *Harv. Int'l LJ, 50*, 61.

National Inquiry into Missing and Murdered Indigenous Women and Girls. (2019). *Reclaiming power and place: The final report of the national inquiry into missing and murdered Indigenous women and girls*. The National Inquiry. https://www.mmiwg-ffada.ca/final-report/

Nunatsiavut Government (2021, June 17). *Process under way to take over child welfare services* [Press release]. https://www.nunatsiavut.com/article/process-under-way-to-take-over-child-welfare-services/

Pihama, L., Tuhiwai-Smith, L., Evans-Campbell, T., Kohu-Morgan, H., Cameron, N., Mataki, T., Te Nana, R., Skipper, H., & Southey, K. (2017). Investigating Māori approaches to trauma informed care. *Journal of Indigenous Wellbeing: Te Mauri Pimatisiwin, 2*(3), 18–31.

Prete, T. (2019). Walking the path of my ancestors: The Siksikastiapi (Blackfoot Confederacy). *Cultural and Pedagogical Inquiry*, *10*(2). https://doi.org/10.18733/cpi29409.

Racine v Woods, [1983] 2 SCR 173.

Royal Commission on Aboriginal Peoples. (1996). *Report of the Royal Commission on Aboriginal Peoples: Vol. 1. Looking forward, looking back.* Canada Communication Group.

Truth and Reconciliation Commission of Canada. (2015). *Honouring the truth, reconciling for the future: Summary of the final report of the Truth and Reconciliation Commission of Canada*. McGill-Queen's University Press.

Turner, A. (2016). Living arrangements of Aboriginal children aged 14 and under. *Insights on Canadian Society.* Statistics Canada Catalogue no. 75-006-X.

United Nations General Assembly. (1951, January 12). Convention on the prevention and punishment of the crime of genocide. https://www.un.org/en/genocideprevention/documents/atrocity-crimes/Doc.1_Convention%20on%20the%20Prevention%20and%20Punishment%20of%20the%20Crime%20of%20Genocide.pdf

CHAPTER 5

Making Connections for Our Children: Indigenous Youth Transitioning Out of Care

Kelly Provost—Miah'nistik'anah'soyii (Sparks in a Fire) and Christina Tortorelli

Setting the Context

This chapter is centred within Treaty 7 Territory in Alberta, Canada. Treaty 7 was signed on September 22, 1877, and covers land located from the Rocky Mountains (west) to the Cypress Hills (east), north to the Red Deer River, and south to the United States border. This land is the traditional territory of the Blackfoot Confederacy: Siksika, Kainai, and Piikani, as well as the Îyâxe Nakoda and Tsuut'ina Nations. Treaty 7 is home to the Métis Nation of Alberta, Region 3. We recognize all First Nations, Métis, and Inuit youth who reside within these boundaries and particularly those who reside in the care of child welfare. Youth are the future leaders in the Indigenous community.

To contextualize further, the writing of this chapter is a collaboration between Indigenous and non-Indigenous colleagues. We use the term

Suggested Citation: Provost, K.—Miah'nistik'anah'soyii (Sparks in a Fire), & Tortorelli, C. (2022). Making connections for our children: Indigenous youth transitioning out of care. In J. Albert, D. Badry, D. Fuchs, P. Choate, M. Bennett, & H. Montgomery (Eds.), *Walking together: The future of Indigenous child welfare on the prairies* (pp. 93–112). Regina, SK: University of Regina Press.

"Indigenous" broadly and inclusively, as it is not our place to determine who is or is not Indigenous. We have grounded our writing in the teachings of the late Mi'kmaq leader Chief Charles Labrador (Acadia First Nation). The Chief's teachings, which were further developed through the work of Albert Marshall, are known as Etuaptmumk (two-eyed seeing). Two-eyed seeing is the weaving rather than the joining of both Indigenous and Western ways of knowing. Two-eyed seeing encourages us to take the strengths of both perspectives and work together to find solutions that have the greatest impact on improving the lives of our people, our cultures, and our world (Iwama et al., 2009).

> *Go into a forest, you see the birch, maple, pine. Look underground and all those trees are holding hands.* (Labrador, as quoted in Kierans, 2003)

It is with two-eyed seeing as a foundation that we have joined together to create an experience for the reader that is impactful, that resonates with Indigenous youth, families, and communities, and that accurately recounts their stories. The content of this chapter is intended to be informative and thought provoking for both Indigenous and non-Indigenous readers. The authors, who are connected through their interest in positive outcomes for youth and their professional experience as leaders in the child welfare context, begin by sharing a bit of their background.

Kelly Provost was born and raised on the Piikani Nation and has been working within the Piikani Child Protection Services since 2001. His Blackfoot name is Miah'nistik'anah'soyii, or Sparks in the Fire. He has worked in all capacities in child welfare on and off reserve and is the executive director of the Piikani Child and Family Services. He attributes the most success to Piikani Blackfoot cultural ways of learning. Kelly and his team are committed to their mission statement: "To deliver strong healthy children, and families through the delivery of Piikani based protection and preventative services" (Piikani Nation Child & Family Services mission statement, n.d.). Kelly is a strong advocate for justice and equity in the provision of services to Indigenous children, youth, and families.

Christina Tortorelli is a non-Indigenous social worker. Raised in Calgary, New Zealand, and Pennsylvania, her home has been in the city of Calgary—or Mohkínstsis, in Blackfoot—for most of her life. Through years of working in the child welfare system in Alberta, Christina has seen the challenges facing youth leaving care. Her experience has generated energy and passion to make a positive difference using personal agency and her academic role as a vehicle for change.

Introduction

Connection defines who we are by grounding us in our history and setting us on a path forward that makes sense in the context of our culture, family, and community.

Connection gives identity, a sense of belonging, and pride. The sharing of connection within Indigenous communities increases the strength of the individual and the community as a whole. The sharing of ancestral beliefs, traditions, values, spirituality, ceremony, healing practices, language, and ways of knowing and being are passed on through stories to new generations.

> *How I really started healing was I turned to culture, I started talking to Elders, listening to their wisdom and their past.* (OCYA, 2020, p. 26)

Storytelling exists in many cultures as a way of passing along knowledge through an experiential process. In Western cultures, storytelling has been diminished. The fast pace of life has overtaken the desire to be still and learn from those who have travelled before us. Western cultures value education using the tools of the written word (books) and the spoken word (films, social media), finding little space for the sharing of lived experience that is real and powerful.

There is a rich history of oral storytelling in Indigenous culture (Wilson, 2016; Warrick, 2012). Indigenous communities are engaged in reclaiming the oral traditions, with Elders demonstrating the importance of history told through stories of lived experience. As Indigenous communities continue to revive their culture after the dismantling of it by European settlers, storytelling as a means of transferring knowledge to the next generation is deeply valued (Hausknecht et al., 2021). The wisdom passed on through Elders helps embed the meaning of being a part of a culture with deep roots to the earth and to one another as a caring community. Elder Kathy Louis shares the importance of storytelling, of deep listening to Elders, as important transmission of traditional teachings and cultural knowledge (National Inquiry into Missing and Murdered Indigenous Women and Girls, 2019). Her wisdom holds true for Indigenous youth in care, illuminating a pathway to engage children and youth on a rich cultural journey.

The story of youth voices begins with understanding how colonial beliefs, embedded in legislation and impacted by worker and agency bias, results in the high involvement of child welfare services in the lives of Indigenous children and families. As we take you on a narrative journey through this chapter, we encourage you to listen with both of your ears and with your whole heart. Embrace the wisdom imparted by youth who are leaving or who have left the care of child welfare. What they share is real, powerful, and critical in altering the pathway for Indigenous youth from one of loss and shame to one of connection and pride in knowing their culture, its history, and its promise.

The Data: Children and Youth in Government Care

The Government of Canada reports that 52.2 per cent of children in foster care are Indigenous, even though Indigenous children in Canada make up only 7.7 per cent of the total child population under the age of fourteen (Statistics Canada, 2016). Focusing in on the Alberta context, as of March 2021 there were 8,260 children aged zero to seventeen in the care of provincial children's services; of those, 5,874 (71 per cent) were Indigenous. Of the total child population in Alberta, Indigenous children aged zero to seventeen make up 10 per cent (Government of Alberta, 2021a). As of July 2021, there were 1,016 children and youth from Treaty 7 in the care of Children's Services across the province (Government of Alberta Children's Services, 2021b). In Saskatchewan, 25 per cent of the child population is Indigenous, and about 65 per cent of children in care are Indigenous (Council of the Federation, 2015). In Manitoba, 23 per cent of the child population is Aboriginal, and about 87 per cent of the children in care are Aboriginal (Council of the Federation, 2015). There is no provincial data in Alberta regarding the number of Indigenous young adults receiving post-eighteen support through the Alberta Support and Financial Assistance Program.

The disrupting of Indigenous families and culture that began with the establishment of residential schools and was followed by the Sixties Scoop (Blackstock, 2007; Johnston, 1983) continues as we witness the numbers of Indigenous children and youth in care increasing. In Alberta we have seen a 2 per cent increase year over year from 2019 to 2021 (Government of Alberta, 2021a). This increase is in direct contrast to the first recommendation of the Truth and Reconciliation Commission of Canada (TRC) (2015), which is to address the overrepresentation of Indigenous youth in care. Instead, more Indigenous youth are in care, their Indigenous roots disrupted, where they face the already challenging task of transitioning to adult life. This is the focus of this chapter.

> *Our children need to come home...we are building relationships in our community for the next generation.* (Harriet North Peigan, Band designate, Piikani Nation, personal communication, June 25, 2021)

Coming home to one's Indigenous family means coming home to a traditional cultural community where the responsibility for raising children does not fall solely to their parents. The community opens its arms and takes pride in providing the lessons of connection to the land, history, and spirituality, forming an identity for each child that has deep intertwined roots. When a child is removed from their parents, they are taken away from everything they know, causing a grief and loss that they struggle to understand (TRC, 2015). The challenges experienced by an Indigenous youth transitioning to adulthood begin here.

Legislation, Policy, and Practice

The origins of child welfare are predicated on the Eurocentric approaches that drove assimilation agendas. All decisions regarding the removal of a child from parental care are to be made in compliance with legislation and policy that set out the requirements to be met and the process to be followed (see the *Child, Youth and Family Enhancement Act* of Alberta, *The Child and Family Services Act* of Saskatchewan, and *The Child and Family Services Act* of Manitoba). Practice guides the assessment of risk and the determination of mitigation factors; ultimately, it informs decisions about the level of involvement required to address child safety. Child welfare legislation, policy, and practice are socially constructed (created by government) to provide the framework by which decisions are made about the lives of children and families in Alberta and other jurisdictions. The numbers of Indigenous children and youth in care now exceed those housed in residential schools, furthering the trauma and extending it to future generations (Bennett et al., 2005).

Indigenous families and communities respect holistic and traditional models that differ greatly from the specialized and often rigid practice models that prevail in most of child welfare (Lafrance & Bastien, 2007). The child welfare worker's inherent biases are layered into assessment and decision-making. A number of studies highlight this phenomenon, in which over-evaluation occurs for some and under-evaluation for others (Enosh & Bayer-Topilsky, 2015; Trocmé et al., 2004; van Krieken, 2010). Enosh and Bayer-Topilsky (2015) asked 105 child welfare workers to review 840 cases of low, high, and ambiguous risk. Results show that when faced with ambiguous and high-risk cases, workers' decisions are influenced significantly by socioeconomic status and race. This means that when a worker is uncertain, increased weight is given to poverty and then to race, increasing the number of children entering care. In the Canadian child welfare context, this over-evaluation applies to the Indigenous child where these biases influence the measure of the need for state intervention. The dynamic fails to consider the effects of previous trauma on generations impacted by government oppression and the removal of children from their families and their culture. Further, Indigenous youth face oppression and systemic barriers created by systems that are supposed to help and support them. These situations are not unique to Alberta and are a function of Eurocentric structures and intentions of government. Blackstock (2015) writes that the federal government "requires First Nations to accept provincial/territorial child welfare laws as a federal funding pre-condition. The funding regimes amplify colonialism as they limit the range and quality of services First Nations can provide, providing minimal funding for culturally based approaches" (p. 8).

This troubling bureaucratic stance serves to continue the trajectory of cultural breakdown in Indigenous families and communities. Del Graff, former Child and Youth Advocate for Alberta, explains, "the facts speak for themselves: Aboriginal children come into care more often, stay in care longer, and are less likely to be returned to their families than their non-Aboriginal peers" (OYCA, 2016, p. 3). As a result, Indigenous youth transitioning to adulthood from the care of child welfare are doing so having experienced limited cultural exposure. This can take two forms: some have no cultural connection, and others have been exposed to generic activities that have little to no connection with their own Indigenous community. For example, young people talk about being asked to wear their Indian dress to participate in school assemblies—a token recognition of Indigenous peoples that is offensive.

Adolescence to Adulthood

As we move to a discussion of the transition from adolescence to adulthood—and specifically the journey from being in the care of child welfare to independence—it is "critically important to keep in mind that developmental tasks are sociocultural constructions" (Roisman et al., 2004, p. 130). The task of the young person during adolescence is to approach adulthood with increasing clarity about who they are, what they believe in, and where and how they fit into society. Indigenous youth find themselves caught in a paradox where they do not know their own culture and all of its unique and wonderful components, nor are they accepted by or comfortable in the Western culture (Bennett et al., 2005).

The critical tasks of adolescence require youth to incorporate their experience of how others see them with their view of self and to envision their future possibilities, placing themselves within culture and society. A journey through childhood that is immersed in family, community, and cultural history, taken in through all of the senses both consciously and subconsciously, has the greatest hope for success. The final report of the National Inquiry into Missing and Murdered Indigenous Women and Girls (2019) noted, "For many people, the importance of healing lies not only in the current generation, but in the future ones, through work with youth" (vol. 1b, p. 32).

Erikson (1960) describes a process of letting go of childhood and taking a leap of faith into adulthood. For young adults, positive results are grounded in the reliability of the adults who support them and in their own connection to family and kin through shared beliefs, values, and perspectives (cited in Hoare, 2013). Youth transitioning from care find themselves with significant gaps in this process, accompanied by negative or ambivalent perceptions of self. Growing up in care presents grave challenges for identity development. Many questions may remain unanswered: Who am I? Where did I come from? Who are my people? What are their beliefs, values, and traditions? Where is my future place in the world? The result is a profound further loss of self, community, and culture.

Choate (2019) notes that from the perspective of Elders, culture is "about the daily interactions with peoples, cultural activity and ceremony, land and language, traditions and connections" (p. 12). A strong connection of youth to their culture, the land, and their spirituality can set them on a positive path. Indigenous leaders, youth, and professionals share stories of Indigenous young people in care who take exceptional risks to get to family on-reserve, confirming that the search for "who I am" is indeed as primary a need as food, shelter, and clothing. As we shift to looking to the future, we will revisit the essential need for belonging, connection through culture, traditional protocols, ceremony, and stories.

Voices of Youth

Youth talk to us through their words, their silence, their poetry, song, and art, and their actions. Quality of life studies (Schalock et al., 2016; Singstad et al., 2021) recommend an individualized approach that focuses on three major areas: personal development, self-determination, and rights. When youth are informed, involved, and respected, the potential for a positive path forward increases. The Office of the Child and Youth Advocate (OCYA) (2016) gathered advice from Indigenous youth across Alberta. What they tell us is critically important and should influence change in the practice of all persons working with Indigenous youth in care moving forward. Elders reinforce the voices of youth by telling us that actions matter, not words but absolutes (Leonard Bastien, personal communication, 2021).

> *Transitions are tough. Help us with our resiliency, make sure young people understand what it means to take care of themselves in a healthy way—life skills, and appropriate ways to cope.* (OCYA, 2020, p. 56)

> *Make sure you are there to support them because they will be vulnerable and fail during transition.* (OCYA, 2020, p. 56)

> *When I want to start a family, who will teach me how (to be a parent) and help me?* (OCYA, 2013, p. 12)

Other contributors to the conversation spoke of the critical importance of immersion in Indigenous culture. In response to the death of "Eli," an Indigenous adolescent male, an Elder offered further wisdom.

> *our traditional ways, they were not lost—just dormant. The opportunities for our people to rediscover our traditions, ways and medicine are ready to be awakened to help people like Eli.* (OCYA, 2020, p. 69)

Loss of siblings is high on the list of concerns raised by youth. In what is termed ambiguous or non-death loss (Mitchell, 2018), children are often separated from siblings as they are placed in multiple foster homes; these siblings yearn for one another and worry about one another's safety. For those who have been caregivers to younger siblings, the separation triggers a profound sense of loss compounded by a continued sense of responsibility that they cannot carry out (Herrick & Piccus, 2009; Riebschleger et al., 2015). Moreover, multiple studies show that when siblings cannot be placed together it is a protective to support their continuing connection in other ways (Kothari et al., 2017; Richardson & Yates, 2014; Wojciak et al., 2018).

Overwhelmingly, youth talk about their families. They are well aware that their families need help to be healthy and safe. As one young person shared,

> *You can't break up families. Everyone I know always goes back no matter what. No matter how bad it was at home, they want to go back. Someone needs to listen to that.* (OCYA, 2016, p. 22)

Further, youth stated that remaining connected to school, community activities, peers, and siblings became even more important when they could not live with their family.

The role of grandmothers rises to the surface. Grandmothers hold a place of reverence in Indigenous culture—they are the cultural bridge builders, the holders of history, tradition, and language. Grandmothers offer wisdom for a better future and embrace grandchildren with their whole hearts. Barnett et al. (2010) identify many of the benefits that grandmothers provide across social, emotional, and financial domains, in parent/child relationships, and with child care. It is grandmothers who can work in the spaces in between to assist parents in making healthy choices. When that is not possible, it is grandmothers who step in to provide care.

Anticipating Transition

Long before they turn eighteen, youth worry about what will happen when they leave child welfare. Uncertainty in terms of support, connection, mentors, and role models weigh heavily on their minds and hearts. In the feedback from youth, knowing and being connected to their Indigenous identity was prominent and gives them direction for the future. Youth shared that whether the relationship with their caregivers was positive or not, they knew a spiritual piece was missing that they struggled to understand. The emotional struggles of adolescence—compounded by trauma, anxiety, and what youth describe as being caught between two worlds (National Inquiry into Missing and Murdered Indigenous Women and Girls, 2019)—can result in emotional dysregulation, acting out, aggression, and running away. As a result, these youth are often labelled as rebellious, disrespectful, or troublemakers. Ironically, externalizing behaviours are common responses to trauma events (CSWE, 2012).

Looking Forward: Hope for the Future

The path forward is one of hopefulness and collaboration where Indigenous communities are fully involved in the leadership of child welfare matters in their communities and for their people. Reconnecting with their children and establishing family and community connections within the context of Indigenous culture and traditions is paramount. Partnering with child welfare agencies and resources off-reserve to find effective and sustainable solutions is prudent.

To better meet the needs of transitioning youth, intentional connection to culture must be initiated at the onset of child welfare involvement, especially when a child or youth is being placed outside the care of their parents. This approach requires open communication and collaborative decision-making not only informed but led by the child's Indigenous community. Mary Plain Eagle, manager of Piikani Child Protection Services, makes a passionate plea for "emotional, spiritual, physical, and cultural safety for Indigenous children to be met in ways that decrease the trauma of removal from family and community, from everything that the child knows" (personal communication, June 25, 2021).

Leonard Bastien/Weasel Traveller is a Blackfoot Elder, consultant, and Traditional Knowledge Keeper. For the past twenty-one years he has worked to connect youth, families, caseworkers, and caregivers involved with child welfare to Indigenous culture, through the Indigenous Children's Services office in the Calgary region of Alberta. With a deep belief in the positive outcomes when children and youth are immersed in Indigenous ways of life, family, and community, Elder Bastien has ensured that case teams make additional efforts to heighten awareness of the necessity of Indigenous cultural connection.

There is a growing list of initiatives that are working—showing promising, positive outcomes for youth. Some are described below. You will notice a focus not only on transitioning youth but on ensuring that cultural and familial connectedness occurs for the youngest children. The intensity of early identity work has a direct and positive impact on youth and adult development; when possible, caregivers should engage birth families as cultural connectors (OCYA, 2016; Degener et al., 2021). Youth transitioning out of the child welfare system into adult life with a host of increased expectations require a solid foundation of cultural identity, the formation of which begins in childhood.

Celebrating the Indigenous Youth's Identity

Identity is built on the foundation of language and culture. Instilling pride in one's identity, whether Indigenous or non-Indigenous, plays a critical role in the formation of each young person's identity and their healthy transition to adulthood. Embrace culture, language, spirituality, and connection through intentional and honourable actions that follow a youth beyond adolescence.

> *No one agency can do that...they have to all come together.* (Elder, as quoted in OCYA, 2016, p. 43)

The cultural significance of last names is deeply rooted in stories, and it is parents, grandparents, and extended family who know these stories. Youth should be supported to seek out their story—a story that instills pride rather than shame. Does my name have a story? Can you share it with me? Are powerful questions connecting the generations with one another?

Naming ceremonies have a tremendous impact and are tied to traditional protocols. The giving of an Indigenous name is one way to welcome a young person back to the community. Assisting a youth in returning to their parents or grandparents and asking them to choose a name further establishes ancestral roots. This process shows young people where they come from as well as traditional practices and their place in generations of history.

Toss out the Western genogram and create an intertwined *family and cultural story*. The use of the Winter Count, a series of symbols created by Indigenous Peoples, offers a traditional approach (Raczka, 1979). Using a natural canvas or white paper to represent the buffalo robe engages youth in illustrating the journey of their life and that of their clan/community history—"always connecting from now to yesterday within culture" (Roy Bear Chief, personal communication, July 2021). The Winter Count is a cultural representation youth can take with them as they transition to adulthood.

> *A small photographic image, drawn on a tanned deer hide, carries a story of the Blackfoot people. Each year thereafter another is added, until the history of the people emerges in what is called a winter count. The image is a reminder of a significant event, a story to be told in detail to future generations.* (Raczka, 1979)

Community and Family Connections

A hopeful approach is to look to the community first, creating lifelong relationships that sustain youth well into adulthood. The reality is that the youth often do not know their culture, and their families may not know all of the story. The rebuilding of culture requires the engagement of everyone who can learn together and offer support to the youth in a safe environment. Youth need both organized and natural opportunities to listen and learn from leaders, Elders, and grandparents about what it means to be Indigenous. Experiencing first-hand how to

TOP: Figure 5.1. Tanned deer hide. "Piikanikoan: A Modern Wintercount," by Ira Provost (Photograph courtesy of Galt Museum & Archives). BOTTOM: Figure 5.2. The Piikani Child and Family Services teepee (Photograph by Kelly Provost).

respect the land, spirituality, and protocols shapes identity, in turn helping to answer the core questions related to "who I am."

The tipi represents another way to think about **community and family connection**. As described by Roy Bear Chief (personal communication, 2021), the tipi poles (fifteen to eighteen or more) that make up the tipi frame represent the youth's family structure, from parents to grandparents and other relatives. The two poles embedded into the ears of the tipi canvas are the youth's strongest connections. The pegs that hold the canvas together represent those supports that ground the youth (e.g., school, friends, activities). The stakes that are pounded into the ground hold the tipi in place, representing the values and beliefs of the youth. The warmth, love, support, guidance, mentorship, safety, and security of being inside the tipi are provided for the youth throughout their lives. This is the environment needed for youth to thrive before they age out of the system. This activity allows the youth to think visually about the important components of their life and to work toward adding those things that are missing (as told by Clement Bear Chief via personal communication with Elder Roy Bear Chief, July 14, 2021).

Sibling Relationships

The importance of sibling relationships cannot be overstated. Thinking about this from the child's perspective offers deep insights into the emotional impact of separation.

> *You miss fussing with your [siblings] and when thunderstorms come you go run, you get in their bed cause you're scared and it's just like, it's not a good feeling at all.* (shared by Ebony, as quoted in Mitchell, 2018, p. 3)

Placing siblings in the same home is ideal. When that cannot happen, starting contact right away and then maintaining it is a powerful strength-based approach. Connection can take many forms. Technology offers additional options for the sharing of stories, photos, play and craft dates, language learning through stories, music, and other areas of interest. When attending in person is an option, the involvement of children/siblings in interesting and age-appropriate community activities builds relationships with safe spaces. Including all siblings (those in care and those who have transitioned out) grows lifelong connections. The experience of a sibling group who met the family's new baby for the first time on their reserve was heartwarming. The worries the siblings had expressed about how the baby was doing were mitigated by spending some highly valuable cultural and social time with their new sibling and his caregiver.

Language and Culture

Creation stories like that of *NAPI and the Rock* (EagleSpeaker, 2017) are embedded in the culture. Many stories are now in readers or in audio formats that can be used in school and at home. Expose youth to cultural teachings through storytelling using the spoken word, art, music, and dance. Explore digital storytelling, a technique that is being used to connect children and youth with Elders, allowing for the capturing of the story and the relationship to be revisited over time.

The Piikani Nation's Blackfoot App (https://piikanicfs.ca/2017/08/22/piikani-paitapiiyssin-app) is an innovative way of engaging youth on their pathway to learning language and culture using technology. Many other apps are also available, with more being developed, allowing adults to support youth in the technological world they live in and to increase interest and grow knowledge. "Culture is not synonymous with country or ethnicity, for example, but rather describes communities whose members share key beliefs, values, behaviors, routines, and institutions" (Jensen, 2015, p. 4).

The Youth's Team

Workers and caregivers play weighty roles in the lives of children in care. They hold a lot of responsibility for the outcomes of youth as they move into their adult lives. Communication with the youth is built from relationships of trust, such that there are times when the young person does not need to speak for the adults to know that help is needed. The creation story of Anitopisi is a metaphor for the role of the **caring adults** who respond when there are vibrations—cries for help—from the children and youth in care. Think about your role and picture a spiderweb of vibrations as you read the story of Anitopisi, as shared by Elder Roy Bear Chief:

> *He instructed Anitopisi to wrap the world, with the people in it, in his web and let them down to the lower world. Anitopisi did as he*

was told and let them down from the upper world through a hole. After the people were lowered from the upper world (spoomootsi) to here below, Anitopisi explained to them that the web would remain with them so that the Creator would know when to help them. Whenever there is trouble or an emergency, one string of the web would vibrate, and this would signal the Creator, who would come to help. Man was told to pattern his life after the web so that they can stay close together and help each other whenever there is a problem, anywhere on the web. When there is no trouble, the web would remain calm; otherwise, it would vibrate and everyone on the web would know and come to help with whatever the problem may be." (as told by Clement Bear Chief via personal communication with Elder Roy Bear Chief, July 14, 2021)

A second and equally important component is to engage early, and often. **Engagement** not only in training but in land-based learning and ceremony is necessary for workers and caregivers. During focus groups led by the Alberta OCYA, it was suggested that cultural mentors be available to caregivers. Natural teaching opportunities on the land augment training and embed a deeper understanding, building compassionate and supportive allyship. Elders recognize that caseworkers and caregivers who accompany children and youth to cultural activities and ceremony become increasingly committed as they understand the cultural dynamics and relationships. This level of involvement allows for deeper meaning, dialogue, and emotional support to occur with the youth. Indigenous youth who succeed are those who live in culturally connected homes, where caregiver connections do not end at age eighteen or when the file closes.

We end this chapter knowing that you have listened with both your ears and have heard the messages of the Indigenous children and youth in care. They know more than we can imagine and have wisdom to share with us about their journey. Their suggestions for improvement have incredible value. We hold them in our hearts as they become adult leaders in our communities.

Every society, in one way or another, lays claim to a territory. Within that claimed territory, a culture arises from the mutual relationship with the land. It is through this mutual relationship with the land

> *that cultural icons, symbols and images, values, customs, ceremonies, stories, songs and beliefs of the people are developed. These in turn, are embodied into the very being of the people.* (Dr. Leroy Little Bear, quoted at Calgary Foundation, n.d.)

Acknowledgements

This chapter would not have been possible without the contributions of the following Blackfoot leaders: Elder Leonard Bastien—Aah baah maah gaah (Weasel Traveller); Elder Roy Bear Chief—Oom ka pisi (Big Coyote); Harriet North Peigan—Immouiskimakii (Curly Haired Woman); and Mary Plain Eagle—Meesomsakayii (Longtime Meek Woman).

Learning Questions

1. We have shared some ideas for working with youth from a Piikani cultural perspective. What steps would you take to develop a cultural plan for youth who come from a different cultural perspective?
2. Think about the events of your life. Who taught you about your family history?
3. What steps could be taken to reduce the numbers of Indigenous youth in the care of child welfare?
4. Thinking about the transition from youth to adult, what emotions could you anticipate a youth in care having as they reach this stage of development?
5. What is one commitment that you can make to ensure that you are listening to and honouring the stories of Indigenous youth and young adults who have experienced the child welfare system?

References

Barnett, M. A., Scaramella, L. V., Neppl, T. K., Ontai, L. L., & Conger, R. D. (2010). Grandmother involvement as a protective factor for early childhood social adjustment. *Journal of Family Psychology*, *24*(5), 635–645. https://doi.org/10.1037/a0020829

Bennett, M., Blackstock, C., & De La Ronde, R. (2005). *A literature review and annotated bibliography on aspects of Aboriginal child welfare in Canada*. First Nations Child & Family Caring Society of Canada.

Blackstock, C. (2007) Residential schools: Did they really close or just morph into child welfare? *Indigenous Law Journal, 6*(1), 71–78.

Blackstock, C. (2015). Social movements and the law: Addressing engrained government-based racial discrimination against Indigenous children. *Australian Indigenous Law Review, 19*(1), 6–19.

Calgary Foundation. (n.d.). *Land acknowledgement*. Retrieved on July 9, 2021, from https://calgaryfoundation.org/about-us/reconciliation/land-acknowledgement/

The Child and Family Services Act, CCSM [1985], c C80 (Manitoba).

The Child and Family Services Act, SS 1989, c C-7.2 (Saskatchewan).

Child, Youth and Family Enhancement Act, RSA 2000, c C-12 (Alberta).

Choate, P. W. (2019). The call to decolonise: Social work's challenge for working with Indigenous peoples. *British Journal of Social Work, 49*(4), 1081–1099.

Council on Social Work Education (CSWE). (2012). *Advanced social work practice in trauma*. Alexandria, VA.

Council of the Federation (2015). *Aboriginal Children in Care Working Group: Report to Canada's premiers*. Council of the Federation Secretariat. Ottawa. https://www.canadaspremiers.ca/wp-content/uploads/2017/09/aboriginal_children_in_care_report_july2015.pdf

Degener, C. J., van Bergen, D. D., & Grietens, H. W. E. (2021). The ethnic identity of transracially placed foster children with an ethnic minority background: A systematic literature review. *Children & Society, 36*(2), 201–219 https://doi.org/10.1111/chso.12444

EagleSpeaker. J. (2017). *NAPI and the rock*. CreateSpace.

Enosh, G., & Bayer-Topilsky, T. (2015). Reasoning and bias: Heuristics in safety assessment and placement decisions for children at risk. *British Journal of Social Work, 45*(6), 1771–1787. https://doi.org/10.1093/bjsw/bct213

Government of Alberta. (2021a). Child Intervention Information and Statistics Summary 2020/21 Q4 data. https://open.alberta.ca/dataset/de167286-500d-4cf8-bf01-0d08224eeadc/resource/62722a62-7679-4045-9736-855cfdc381c9/download/cs-deaths-of-children-youth-or-young-adults-receiving-child-intervention-2021-04.pdf

Government of Alberta Children's Services. (2021b). Retrieved from field operations data on July 6, 2021.

Hausknecht, S., Freeman, S., Martin, J., Nash, C., & Skinner, K. (2021). Sharing Indigenous Knowledge through intergenerational digital storytelling: Design of a workshop engaging Elders and youth. *Educational Gerontology, 47*(7), 285–296. https://doi.org/10.1080/03601277.2021.1927484

Herrick, M. A., & Piccus, W. (2009). Sibling connections: The importance of nurturing sibling bonds in the foster care system. In D. N. Silverstein & S. L. Smith (Eds.), *Traumatic separations and honored connections* (pp. 27–42). Praeger.

Hoare, C. (2013). Three missing dimensions in contemporary studies of identity: The unconscious, negative attributes, and society. *Journal of Theoretical and Philosophical Psychology*, *33*(1), 51–67. https://doi.org/10.1037/a0026546

Iwama, M., Marshall, M., Marshall, A., & Bartlett, C. (2009). Two-eyed seeing and the language of healing in community-based research. *Canadian Journal of Native Education*, *32*(2), 3–23.

Jensen, L. A. (2015). Theorizing and researching moral development in a global world. In L. A. Jenson (Ed.), *Moral development in a global world: Research from a cultural developmental perspective (pp. 1–19)*. Cambridge University Press.

Johnston, P. (1983). *Native children and the child welfare system*. Canadian Council on Social Development in association with James Lorimer.

Kierans, K. (2003, May 18). Mi'kmaq craftsman preserves 'old ways.' *Halifax Sunday Herald*, C4.

Kothari, B. H., McBeath, B., Sorenson, P., Bank, L., Waid, J., Webb, S. J., & Steele, J. (2017). An intervention to improve sibling relationship quality among youth in foster care: Results of a randomized clinical trial. *Child Abuse & Neglect*, *63*, 19–29. https://doi.org/10.1016/j.chiabu.2016.11.010

Lafrance, J., & Bastien, B., 2007. Here be dragons! Reconciling Indigenous and Western knowledge to improve Aboriginal child welfare. *First Peoples Child & Family Review*, *3*(1), 105–126. https://doi.org/10.7202/1069530ar

Mitchell, M. B. (2018). "No one acknowledged my loss and hurt": Non-death loss, grief, and trauma in foster care. *Child and Adolescent Social Work Journal*, *35*(1), 1–9. https://doi.org/10.1007/s10560-017-0502-8

National Inquiry into Missing and Murdered Indigenous Women and Girls. (2019). *Reclaiming power and place: The final report of the national inquiry into missing and murdered Indigenous women and girls*. The National Inquiry. https://www.mmiwg-ffada.ca/final-report/

Office of the Child and Youth Advocate Alberta. (2013). *Where do we go from here? Youth aging out of care: Special report*. https://www.ocya.alberta.ca/wp-content/uploads/2014/08/SpRpt-2013Apr10_Youth-Aging-out-of-Care.pdf

Office of the Child and Youth Advocate Alberta. (2016). *Voices for change: Aboriginal child welfare in Alberta: A special report*. https://www.ocya.alberta.ca/wp-content/uploads/2014/08/SpRpt_2016July_VoicesForChange_v2.pdf

Office of the Child and Youth Advocate Alberta. (2021). *Mandatory reviews into child deaths: April 1, 2020–September 30, 2020*. https://www.ocya.alberta.ca/adult/news/mandatory-reviews-april-1-2020-september-30-2020/

Piikani Nation Child & Family Services. (n.d.) Mission statement. http://piikanicfs.ca/

Raczka, P. (1979). *Winter count: A history of the Blackfoot people*. Oldman River Culture Centre.

Richardson, S. M., & Yates, T. M. (2014). Siblings in foster care: A relational path to resilience for emancipated foster youth. *Children and Youth Services Review*, *47*, 378–388. https://doi.org/10.1016/j.childyouth.2014.10.015

Riebschleger, J., Day, A., & Damashek, A. (2015). Foster care youth share stories of trauma before, during, and after placement: Youth voices for building trauma-informed systems of care. *Journal of Aggression, Maltreatment & Trauma, 24*(4), 339–360. https://doi.org/10.1080/10926771.2015.1009603

Roisman, G. I., Masten, A. S., Coatsworth, J. D., & Tellegen, A. (2004). Salient and emerging developmental tasks in the transition to adulthood. *Child Development, 75*(1), 123–133. https://doi.org/10.1111/j.1467-8624.2004.00658.x

Schalock, R. L., Verdugo, M. A., Gomez, L. E., & Reinders, H. (2016). Moving us toward a theory of individual quality of life. American Journal on Intellectual and Developmental Disabilities, *121*(1), 1–12. https://doi.org/10.1352/1944-7558-121.1.1

Singstad, M. T., Wallander, J. L., Greger, H. K., Lydersen, S., & Kayed, N. S. (2021). Perceived social support and quality of life among adolescents in residential youth care: A cross-sectional study. *Health and Quality of Life Outcomes, 19*:29. https://doi.org/10.1186/s12955-021-01676-1

Statistics Canada. (2016). *Reducing the number of Indigenous children in care (2016)* [Infographic]. https://www.sac-isc.gc.ca/eng/1541187352297/1541187392851

Trocmé, N., Knoke, D., & Blackstock, C. (2004). Pathways to the overrepresentation of Aboriginal children in Canada's child welfare system. *Social Service Review (Chicago), 78*(4), 577–600. https://doi.org/10.1086/424545

Truth and Reconciliation Commission of Canada. (2015). *Honouring the truth, reconciling for the future: Summary of the final report of the Truth and Reconciliation Commission of Canada*. McGill-Queen's University Press.

van Krieken, R. (2010). Childhood in Australian sociology and society. *Current Sociology, 58*(2), 232–249. https://doi.org/10.1177/0011392109354243

Warrick, G. A. (2012). Buried stories: Archaeology and Aboriginal peoples of the Grand River, Ontario. *Journal of Canadian Studies, 46*(2), 153–177.

Wilson, J. (2016). Gathered together: Listening to Musqueam lived experiences. *Biography (Honolulu), 39*(3), 469–494. https://doi.org/10.1353/bio.2016.0056

Wojciak, A. S., McWey, L. M., & Waid, J. (2018). Sibling relationships of youth in foster care: A predictor of resilience. *Children and Youth Services Review, 84*, 247–254. https://doi.org/10.1016/j.childyouth.2017.11.030

CHAPTER 6

Child Advocacy Work in Alberta: The Importance of Children's Voices on Critical Issues

Del Graff and Arlene Eaton-Erickson

Introduction

The Office of the Child and Youth Advocate Alberta (OCYA) is an independent office of the Legislative Assembly of Alberta mandated to work with vulnerable young people. The OCYA provides individual advocacy for children and youth receiving "designated services," as defined under the *Child and Youth Advocate Act* (2011). This includes young people receiving or attempting to access services under the *Child, Youth and Family Enhancement Act* (2000) and the *Protection of Sexually Exploited Children Act* (2000) as well as young people who are involved with the youth justice system. The OCYA also provides access to independent legal representation for young people receiving child intervention services, offers public education, and conducts investigations into the serious injuries and deaths of young people receiving designated services. The OCYA is child and youth focused, and its services are rights based. The essence of the

Suggested Citation: Graff, D., & Erickson, A. E. (2022). Child advocacy work in Alberta: The importance of children's voices on critical issues. In J. Albert, D. Badry, D. Fuchs, P. Choate, M. Bennett, & H. Montgomery (Eds.), *Walking together: The future of Indigenous child welfare on the prairies* (pp. 113–133). Regina, SK: University of Regina Press.

OCYA's work is about engaging with children and youth, their communities, and others to address issues identified by and affecting young people.

Established in 1989, the OCYA provides direct advocacy services external to the child welfare system. On April 1, 2012, it became an independent legislative office with the proclamation of the *Child and Youth Advocate Act*. The Act enables the OCYA to carry out duties impartially and allows for greater independence. The Child and Youth Advocate reports to the Alberta legislature through the all-party Standing Committee on Legislative Offices.

The OCYA provides feedback primarily to Alberta's legislature and the ministries of Children's Services, Justice and Solicitor General, Health, and Education. This feedback, which is provided informally on a continuous basis, is formally conveyed through written reports. The government is expected to respond to the recommendations of the OCYA in published reports, including annual reports, investigative reviews, and special reports.

This chapter will introduce readers to the work of the OCYA in Alberta, discuss the importance of children's rights, and highlight some of the individual and systemic advocacy work of the organization. We will also discuss the overrepresentation of Indigenous children in the child welfare system and provide some thoughts about how we can collectively move forward.

> *Children in care want and deserve love, loyalty, and respect.* (young person)

> *You can't break up families. Everyone I know always goes back no matter what. No matter how bad it was at home, they want to go back. Someone needs to listen to that.* (young person)

About the OCYA

In 2019, the OCYA celebrated its thirtieth anniversary. This was an important time for the OCYA to pause, reflect, and consider future directions. The office held collective conversations, reflected on advocacy work with children and youth, and considered ongoing conversations with stakeholders. This work resulted in a commitment to three strategic priorities that are embedded in the work the organization does as we serve children and youth across Alberta.

1. We are guided by both individual and collective rights.
2. We are a model of youth participation.
3. We are meaningfully involved with communities.

OCYA Mission: We stand up for young people.

They taught me things about my rights and gave me the confidence to stand up for myself. (young person)

They helped me find words to advocate for myself. (young person)

OCYA vision: Our vision is that young people in Alberta succeed in their lives and communities. Success is defined by children and youth based on what is important in their lives, and children and youth identify the communities that are important to them.

OCYA Practice Framework

Our *Advocacy Practice Framework* (OCYA, 2019) provides guidance for how we develop, deliver, and support a range of advocacy services under the *Child and Youth Advocate Act*. It also provides a shared understanding of our values in our efforts to represent the rights, interests, and viewpoints of young people. The practice framework identifies a range of child and youth advocacy services through three continuums: individual to collective, direct to indirect, and prevention to intervention. For the OCYA, aiming to achieve a balance within these continuums is critical to effectively advocate with and for young people.

In working with young people, communities, and stakeholders, our practice areas reflect four key concepts.

1. **Principled:** The work that we do is guided by the rights of young people and is done with integrity and respect.

2. **Holistic:** We work with children and young people within the context of their lives and lived experiences, to learn and understand who children and young people are, who the people they love and care about are, what is important to them,

and what makes them unique. Fundamentally, the physical, mental, emotional, and spiritual well-being of young people is critically important. The OCYA recognizes that when families and communities are recognized and supported, children and young people thrive.

3. **Relational:** The OCYA values relationships with young people, families, stakeholders, and communities. Through reciprocity, the OCYA works hard to build and maintain these relationships and to repair and rebuild, as necessary. We recognize the value of relationships for young people, particularly in times when they might be separated from their families and communities. Likewise, the OCYA supports young people to maintain strong relationships with those people who are important to them and model how to maintain, build, and repair relationships.

4. **Balanced:** Most critical in the OCYA's approach and response to both opportunities and challenges is balance. This is essential as we continuously learn, reflect, and build as an organization. Advocates listen respectfully and respond in ways that ensure openness—both now and in the future.

While the four key concepts are aspirational, this framework is a tool that allows us to reflect on our current practices and provides us with direction for improvements and the development of new practices.

The Rights of the Child

The overall work of the OCYA is guided by the rights of the child. Several important United Nations (UN) documents outline both the individual and the collective rights that children have. Rights documents are important because they influence legislation and regulations. When a country signs on to a rights document, it is committing to incorporating these rights into its laws and ensuring the laws are compatible with the rights of citizens.

The United Nations Convention on the Rights of the Child (UNCRC), passed in 1989, is the most widely adopted instrument of its kind in history. Canada ratified this convention in 1991, and the Government of

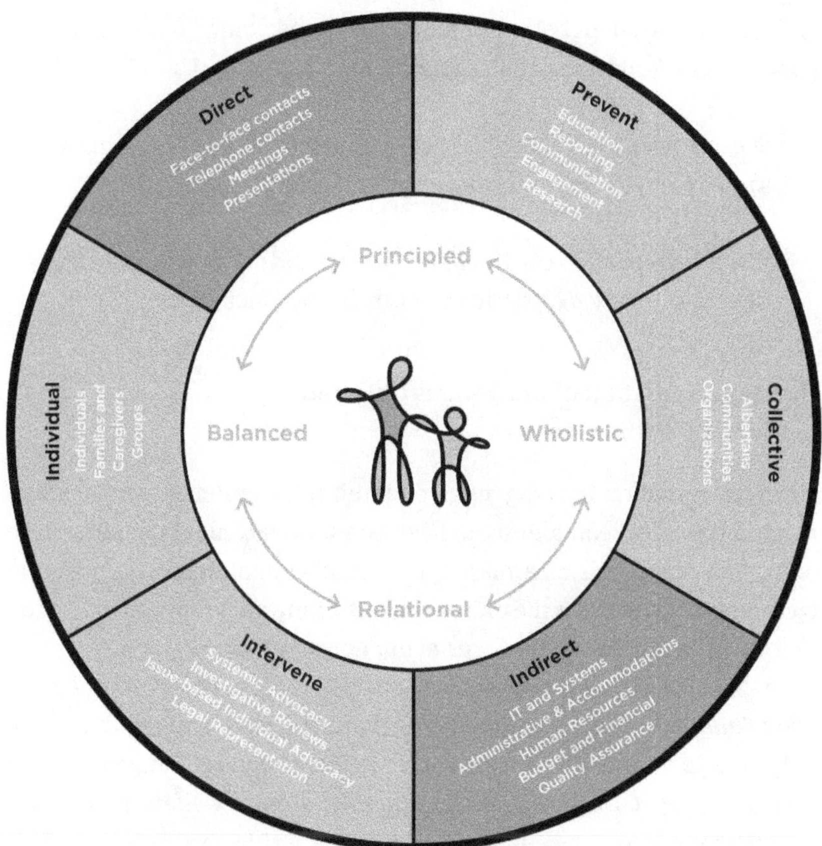

Figure 6.1. Advocacy practice framework. (OCYA, 2019)

Alberta endorsed it in 1999. The UNCRC covers aspects of children's lives that are necessary for them to grow up and develop into healthy adults. This Convention includes fifty-four articles that address children's rights and state responsibilities. Under the UNCRC, children have the right to know what their rights are, and adults have a responsibility to educate young people about their rights.

In addition, there are specific protections provided for vulnerable populations such as children with disabilities (the UN Convention on the Rights of Persons with Disabilities) and Indigenous children (the UN Declaration on the Rights of Indigenous Peoples, or UNDRIP) (UN General Assembly, 2007a, 2007b). UNDRIP established a "universal framework of minimum standards for the survival, dignity and well-being of the Indigenous people of the world." (UN DESA, n.d.). Given the overrepresentation of Indigenous children and youth in both the child welfare and youth justice systems in Canada, this rights document is foundational to the work we do.

> *She was open to listening to us. She would tell us, 'Don't be afraid to share what you want—you have rights.'* (young person)

> *When I was put into child welfare, I wasn't told my rights. I have the right to know my rights.* (OCYA Youth Council member)

Overrepresentation of Indigenous Children in the Child Welfare System

Overrepresentation of Indigenous children in government care systems is not a new problem, and there has been little meaningful change. The OCYA first raised this as an issue in its first Annual Report in 1990 and continues to raise this issue every year. It is a long-standing systemic issue, and one that remains at the focus of our advocacy efforts.

In 2016, the OCYA published a special report, *Voices for Change: Aboriginal Child Welfare in Alberta*. At that time, we identified that while only one in ten children in Alberta was Indigenous, Indigenous children made up 69 per cent of the province's child welfare population. Overrepresentation has only increased in the last five years, and in 2021, 71 per cent of children in Alberta's child welfare system are Indigenous (OCYA, 2021). The OCYA is acutely aware that Indigenous children come into care more often, stay in care longer, and are less likely to be returned to their families than their non-Indigenous peers. It has been this way for many years (OCYA, 2016).

The goal of writing the *Voices for Change* report was to develop findings and recommendations that would improve Indigenous children's and families' experiences and outcomes with the child welfare system, push Indigenous child welfare to a greater level of practice excellence, and collectively influence government and others to change their relationship with First Nations and Métis peoples regarding child welfare. We spoke to 746 individuals (young people, Elders, caregivers, service providers, and community members) to hear their stories, lived experiences, and perspectives on this issue. We heard that the legacy of colonization, residential schools, and the Sixties Scoop continues to impact Indigenous families and communities. We heard about the importance of love, stability, safety, and connection to family and community. We heard about the importance of enabling young people in care to learn about who they are and where they come from, who their family members and communities are, and why they were brought into care (even if this story is difficult). Connection to and the acknowledgement of Indigenous identity was one of the most prominent topics that was brought up. We heard about young people feeling like they had lost themselves when they came into care, who "forgot they were Aboriginal" (OCYA, 2016, p.23).

After gathering the information, we met again with stakeholders to confirm what we learned. We identified eight recommendations in four areas where improvements should be made in the child welfare system:

1. Legislation, governance, and jurisdiction
2. Resources, capacity, and access
3. Program and service delivery
4. Outcomes and accountability

Since the *Voices for Change* report was released in 2016, the overrepresentation of Indigenous children in care has increased.

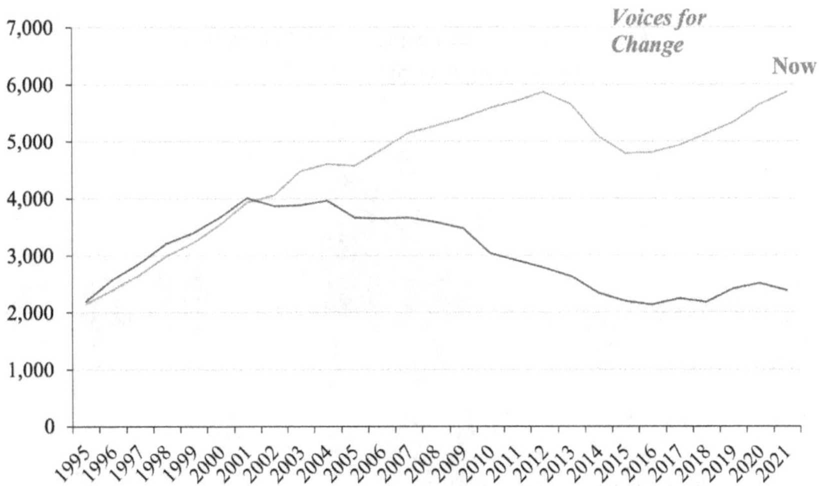

Figure 6.2. Indigenous and non-Indigenous children in care in Alberta.

In addition, the more intrusive the child intervention system is in the lives of young people, the more Indigenous young people are overrepresented. This was true in both 2016 and 2021—in fact, this trend has worsened for Indigenous young people.

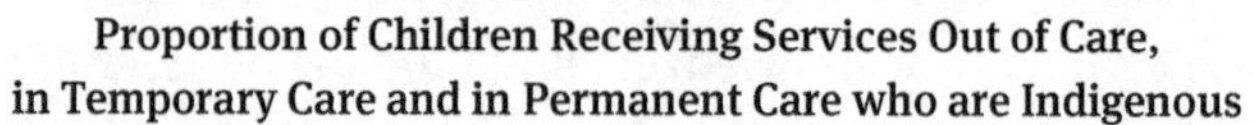

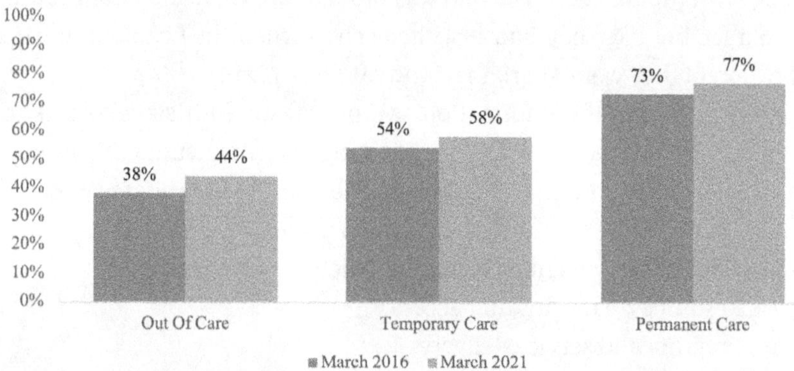

Figure 6.3. Proportion of children receiving services out of care, in temporary care, and in permanent care who are Indigenous.

Finally, the percentage of young people in care served by delegated First Nations agencies (DFNAs) in each of the treaty areas has decreased over time, which is incongruent with advancing the inherent rights of these agencies to provide services to their own children.

Percentage of Young People in Care Belonging to each Treaty Area Served by DFNAs

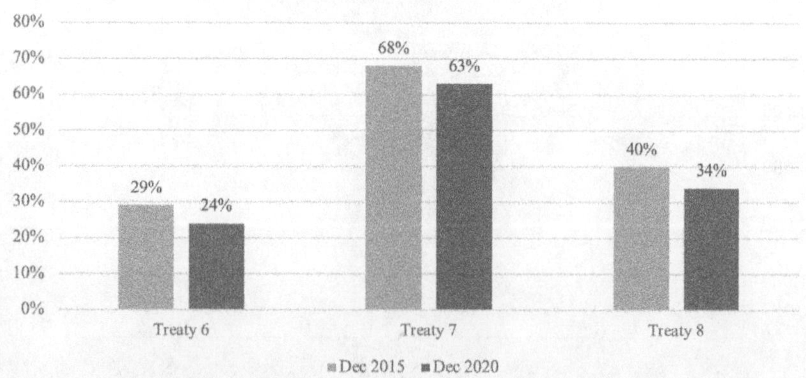

Figure 6.4. Percentage of young people in care belonging to each treaty area served by delegated First Nation agencies (DFNAS).

The number of Indigenous children involved in the child welfare system continues to rise. Overrepresentation continues, and First Nations children are being served less by DFNAs. It is getting worse, not better—we still have work to do.

Individual Advocacy for Indigenous Young People

According to Article 30 of the UNCRC, "You [children] have the right to practise your own culture, language, and religion. Minority and Indigenous groups need special protection of this right" (UNICEF, n.d.). Article 12 says, "You have the right to give your opinion, and for adults to listen and take it seriously" (UNICEF, n.d.).

The first and best advocacy option for most young people is a natural advocate, such as a family member, friend, or other adult who is involved in their life. When this is not an option, the OCYA can help. Being an advocate is a privileged role, and our work is always focused on the young person. We assist them to have their voices heard (individually and collectively), and we attempt to create space where decision-makers can consider their voices and lived realities when they make decisions about practice, policy, and legislation. Advocacy can be understood as using voice or acting as the voice of another (Conley Wright & Jaffe, 2014, p. 3). Child advocacy work is social justice work and aims to empower young people so that they can advocate for themselves. Advocacy "promotes equality, social justice, and social inclusion. It can empower people to speak up for themselves. Advocacy can help people become more aware of their own rights, to exercise those rights and be involved in and influence decisions that are being made about their futures" (Lee, 2007, as cited in Dalrymple & Boylan, 2013, p. 2).

At the OCYA, advocacy has historically been focused on the rights of an individual young person. We strive to hear what the child is saying and, as much as possible, have the child participate in decisions that affect them. If the child is able, they are provided every opportunity to identify their issues and their desired solution (OCYA, 2018). A key component of advocacy work is ensuring that young people know they have rights, have the skills to navigate complex systems, and engage in dispute resolution. A critical question to ask in advocacy work with young people is how we as helpers are supporting their ability to self-advocate more effectively.

There has been a shift in the OCYA to consider rights more wholistically, to focus on both the individual and collective rights of young people. As an organization, this has been a significant learning opportunity and is one of our three strategic priorities. We have developed an internal committee focused on this learning through considering and gathering information on the following questions:

- What are collective rights?
- How do these differ from individual rights and how are they interconnected?
- How are group rights different from individual collective rights?
- In our work, how do we balance this?

There are challenges for us to work through as we consider how these factors impact the advocacy work we do. For example, how do we advocate with a young person when what they want is not in alignment with what their family/community/Nation wants for them? It is difficult when there are strong competing points of view as to what is in a young person's best interest. These circumstances are challenging for everyone involved in the young person's life.

When the work we do is child centred, it cannot be "win or lose." Our goal is for young people to be successful in their lives and communities, and we see the intersection between our advocacy work and the spaces in which young people live, play, and work. It is important to create space where a young person's wishes and perspectives can be heard and to create an understanding about the importance of involving young people in decisions about their lives. This process involves identifying the people and communities important to the young person and involving them in the advocacy process. It is important to ensure the engagement of the young person (in whatever way possible given their age and stage of development) and their community/communities, with consideration of both individual and collective rights. This can be difficult and emotional work, and it is imperative that children remain at the centre of both the work and the decisions being made.

The majority of the young people the OCYA works with are Indigenous. It is important to us to ensure that Indigenous young people (and all young people) are aware of their rights. In child-friendly language, Article 8 of the UNCRC tells young people, "You have the right to an identity," and Article 30 states, "You have the right to practise your own culture, language and religion. Minority and Indigenous groups need special protection of this right." (UNICEF, n.d.). Identity is a person's concept of self, and knowing who we are "connected to is essential to knowing who we are" (Barker, 2020, p. 68). There are many aspects that make up identity (heritage, religion, beliefs, culture, disability, etc.), and together they help shape a young person's worldview and their connection to others and to where they belong. As Barker (2020) states, "The development of a positive identity comes through having experiences with those who are like you and with meaningful exposure to your culture and language. To learn who they are, foster children must learn an Indigenous way of thinking, acting, speaking, and doing" (p. 68). When advocates support children and youth to explore their identity, connections can be made to their communities. Other times, exploring identity is about planting seeds to support youth in their journey of reconnecting to where they came from.

The OCYA recognizes that when children and youth come into care their lives often become fragmented in unanticipated ways. This fragmentation can impact a young person's identity and their sense of safety. Some of the children and youth the OCYA works with struggle with self-identity, and in our work, we do everything possible to support activities that promote both identity and connection. It is "incumbent on us all to ensure that Indigenous children receive and internalize positive messages about who they are and where they are from" (Barker, 2020, p. 61). For example, the OCYA worked with a young woman who was deeply disconnected from her Indigenous culture and wanted nothing to do with her history or her culture. Through many conversations and intentional connections to community members, this young person was able to connect with a mentor and teacher. This mentor developed a relationship with the young person and gently supported her in this journey. This young person now identifies as a strong Indigenous woman, participates in ceremony, and works as an advocate for other Indigenous young people.

In another case, a young man who was involved with supporting the work of our organization had a strong sense of identity as a First Nations young person. He supported other young people and helped build relationships based on belonging and purpose. He also helped the OCYA to consider different ways young people express their identities, and he demonstrated this through the strength and clarity of his own identity. What helped this young man was the support provided by his family, his community, his Elders, and his Nation as he transitioned through his own identity formation. He was actively engaged in learning about who he was, and he was able to approach the connections to his culture with the support of many caring adults in his life. He belonged to a group of people from his Nation who sang and drummed together, and this evolved into a community that was a huge support in his life. He is a highly respected member of his community, where he is now a father and is raising his young family.

The work of the OCYA is about listening and hearing the voices of children and youth. When a young person does not feel heard and does not feel like their voice matters to anyone, and they are able to experience what it is like to be heard—to have someone in their corner—a light goes on for them. When that happens, our work is not just about the individual young person but also about their siblings, the people they love, and the people who love them. When young people experience being heard, when they feel like they belong, those connections are strengthened, and it makes a difference. When young people are taken seriously, when their needs and rights are attended to, advocacy becomes profoundly impactful. When a young person recognizes that they have the right to be who they are, to live in their cultural ways, and to embrace their identity, and that it is safe for them to have a voice and be a full participant in their own life, it can be transformative. It speaks to how they conceptualize themselves and their place in the world.

Transformative system change needs to occur in child welfare. We believe that systems can be adaptable and can change, so that young people can strengthen their connections with helpful support from family, friends, and the communities in which they feel a sense of belonging.

> *They handled the situation in a way that taught me how to advocate for myself.* (young person)

> *[My advocate] made sure I was heard and made sure I was okay with the decisions or if I have any questions. My advocate was totally in my corner.* (young person)

Systemic Advocacy for Indigenous Young People

Systemic advocacy is about working toward broad changes in policy, practice, and legislation that will benefit many young people now and in the future. The OCYA's independence from government has provided a great deal of autonomy in identifying systemic issues and advocating for systemic change, reporting, and making recommendations to government about how to improve systems that serve young people.

The OCYA invites young people, Elders, Knowledge Keepers, community members, and various experts to participate in processes so we can receive their guidance, knowledge, and information. It is critically important that they help us to understand the circumstances of their lives, their children, and their communities. Through conversations and shared knowledge, the OCYA is empowered to make sound recommendations that we anticipate government will hear, act upon, and be accountable for. Making recommendations to government is one of the most important ways we can advocate at a systemic level.

Child advocates across Canada do not have the authority to issue orders for government or to impose binding recommendations requiring government action. Provincial and territorial child advocates are required to provide information that supports the basis for the recommendations we make, and governments are required to provide a response to our recommendations. In Alberta, there is no requirement for government to be accountable to any public body for the actions taken in response to our recommendations. We believe that the OCYA should be bound to be publicly accountable for the recommendations we make to government to improve systems that serve young people. We also believe the government should be bound to be publicly accountable for what it does in response to our recommendations. We believe that the notion of binding accountability is going to be even more substantive in the future.

The OCYA has authored many reports that address systemic issues and the barriers that young people in Alberta experience. These reports have focused on the overrepresentation of Indigenous children in the child welfare system; young people transitioning out of government care; LGBTQ2S+ young people in the child welfare and youth justice systems; the use of pepper spray and seclusion on young people in youth justice facilities; and most recently, the opioid crisis. Given the disproportionate number of Indigenous young people in both the child welfare and youth justice systems, the issues discussed in each of these reports disproportionately impact Indigenous young people. We hear from young people that systemic changes are needed for them (collectively) to be healthy and successful in their lives and communities.

It is our belief that systems can change, but this change is often difficult and slow. For those serving young people, like the OCYA, it means being self-reflective about our beliefs, our motivations, and our capacity for change. It involves examining our work and the work of our organizations—looking at our practice and policies and seeing how they intersect and support the rights of the children and young people we serve. It means allowing our work (individually, organizationally, and collectively) to be challenged and encouraged by the rights, experiences, and voices of young people. It is important for us to engage in collective conversations about the challenges we experience in advocating for young people and how we adapt our work to remain relevant to the current realities facing young people and their communities.

> *If you have success without sacrifice, it's because someone sacrificed for you. If you sacrifice without success that means someone will succeed after you. So, just because I have sacrificed, I feel like some people who grow up in the same situation are going to succeed.* (young person)

Self-Governance and Moving Forward

It is clear, after thirty years' experience in advocating for children and youth, that while governments speak about full and equal partnerships, and have, at times, made progress along this path, decision-makers continue to remain committed to a "dominion over" relationship to First Nations, Métis, and Inuit peoples. This "dominion over" relationship is characterized by government co-operation until there is a conflict or disagreement that is too challenging to resolve, and then government exercises authority over Indigenous people. It has been this way since colonization, continuing to perpetuate the institutional racism that Indigenous people experience across government systems. Until government is willing to shift from a "dominion over" relationship, this injustice will remain a challenge, and any relationship that is full and equal will remain elusive.

It is critical to ensure that self-determination for Indigenous people in relation to child welfare is a priority. Our belief is that to be effective, First Nations, Métis, and Inuit people must be able to govern, develop, and deliver child welfare services to their own children in their own ways. As Dion et al. (2020) state, "There is an over-representation of the Western ways of knowing in Indigenous child welfare" (p. 97). It is critical to enable an Indigenous worldview rather than the prevailing Western worldview for Indigenous people, particularly in relation to the welfare of their children.

Blackstock (2009) reminds us that social work has a great deal to learn about Indigenous culture, particularly in relation to the care, safety, and well-being of Indigenous children. Governments must engage with Indigenous communities in a renewed and respectful relationship based on equality and full partnership. One of the biggest challenges in the relationship between government and Indigenous people has been shifting control of child welfare back to Indigenous communities. With *An Act respecting First Nations, Inuit and Métis children, youth and families*, which came into force on January 1, 2020, there is some hope of a path for governance of child welfare to return to Indigenous communities. While several outstanding issues remain, this federal legislation "affirms the right to self-determination of Indigenous people, including the inherent right of self-government, which includes jurisdiction in relation to child and family services" (Act, 2019, preamble).

One of the core recommendations made by OCYA in the *Voices for Change* report states that supports to Indigenous children and families must be delivered with a strengths-based approach that reduces risk to child safety and well-being. It is critical to establish an Indigenous authority for statutory services and to identify and adopt practice standards consistent with the interests of Indigenous people. The current system is not structured to support this approach and fundamental change is required to shift practice, to promote strengths-based approaches, and to find ways to support better outcomes for children.

The act of child protection comes at a cost. While a child may be protected from certain risks, there are significant consequences to that action. The child welfare system often pushes people to do what they are not good at, as opposed to building on what they are good at (strengths based), and there is often only a single and limited view of what qualifies as success from the current legislation that guides workers. The OCYA acknowledges there are times when it is not safe for a child to be with their parents. We must continue to ask how to keep children connected to their families, community, and culture because all of those things contribute to the children's physical, mental, emotional, and spiritual well-being. It is critical to consider the implications beyond physical safety and to ensure that the well-being of the child or young person is considered in a wholistic way. As Makokis et al. (2020) state, "Child welfare legislation can begin honouring an Indigenous worldview by not solely privileging cognitive, emotional and physical health, but also by honouring spiritual well-being" (p. 40).

The following comments, from three young people, raise the importance of both individual and collective rights and responsibilities in recognizing cultural obligations for Indigenous young people and their families:

> *I was happy when I was first in care to be with my siblings, but over time my caseworker did not make it a priority to stay in contact with family. When I came back in my teens, it was like I did not belong. I came back to the reserve and people did not even recognize who I was.* (young person)

> *When I was in care, I forgot who I was and where I came from. I remember wanting to be white and being ashamed of who I was. I hope that no child ever has to feel like that ever, no matter what their background is.* (young person)

> *I wasn't proud to be Native. I thought that I was assimilated. I don't know what it means to be Native.* (young person)

We all must contend with the history of colonization and the challenges of government systems. We believe the OCYA plays a role in that process, and we need to continue to listen, learn, and act. We will continue to be guided by individual and collective rights and to ensure that we are meaningfully involved and engaged with communities and First Nations.

Our strategic priorities—individual and collective rights, a model of youth participation, and meaningful involvement with communities—are critical in moving forward. Each priority provides direction for advocacy work in the future and implies necessary change. These priorities can be conceptualized as a braid of three strands. The work that we do is interconnected—we cannot move one priority forward without the others. We cannot talk about engaging young people without understanding individual and collective rights. We cannot engage communities without involving young people in that process. Intersectionality is an important frame for this work—it assists us in walking alongside children and youth to ensure that they can be successful in their lives, in their relationships, and in their communities.

Conclusion

Some of the most challenging questions for the OCYA (and we are not alone) are related to the future of child welfare for First Nations, Inuit, and Métis children, youth, and families. As advocates for children and youth, do we have a role to play in changing the landscape of child welfare with Indigenous people? If so, how might our role as advocates for young people need to change? How do we need to think about our own transformative change as the child welfare system undergoes a transformation at the levels we have been discussing? The questions can be clearer than the answers.

In writing this chapter, it is important to us that our conclusions come from a more personal place. Here is what each of us wants you to know.

Arlene Eaton-Erickson

As a social worker and advocate for twenty-five years, I find myself in a place of unlearning, listening, and reflecting. I have had to spend time reconciling my work as a protection worker and as a helper who believed "I know best"; I now know that this is not true. What I do know is that I am profoundly grateful for the calling in my life to walk alongside these amazing, strong, and resilient young people who teach me every single day. I have a depth of love and hope for these young people that has me reflecting daily on what allying looks like and how I decolonize my life and my work. I echo the words of Barker (2020): "The stories (young people) tell you...are sacred stories. Story-listeners all carry responsibilities. Once you have been told, you know. Once you know, you are responsible" (p. 97).

Del Graff

There is a saying that when it comes to waves of systemic change, we really only have three options: lead, follow, or get out of the way. I have learned that what is important about these options is characterized by the last line in a well-known prayer, the Serenity Prayer: that is, "the wisdom to know the difference." The best way I know of to sort out the difference is to look closely at what I believe. As a Métis person, and after almost forty years of professional practice, I believe in my heart three things that, in my view, are undeniable truths:

- First Nations, Métis, and Inuit people have the inherent right to raise our own children.
- First Nations, Métis, and Inuit people are the most able people to raise our own children.
- First Nations, Métis, and Inuit people, with the governance, resources, services, and accountability we need, have the greatest natural capacity to provide for the welfare of our own children.

It is becoming clearer that the best ways for us to represent the rights, interests, and viewpoints of Indigenous children and youth is to support and advocate for the transformation of the child welfare system toward these undeniable truths. At the national closing event for the Truth and Reconciliation Commission in June of 2015, the Canadian Council of Child and Youth Advocates presented its Declaration of Reconciliation. It was my privilege to read the Declaration at the closing ceremonies. It stated,

> *Our Council of Advocates will continue to work towards the reconciliation initiated by the Truth and Reconciliation Commission process. We will be vigilant in ensuring that the rights of Aboriginal children are respected. We will continue to work to engage with Aboriginal children and youth.*
>
> *The healing journey, and the path to reconciliation, includes the involvement of youth in defining their own future. This is a journey that must be taken by all Canadians. By appreciating the past and hearing and learning from and about each other, trust and respect can be built. We will work to support Aboriginal children and youth to speak out, have their voices heard, and have their best interests*

reflected in how our nation's future unfolds. (Canadian Council of Child and Youth Advocates, 2015, p. 2)

This means we need to do all we can to support First Nations, Métis, and Inuit people to exercise our inherent rights, our abilities, and our capacities to raise our children and youth in the good ways and on the lands that we share.

Learning Questions

1. Why is it important to understand children's rights? What could some of the consequences be if young people do not know their rights?
2. Were you surprised to learn that the overrepresentation of Indigenous children in Alberta's child welfare system has increased over the last five years? What changes do you think need to occur (in legislation, policy, practice) to address this issue?
3. How do you define advocacy? Do you think it is important for people to have a shared understanding/definition of advocacy? Why or why not?
4. In your role (as a helper, student, academic, or community member), how do you support others to self-advocate more effectively?
5. *An Act respecting First Nations, Inuit and Métis children, youth and families* came into force on January 1, 2020. How do you think this piece of legislation will impact the overrepresentation of Indigenous children in the child welfare system? How does this piece of legislation impact you and the work you do?

References

An Act respecting First Nations, Inuit and Métis children, youth and families, SC 2019, c 24. https://laws.justice.gc.ca/eng/acts/F-11.73/page-1.html

Barker, C. (2020). Miyawâta: Family teachings on Turtle Island. In L. Makokis, R. Bodor, A. Calhoun, & S. Tyler (Eds.), *ohpikinâwasowin/Growing a child: Implementing Indigenous ways of knowing with Indigenous families* (pp. 43–70). Fernwood Publishing.

Blackstock, C. (2009). The occasional evil of angels: Learning from the experiences of Aboriginal peoples and social work. *First Peoples Child & Family Review*, *4*(1), 28–37. https://doi.org/10.7202/1069347ar

Canadian Council of Child and Youth Advocates (2015, June 1). *Declaration of reconciliation*. http://www.cccya.ca/Images/english/pdf/Declaration_of_Reconciliation_En.pdf

Child and Youth Advocate Act, SA 2011, c C-11.5. http://www.qp.alberta.ca/documents/Acts/c11p5.pdf

Child, Youth and Family Enhancement Act, RSA 2000, c C-12. http://www.qp.alberta.ca/documents/Acts/c12.pdf

Conley Wright, A., & Jaffe, K. (2014). *Six steps to successful child advocacy: Changing the world for children*. Sage Publishing.

Dalrymple, J., & Boylan, J. (2013). *Effective advocacy in social work*. Sage Publishing.

Dion, A., Tyler, S., Pace, C., & Delver, K. (2020). Ayahpatisi: Practice as ceremony. In L. Makokis, R. Bodor, A. Calhoun, & S. Tyler (Eds.), *ohpikinâwasowin/Growing a child: Implementing Indigenous ways of knowing with Indigenous families* (pp. 92–112). Fernwood Publishing.

Makokis, L. Bodor, R., Calhoun, A., Tyler, S., McLellan, A., Veldhuisen, A., Kopp, K., McLeod, S., & Goulet, S. (2020). Iyiniw tâpwêwin ekwa kiskeyitamowin. In L. Makokis, R. Bodor, A. Calhoun, & S. Tyler (Eds.), *ohpikinâwasowin/Growing a child: Implementing Indigenous ways of knowing with Indigenous families* (pp. 13–40). Fernwood Publishing.

Office of the Child and Youth Advocate (2016). *Voices for change: Aboriginal child welfare in Alberta: A special report*. https://www.ocya.alberta.ca/wp-content/uploads/2014/08/SpRpt_2016July_VoicesForChange_v2.pdf

Office of the Child and Youth Advocate (2018). *Advocacy services: Policy and procedure manual*. https://www.ocya.alberta.ca/wp-content/uploads/2014/08/PolMan_2018Aug_AdvServices.pdf

Office of the Child and Youth Advocate (2019). *Advocacy practice framework*. https://www.ocya.alberta.ca/wp-content/uploads/2019/11/OCYA_AdvocacyPracticeFramework_Final_web.pdf

Office of the Child and Youth Advocate (2020). *Annual report: 2019–2020. 30th anniversary edition*. https://www.ocya.alberta.ca/wp-content/uploads/2018/11/2019%E2%80%932020-OCYA-Annual-Report.pdf

Office of the Child and Youth Advocate (2021). *Voices for change data update* [Unpublished internal document].

Protection of Sexually Exploited Children Act, RSA 2000, c P-30.3. http://www.qp.alberta.ca/documents/Acts/P30P3.pdf

UNICEF. (n.d.). *The convention on the rights of the child in child friendly language*. Retrieved September 1, 2021, from www.unicef.ca/sites/default/files/2016-11/crc_poster_en.pdf

United Nations Department of Economic and Social Affairs. (n.d.). United Nations declaration on the rights of Indigenous Peoples. Retrieved September

1, 2021, from https://www.un.org/development/desa/indigenouspeoples/declaration-on-the-rights-of-indigenous-peoples.html

United Nations General Assembly. (1989, November 20). Convention on the rights of the child (UNCRC). A/RES/44/25. https://www.ohchr.org/en/professionalinterest/pages/crc.aspx

United Nations General Assembly. (2007a, March 30). Convention on the rights of persons with disabilities and optional protocol. A/RES/61/106. https://www.un.org/disabilities/documents/convention/convoptprot-e.pdf

United Nations General Assembly. (2007b, September 13). United Nations declaration on the rights of Indigenous peoples. A/61/L.67. https://www.un.org/development/desa/indigenouspeoples/declaration-on-the-rights-of-indigenous-peoples.html

CHAPTER 7

Grassroots of Child Welfare Advocacy for Indigenous Children in Alberta: The Creating Hope Society

Bernadette Iahtail

> *Where are our artisans, our weavers, fishermen, medicine people, dancers, shamans, sculptors, and hunters? For thirty years, generations of our children, the future of our communities, have been taken away from us. Will they come home as leaders knowing the power and tradition of their people? Or will they come home broken and in pain, not knowing who they are, looking for the family that died of a* BROKEN HEART?
>
> —Suzanne Fournier and Ernie Crey, *Stolen from Our Embrace*

Introduction

Grassroots child welfare advocacy for Indigenous children involved in the child welfare system in Alberta is a growing movement whose voice will not be silenced. The Creating Hope Society (CHS) began in March of 2006 with a bold vision: "An Aboriginal Home for Every Aboriginal Child by

Suggested Citation: Iahtail, B. (2022). Grassroots of child welfare advocacy for Indigenous children in Alberta: The Creating Hope Society. In J. Albert, D. Badry, D. Fuchs, P. Choate, M. Bennett, & H. Montgomery (Eds.), *Walking together: The future of Indigenous child welfare on the prairies* (pp. 135–148). Regina, SK: University of Regina Press.

2025." When CHS began, 2025 seemed far away—now it is just around the corner. It was anticipated that the care and protection of Indigenous children would have evolved over the past decade and that this vision would have been fully supported. CHS is a non-profit society that was established to recognize the 1960s and 1970s child welfare "scoop" of Aboriginal children as a continuation of the residential school era. The growing number of Indigenous children in care has more recently been described as the Millennium Scoop and the number of children in out-of-home care has surpassed that of the Sixties Scoop. Voices of survivors are at the heart of CHS, and key principles guiding the journey of this organization include building on the resiliency of survivors, remembering the past while moving forward into the future, and learning from and acknowledging the past while continuing to forge ahead. CHS is a learning and educational organization that is deeply involved in the community, providing hope and supports to children and families through various cultural events. It created the program "Knowing Your Rights: Understanding Child Welfare" and provides direct advocacy and support to children and families navigating the child welfare system.

The Work of the Creating Hope Society

At the heart of the Creating Hope Society are key initiatives that place family and culture at the centre of the programs it offers. Initiatives and programs include Aboriginal Fathers Love Their Children Too!, the Aboriginal Mothers Advocacy Program (AMAP), Resiliency Within, Creating Safe Paths for LGBQT2S, and Story Telling: Empowering People. This chapter will profile the work of CHS in relation to its direct front-line advocacy and support of children and of families whose children are often apprehended. Narratives around cultural safety and family support will be central in this chapter. The voice and vision of CEO Bernadette Iahtail, CHS co-founder and Sixties Scoop survivor, will illuminate and illustrate the need for Indigenous voices every step of the way in the child welfare system.

I could see that what happened to us as children was happening to our children and grandchildren. I am a survivor of the Sixties Scoop, and I recognized that what I had experienced was still occurring but under the guise of child protection. Today there are more Indigenous children in care than ever. Our vision at CHS is to return children back home. We also had a dream of an Aboriginal home for every Aboriginal child in care by 2025. I started getting calls from grandmothers asking me to help them before they lost their grandchildren to child welfare. And that is where the advocacy began. A social worker called and said, "I am not supposed to call you or refer you any clients, but I love your declaration. I have a grandmother whose grandson was apprehended—can you go and see her?" I went to see the grandmother, and when I walked into her two-bedroom apartment the first thing I could tell was that the home was child oriented and that she had everything in place for that child. I asked the grandmother for more information, and she told me that the caseworker had not seen her in six months. She said there was conflict between the kinship worker and the caseworker and there were a lot of barriers for her, so it was then that I started calling. First I called the case worker, but to no avail—I was not getting the answers I was looking for. Then I reached out to the supervisor and then called the manager.

The next step was to do a file audit to see what was going on, and this is how we found out that the caseworker had indeed not seen the grandmother in six months. The caseworker decided that the child had to be removed because the father had gone to pick up the child at a daycare, when he wasn't supposed to have a relationship with the child. It was this decision that led to the grandmother contacting CHS. What we heard next was shocking. The caseworker told the grandmother, "Oh, that kid is so cute I could have him adopted out in no time." The caseworker was constantly putting the grandmother in a situation where she felt insecure, and she felt scared. Hearing this grandmother's voice is what really started our advocacy for families and grandmothers. We witnessed how caseworkers were working with families who were trying to keep their kids in kinship care, who wanted their grandchildren living with them, and who were facing so many barriers.

When we started CHS in 2006, we had parents coming to us whose children had been in care for ten years and saying, "I want them back. What do I need to do? I went back to school, I went to treatment, what else can I do?" The report *"Jumping through Hoops"* by Marlyn Bennett was published in 2008, and this work was deeply influential in the work of CHS. Focused on the experiences of Indigenous mothers with the child welfare system, Bennett stated, "The burden of dealing with child welfare must be shared and it is hoped that governments will recognize that only when Aboriginal mothers, fathers, families and communities are given adequate resources for health, education, housing, respite and supports will we see healthier and safer Aboriginal children" (p. 7).

Initiatives such as family group conferencing were underway at the time in British Columbia, and it was hoped that other provinces would adopt such approaches. We wanted to work with caseworkers on the issue of returning children to their families, and caseworkers were telling us that their job was to get children back home. CHS understood that many of our families were the second or third generation of recipients of child welfare services. What helped us do this work was listening to people's stories—listening to the stories of Sixties Scoop survivors and listening to what people went through in life, hearing them explain why they struggled with addiction, codependency, and alcoholism. I do not know any parents who do not love their children. Too often, we discovered that parents who had not healed from their trauma were facing major challenges in parenting, so it was critical to support pathways for families to engage in healing.

The Truth and Reconciliation Commission

I attended the Truth and Reconciliation Commission (TRC) conference in 2014 and presented *Broken Hearts: For Families*, a documentary on families involved with the child welfare system. After the question-and-answer period, I realized that the Sixties Scoop and the foster care system had replaced residential schools and were continuing to keep children separate from their parents. I learned that in 1874 the Canadian government and the churches of Canada had decided that the churches would set up and run residential schools for as many Native children as possible, "to kill the Indian in the child," and this was like a thunderstrike to my heart and mind. I listened to their stories, which were so like the stories of those who experienced the hurts and woundedness of being involved in the child welfare system: loss of communities, loss of language, loss of identity, loss of family, loss of culture, feelings of abandonment, loss of relationships, loss of kinship, experiences of racism, and mental, physical, emotional, and spiritual abuse.

Telling stories is an outlet. For many Indigenous Nations, it was part of survival. Yes, we all love our children, but what happened to them, the ways in which they were traumatized by the Canadian colonial agenda (and child welfare in particular) has led to a lot of unresolved issues. It has contributed to attachment disorders. Parents often did the best they could do, but they were not always able to get it right because of a lack of parenting skills, lack of resources, unresolved grief, and poverty—and that's often when child welfare gets involved. Parents are struggling and dealing with their own trauma. For parents, losing their children is devastating. So many parents worked so hard to get their children back, and they really wanted to get their children back. For some parents I worked with, it took up to ten years.

Indigenous Pedagogy: Storytelling

There is one story that I will never, never forget, and it brought me to tears. CHS interviewed families who were raised in the child welfare system. One woman we interviewed, a grandmother, had grown up in care. I remember she brought her grandson with her, and he was sticking to her like glue, just right beside her, and this woman was a double amputee. She told us a story about her life: that she had been put in a foster home when she was thirteen years old and the foster family lived way out in the country somewhere, and the foster parents were very abusive to her. She ended up running away; it was the middle of winter, and she got lost in the bush. When they found her, she had frostbite on her legs, and her legs had to be amputated—she was thirteen at the time. She was in the hospital for about six months until they found her another home to go to. She was taken to live with the new foster parents. She continued her story, and I recall her voice with a shiver. She said, "I wish I would have met this family when I was in my first foster home because I would still have my legs." And it was unbelievable to think that she was taking care of all her grandchildren and doing the best she could. I know that sometimes we are a better grandparent than a parent because we have gone through it with our own children and have learned. And now grandmothers are taking care of their grandchildren and even great-grandchildren.

In terms of addictions, it is critical to recognize that healing opportunities are available, and there are many pathways to support. Whether a person gets help from attending a support group or by seeing a therapist, a counsellor, or an Elder, or by going to a ceremonial sweat, a variety of tools exist that they can use on their healing path. Once an individual works with their addiction, another layer is uncovered in the healing toward wholeness. There are opportunities for healing and a wide array of wellness tools that can support the journey toward health and recovery. This grandmother was just amazing, but it broke my heart when she told me her story. I have been privileged to do this work and hear the stories of many mothers, grandmothers, fathers, and grandfathers.

The First Decade of the Creating Hope Society

The first decade of CHS, from 2006 to 2016, was a challenge. We were always trying to get grants and trying to fund research with families who were involved with child welfare and were also part of the success group. We wanted to know what worked best for families involved with child welfare. We recognized that so many of our families who have been involved with child welfare for years had no knowledge of how to navigate the system, no way to access a lawyer, a children's advocate, or even somebody who could speak on their behalf. As a result of this recognition, we began a new project: a documentary called *Broken Hearts*, whose focus was on the voices of parents and grandparents sharing their stories. We also developed a booklet called *Knowing Your Rights*. One of the most profound experiences in doing this work was recognizing that there were wonderful people who really wanted to work with us and help us with our vision and goals. Dr. Raven Sinclair, Steve Gold, Colleen Courtoreille, Jean Lafrance, and Dorothy Badry all got involved in our work early on. I felt supported, and I had a team who was really working toward figuring out ways to best support families and to do the work that we needed to do in communities to advocate for children and families. We had a vision—a way forward. We wanted to help families to find ways to navigate the child welfare system.

We had a partnership with the Multicultural Health Brokers in 2010, and Teresa Woo-Paw, former MLA from Calgary, called me with a concern about immigrant children's contact with the child welfare system, as she recognized this had already happened to Indigenous children. She asked if CHS could work with these immigrant families, help them, guide them, and we agreed and developed a partnership with multicultural health workers. Through this work we began to see parallels and similarities between immigrant children and our Indigenous children. We did not know the histories of many of the immigrant cultures we came into contact with, so we had to learn. We developed the Aboriginal Mothers Advocacy Program (AMAP), which supported our vision of returning children back home. Our primary vision and goals were to stop children from being apprehended and to work with families directly.

The CHS team had a meeting with a CEO from what was called the Aboriginal Leadership Team in Children's Services. They asked how CHS did this work and where our funding came from. I indicated that we received funding from the federal Department of Justice. We had received $75,000 to be able to start the AMAP program and get it off the ground. And the CEO said, "If you continue this work, I'm going to give you $70,000," and that's how we got started with funding from Children's Services. I had not expected funding from Children's Services because I had a chip on my shoulder about Children's Services. I grew up in the child welfare system, and that is part of my legacy. However, Director Carol Anne Patenaude and I sat down, and we talked for a couple of hours, and she listened to my story. Brian Kelly, a manager, also sat down and just listened to me and Carol Anne talking, and he said that Children's Services wanted to support the AMAP project. These conversations led to a meeting with the Minister of Children's Services at the time, and I shared with her a copy of my documentary *Broken Hearts* and the *Knowing Your Rights* booklet. I also gave her a gift of tobacco, and we had tea. Patenaude stated that she was grateful for the work we were doing at CHS; she said our work was bridging gaps and that nobody understood very well the true impact of the Sixties Scoop and the effect of the residential schools. TRC Commissioner Wilton Littlechild told me, "You know what you are doing, Bernadette, you're bringing the heart back to the family." He said, "For years our government has always taken the heart of your families, your children, and you're bringing them back to the home fire" (personal communication). Those kinds of comments were so meaningful and supportive, and they let me know that I was doing a good job. There had been many obstacles to overcome along the way, even in starting the organization. I knew that I had people's ears and that people were listening. There were some individuals who were not supportive of CHS and what it stood for, but we had a powerful group of First Nations people who understood that this work needed to be done and who worked with us and walked with us on this journey. We chose to work with people who shared our vision for a new way of supporting Indigenous families involved in child welfare.

In our work in AMAP, which ran for more than ten years, we were involved in the return of over 435 children back home, and we were able to help stop the cycle of some families' involvement with child welfare. One of the most important things that CHS does is to acknowledge when children go back home to their families. We hold what we call the "Welcome Home Ceremony," a blanket ceremony. When you think about families who have worked so hard to keep their children and when you acknowledge all of the hard work they have done, it makes a difference. We have seen parents go to treatment, go back to school, succeed in getting stable housing—all to get their kids back from the child welfare system. We need to recognize the hard work that these parents have done to bring their children back into the circle. We need to get around them, to honour them, and sing to them. In our lifetime we do not give enough recognition to the parent(s) who have worked to make a difference in the lives of their children and youth. Parents have done so much work to create a healthy, loving home fire.

Aboriginal Fathers

Our work with Aboriginal fathers has been important for CHS. If fathers were fully recognized as parents, fewer children would be in care. Another important area of our work has been with fathers who wanted their children returned to their care, particularly when mothers were not around. One dad said, "You know my kids have been in child welfare for three to four years and the mom is not around." Fathers started asking us to help them gain access to their children in care, so we started looking around for funding. Our first project, which was funded by Homeward Trust Edmonton in 2014, was to do research about Aboriginal fathers and homelessness. Through this work we saw how fathers' own cycle of child welfare involvement and the pain associated with this contributed to homelessness. Fathers love their children too—that idea became important in our work. There was one story I heard about a father. When the father knew that the caseworker was taking his kids to visit their mom, he would stand underneath the tree outside just to see his kids going into the house and coming out of the house. It broke my heart hearing stories like this, so we continued doing our work for these fathers, mothers, and children. We received funding from Alberta's Human Rights Education and Multiculturalism Fund for the "Aboriginal Fathers Love Their Children Too!" project and held a conference about Aboriginal fathers and child welfare. It was an amazing conference, attended by over a hundred men from Calgary, Edmonton, and all over Alberta who wanted to be there. We even had people from Saskatchewan coming because they had similar issues with the child welfare system.

With the funding we received for this project, CHS collaborated with fathers as well as several community partners to produce a comprehensive literature review, documentary, and resource booklet. Research findings from Phase 1 clearly indicated that Aboriginal fathers in Alberta continue to be discriminated against, and that this is in many respects a consequence of systemic racism in the child welfare system. Aboriginal fathers informed us that they are often excluded from "family meetings" and that even when they are included, they feel misunderstood, belittled, and not respected in their interactions with child welfare workers.

We produced a documentary, also titled *Aboriginal Fathers Love Their Children Too!* We were approached by Pro Bono Canada, who helped by providing the support of two practicum students in law, supervised by lawyer April Kellet, to help facilitate the development of the *Knowing Your Rights* booklet for dads and the creation of a dads' resource booklet.

It was amazing to get this level of support. We held a huge Sharing Circle to talk about dads, and sixty-five people showed up. I told the people there that I would like to hear a story about their dads: How was your dad involved with you? What kind of influence did he have? It was such a wonderful Sharing Circle, and there were people who were crying and said, "You know, I never really thought about my dad. I thought about my mom, you know, what a strong pillar [she was], but I never really thought about my dad." We recognized that many people did not have relationships with their dads, and we questioned them: Why don't we look at the paternal side of your family? We wondered what barrier was there, and when we started to look at child welfare involvement in families, we realized we usually only looked at the maternal side of a family, not the paternal side. This led to a new conversation about the primary focus on mothers and limited focus on fathers in these circumstances with child welfare. One of the things I remember asking Minister David Hancock was,

"Tell me a story about your dad," and he said, "My dad was my hero, he was my mentor." So, everyone from the minister to the conference participants, regular people, shared stories about their dads. This helped us in CHS's work with dads, and in some cases, some fathers had their children returned to them. This became an important focus of CHS's work. However, one of the biggest challenges facing Indigenous families is that they all tend to be viewed the same way. The child welfare system tends to put the same blanket on Indigenous families. A couple of families we are working with, who are not alcoholics or drug addicts, are expected to go for the drug tests because it is assumed they have addiction issues. We now know this is systemic racism.

We have struggled to maintain some of our programs. For example, AMAP has no funding, so we continue to look for funding to run that program. We are updating the *Knowing Your Rights* booklet. A lot of changeovers have taken place in the child welfare ministry. One of the key roles of CHS is not only to support people but to support their hopes and dreams of having their children back in the family. Another role is to support advocacy and provide education to families, so they know their rights within the child welfare system.

I remember a time when I had no clue what my rights were as an Indigenous person. I didn't even know about Indian Affairs until I was thirty-six years old, and I had to educate myself around Indigenous issues. In my work at CHS, I had always wanted people to know that they have rights. I want people to know that they have the right to be here, they have the right to have their kids, they have the right to be able to care for their kids. I focus on the work of helping families navigate systems and really understanding how navigation works. One thing that I really love about the work is creating allies, and I have allies in the community, in the universities, and in different levels of government.

Impact of the COVID-19 Pandemic

Recently, a young man who had just got out of jail was referred to CHS. The referral source said he was an angry person, and they refused to work with him. Well, I spoke with him on the phone, and he was kind. He was so polite with me, and I don't think he even knew who I was. I was just asking him simple questions, like, how can I help you? I told him I was sorry for the things he was going through and asked him what I could do for him right now. He told me had just got out of jail and was tested for COVID-19. He said, "I can't see my family because of isolation and people are sending me forms to fill out and I don't know even know how to print them." I told him to email them to me and I would make sure we printed the forms and dropped them off at his door for him to sign and that we would scan them and email them to the income supports. Just simple little things like these help people to know that their voice matters and that you can be present for someone who needs help. This man was identified as just an angry guy, but he did not appear like that to me, and I would not blame him for being angry after just getting out of jail, being isolated, and having no food and no way to see his family. He really wanted to see his kids, and his family had paid his first and last month's rent.

We have done a lot to help families dealing with COVID-19. We have had families lose jobs and get behind in their rent. We have been able to provide meals, face masks, and sanitization supplies. We had to move our programs online and that has been challenging. We do our best to support people in knowing their culture, and it is challenging to do this work over Zoom. We offer a program where people can learn about parenting and they can read about culture. We have Elders coming online and providing teachings. This is one of the things that we are able to do on Zoom since we cannot meet with people in person.

Another important activity for CHS is hosting events, which have all been put on hold because of the COVID-19 pandemic. Children's Services and the United Way have helped some families get iPads and tablets, which have helped children in care to facilitate and maintain some contact with their families despite the restricted visits that are due to the pandemic. We have tried to reach out to children and families, to have conversations, and have struggled to stay fully connected to Children's Services during the pandemic.

Children Who Have Died in Care

The role of CHS regarding children who have died in care is critical in the community. We know that information on the deaths of children in care has been somewhat limited since the start of the pandemic, and it just seems like everything has gone silent. Every year we used to do the Blanket

Remembrance for children who died within the child welfare system. We used to have community Round Dances and connect with families. We would hold a Pipe Ceremony to recognize those children who died in care. I grew up during the Sixties Scoop and was removed from my family, and there were so many of us who lost contact with our siblings. In some cases, we found out later that they had died. Where I grew up, we were eleven children who became part of the child welfare system, and out of eleven, only four of us are still alive. It is important to ask, Who is recognizing these children who died in care? Who is acknowledging them right now? And one of the biggest concerns about these children is that they never knew why they were in care. Many questions may be raised: Why was I fostered or adopted? What is my history? Who is my family? Where is my community? So many individuals do not know their history, they do not know their families, and they do not know their community. They experience all these losses, and we absolutely need to recognize children who have died in child welfare because it affects everybody in the Indigenous community. It hurts everybody, and it is part of our work at CHS to recognize these children. We were given a set of trees on a walkway at Central McDougall Park in Edmonton, and a plaque that states these trees are dedicated "to the children who died in the Child Welfare and Residential School systems, for those who never returned, and to celebrate and honor all children of today and of the future." We remember those children with a Pipe Ceremony on a regular basis.

Creating Hope Society: Going Forward

In the second decade of our work, CHS continues to receive funding, and there is still a lot of work to do. We want to focus on families involved with the intervention side of child welfare, and right now there are many barriers. Child welfare programs have changed, and we are trying to see how CHS fits within a changing system. We need to continue to do advocacy work for children and families and to continue AMAP, which is currently on hold. We are still getting calls regularly from families whose children have been apprehended or who cannot access visits with their children. They reach out to CHS and ask us to help with these problems; in turn, we ask what the service plan is and what kind of cultural support is required. It has been very difficult during the pandemic to provide the kinds of supports we used to, but we can still provide families with emotional, spiritual, and mental health support. We feel the advocacy role has become more challenging.

I would like to see a CHS network across Canada. We have been asked to open different chapters, but for this to happen would take a lot of intensive work on the ground, and we are a small organization. When CHS started, I knew I needed to step up to the plate for children and families, and when I think about my declaration of an Aboriginal home for every Aboriginal child in care by 2025, I realize that was such a powerful message. I would like to think that this declaration is a right for every child and that the willingness exists to make it happen. I wish this for our children if they cannot be with their own families. I wish everyone would have the mindset that they would do everything possible to support Indigenous children and families in being together. With so much restructuring in Children's Services, we feel there are gaps in our connections that need to be worked on. We will continue to do our advocacy work—to hold meetings and ask questions with and on behalf of children and families. For me it is important to continue working with our families, and we cannot lose sight of the knowledge that our families love their children. We all love our children, and we need to understand that healing does not happen overnight. It can be difficult to meet child welfare intervention timelines, and we need some flexibility when we work with families. Some people may go to treatment ten times, or experience family violence, or suffer from mental health problems, and it takes time to heal from inherited trauma. Some of these problems may require ongoing support.

Conclusion

The Creating Hope Society is a small organization, but we are mighty. We want to make sure that children are recognized and that they have the right to be part of their families. We know that sometimes there are families who are not able to parent, but they still love their children. Eventually, I would love to see a home where a child can live and that becomes the child's home—a place they never have to move away from. Children in care often have to move and this cycle must change. My vision is that we build a home for a child and that perhaps kinship carers or foster parents move in, but the child never moves out. It is their home. Secure attachment to place and people is so important. In this home, the child would be able to attend the same school, go to the same corner store or the local arena, and get to know their community. All these things are so important—we need to stop moving children to places where they have to start all over again.

Learning Questions

1. What is the impact of the Sixties Scoop on child welfare today?
2. What are three ways that you can educate yourself about the history of child welfare and colonization?
3. In what ways can you promote and support new narratives about Indigenous children and families in Canada?
4. What do you think is the most important thing for you to learn about in relation to child welfare and its role in Indigenous families in Canada?
5. What actions can you personally undertake that contribute to supporting, improving, and creating hope for Indigenous children in Canada?

References

Bennett, M. (2008). *"Jumping through hoops": A Manitoba study examining the experiences and reflections of Aboriginal mothers involved with child welfare and legal systems respecting child protection matters*. Ka Ni Kanichihk.

Creating Hope Society. (2009, July 2). *Broken hearts: Rights for Aboriginal families with children in care*. [Video]. YouTube. https://www.youtube.com/watch?v=reRKqaPjkxg

Creating Hope Society of Alberta. (n.d.). Knowing your rights: Understanding child welfare. Online: https://www.creatinghopesociety.ca/knowing-your-rights-understanding-child-welfare/

Fournier, S. & Crey, E. (1997). *Stolen from our embrace: The abduction of First Nations children and the restoration of Aboriginal communities*. Douglas & MacIntyre.

PART III

Research

CHAPTER 8

Walking Courageously: The Voices of Indigenous Child Welfare Workers in Manitoba

Eveline Milliken and Linda Dano-Chartrand

Introduction

It has long been understood that Indigenous peoples' interactions with Canadian social systems have been painful. Those interactions are described in the final report of the Truth and Reconciliation Commission of Canada (2015), the final report of the National Inquiry into Missing and Murdered Indigenous Women (2019), and the works of Trocmé et al. (2001, 2004), Bala et al. (2004), Blackstock (2011), Kinequon (2009), Gray et al. (2013), and Hughes (2013). Sinclair et al. (2004), Blackstock et al. (2007), Kufeldt and McKenzie (2011), and Krugel (2018) document the hardships that Indigenous people have experienced particularly with child welfare systems. Relationships between child welfare systems and Indigenous children, parents, and communities have been explored with respect to residential schools, poverty, ill health, incarceration, and inadequate housing.

Suggested Citation: Milliken, E., & Dano-Chartrand, L. (2022). Walking courageously: The voices of Indigenous child welfare workers in Manitoba. In J. Albert, D. Badry, D. Fuchs, P. Choate, M. Bennett, & H. Montgomery (Eds.), *Walking together: The future of Indigenous child welfare on the prairies* (pp. 151–172). Regina, SK: University of Regina Press.

The report *Truth and Reconciliation Commission of Canada: Calls to Action* (TRC, 2015, p. 1) prioritize attention to Indigenous culture in the child welfare system. Of five recommendations related to child welfare, three explicitly emphasize the importance of culture:

1.ii. "Providing adequate resources to enable Aboriginal communities and child-welfare organizations to keep Aboriginal families together where it is safe to do so, and to keep children in *culturally appropriate environments* [emphasis added], regardless of where they reside."

1.iii. "Ensuring that social workers and others who conduct child-welfare investigations are *properly educated and trained about the history and impacts of residential schools* [emphasis added]."

4.iii. "Establish, as an important priority, a requirement that placements of Aboriginal children into temporary and permanent care be *culturally appropriate* [emphasis added]."

Missing from this literature is the experience and perspective of Indigenous social workers working within child welfare systems. Given that transforming child welfare systems per the TRC's calls to action depends on Indigenous social work leadership, it is imperative to consult with Indigenous child welfare workers, to listen to their experience inside the system, and to learn from their insights. One could well assume that they face additional pressures, contested values, and increased tensions in their mandated agencies. Anecdotally, Kinequon (2009) indicates,

> *I see First Nations social workers come into this social work environment...with fire in their eyes and a passionate desire to make changes for First Nations children. Over time you see the passion begin to fade as they struggle within the bureaucracy and become consumed by a system....Eventually, the flame fades and it's difficult to watch as people leave First Nations social work tired and burnt out.* (p. 9)

In the spirit of "not about us without us," Eveline Milliken developed this chapter with Linda Dano-Chartrand. Milliken is a long-time associate professor at the University of Manitoba Inner City Social Work Program (ICSWP). She acts as director for this program, which seeks to increase access to social work education for Indigenous students (Clare, 2013). While Celtic in lineage, she was born and raised in Treaty 3 territory, where she has sat with Elders in ceremony since her early teens.

Dano-Chartrand is the former director of programs for an Indigenous child welfare agency, clinician supervisor for Wiijii'idiwag Ikkwewag Restoring the Sacred Bond Birth Helper Program, and trainer for 7 Sacred Ways of Healing Trauma through Mind, Body and Spirit. She now works as an Anishinaabe Knowledge Keeper for the ICSWP. She accepted tobacco to co-author this chapter because of her work and positive relationship with Milliken for over twenty years, noting that "I believe my twenty-two years in child welfare and thirty-seven years in the helping field with Indigenous people...have taught me that hearing the voices from helpers in the field contributes towards health and wellness for children, youth, families, communities."

This chapter was written, with gratitude, on Treaty 1 land—the traditional territories of Cree, Ojibway, Oji-Cree, Dakota, Dene, and Métis Peoples. The authors thank the co-researchers for their courage, trust, and generosity in sharing their experiences. When appropriate, tobacco was passed.

The Research

The thirteen Child and Family Services (CFS) social workers who shared their experiences identified as Indigenous (Anishinaabe, Cree, Métis, and Dakota). All had a bachelor of social work (BSW) or master of social work (MSW) degree. All had worked within one or more of the four child welfare authorities mandated in Manitoba (the General Authority, First Nations of Northern Manitoba Authority, Southern First Nations Network of Care, and the Métis Child, Family and Community Services Authority). Some had worked in all four. At the time of the conversations, individual employment in the child welfare role ranged from three to more than twenty years. Following Research Ethics Board protocols, the identities of the respondents are known only to Milliken.

Indigenous co-researchers were asked about their sense of "cultural safety." This concept, arising from the healthcare context of Aotearoa

(New Zealand), was offered as a gauge by which co-researchers could assess their work environment. It refers to "actions which recognize, respect and nurture the unique cultural identity needs of marginalized peoples and safely meet their needs, expectations and rights" (Polaschek, 1998, p. 452). Cultural safety has a communal sense in that the culturally safe individual "is given active reason to feel hopeful that her/his needs and those of her/his family members and kin will be accorded dignity and respect" (Ramsden, 1997, in Fulcher, 1998, p. 333). Milliken (2008, 2012) identifies three key contributors to this sense: being surrounded by similar others who shared one's values and experiences; belonging to a community in which one felt included and valued; and being respected for all aspects of one's humanity (physical, emotional, spiritual, and intellectual). Cultural safety shifts the locus of power, authority, and agency from the service provider to the service user, that is, from the person with the most power to the person with less. To develop a culturally safe space, Tervalon and Murray-García (1998) contend, the privileged must exercise cultural humility, "a lifelong commitment to self-evaluation and critique to redress power imbalances, and a commitment to developing mutually beneficial and non-paternalistic partnerships with communities on behalf of individuals and defined populations" (p. 123).

Co-researchers were invited to share experiences of feeling culturally safe or unsafe within child welfare work. They were asked the following questions:

1. What is your definition of cultural safety/cultural humility?
2. What might be challenges facing an Indigenous social worker within a mandated child welfare system?
3. Given the history of social work involvement in the Sixties Scoop and the current high number of Indigenous children in care, is it possible to make a difference for families caught in mandated systems?
4. Is there such a thing as Indigenous child welfare practice? If so, what characteristics would you ascribe to this way of practising?
5. How can social work education contribute to transforming child welfare practice to be more culturally safe?

Methodology

As with all grounded theory (Charmaz, 2014), co-researchers were free to respond to questions in their own way. Their observations were recorded and transcripts were later returned to them to confirm accuracy and ensure they endorsed giving their words to this project. Commonalities among the thirteen unique responses were identified and themes developed that were reviewed with co-author Dano-Chartrand, to understand their importance and reduce cultural bias in their interpretation.

Findings

The co-researchers' descriptions of cultural safety were consistent with the definitions provided above by Polaschek, Ramsden, and Milliken. Their definitions were holistic; that is, they related to all aspects of their identity:

- "For me personally the term 'cultural safety' means to be able to feel safe in...in an environment where you're able to express yourself emotionally, spiritually, mentally, and physically, the four aspects of who we are as Aboriginal people."

- "When I hear the phrase 'cultural safety,' the first thing I think about is...feeling free to be yourself, without fear...being able to identify who I am culturally."

They identified positive and negative community influences on their sense of cultural safety:

- "Belonging...before, I [was] always having to adapt to my environment wherever I was, whether it was at school, with my friends in their homes, fear of people judging me, my skin or who my families were or our history, all those messages...I could let people see who I was and it wasn't a bad thing. I felt I belonged."

- "I feel safe to express myself and my teachings, my language, my beliefs, my values, my understanding and concepts of the world freely, without feeling oppressed or suppressed."

Five positive themes were discerned from the conversations. These themes, identified by both presence and absence, were

1. the opportunity and ability to participate in cultural practices;
2. resilience of the families worked with;
3. supportive colleagues and leadership;
4. social work education that was decolonizing; and
5. access to culturally appropriate resources.

A sixth, exclusively negative theme, identified as "tensions," was evident across all the other themes. Indigenous social workers felt caught between worldviews and systems. These tensions were present throughout the work environment and could diminish the sense of cultural safety.

Indigenous cultural practices in the workplace was the first theme identified as sustaining. The practices mentioned included smudging, sweat lodge and other ceremonies, sacred medicines, prayer, and Sharing Circles. For those who saw these as an integral part of their culture, these practices helped them cope with the stress of the job:

- "[Cultural practices] gave me healing."

- "It made our actual job more bearable....The challenge was: scheduling, and quality time to spend, 'cause if you have a Sharing Circle, you don't know how long it's gonna take...but then you have to go to Court or you've got an apprehension, but when we came into a Circle, we felt that was what social work was for, those that understood culture."

- "We always prayed; sweats were available; our team days were completely culturally safe."

Organizational support for these practices and worldview was greatly appreciated:

- "Medicines are available—we didn't have to have permission...You could go in and smudge and just sit there for fifteen minutes."

- "They allowed us to do cultural practices like sweat lodges and other ceremonies as a team-building day. They recognized it as building the strength through the organization as a team, so HR was promoting that."

- "The other thing was...definitions of family, like in regards to our bereavement: recognition of our extended family."

Conversely, resistance to these practices was a source of tension for the CFS workers:

- "I couldn't smudge—people said they had asthma or a cough or whatever."

- "We were told we had to smudge in the parking lot—do you know how that makes you feel?...Then they told us the drums bothered them too...so out they go."

- "I've only worked for First Nations organizations. In one agency I saw staff going around the office spraying Lysol where I had just smudged...that was really difficult."

When working with families from one's own and other Indigenous communities, their resilience was the second theme identified as contributing to a sense of cultural safety. To be sure, families in contact with the child welfare agency could be anxious and sometimes resistant. However, the sense of shared identity within community often resolved into a feeling of satisfaction and good relations among the co-researchers:

- "Initially, when there's conflict and the whole reason they're involved with our agency...you do get that resistance. You know there's always gonna be that, but at the end of our relationship, it always seems to be a positive one."

- "I love what I do, but I'm 'CFS.'...The sense is that everybody hates us. One person said, you're not allowed in my home. I don't like CFS. At the beginning, they're very negative....I'm willing to accommodate: 'It's give and take and you need to be that way.' Then they just say 'no big deal; c'mon over.'"

However, familiarity could also breed tension; shared Indigenous identity could work against trust:

- "The people in the community maybe didn't want to do some stuff—they didn't want bad relationships in the community and I get that—so they'd fly someone in to do it—I had to do that once and I didn't know why they wanted the apprehension—so I felt awful, I couldn't explain why I was doing this really serious thing."

- "A lot of people are related....Things can get difficult....You can be talking about someone's cousin."

- "[The response from the community is] Mixture: 50 per cent of the families, when I meet them, their first question is, are you Aboriginal? I say yes, I am; some families say to me, I'm glad because you get it then. On the other hand, I've had a few [Indigenous families] say, absolutely not! I don't want an Aboriginal worker."

As a result of colonization in general and residential schools in particular, many Indigenous people have a loyalty to a Christian faith that historically has not welcomed traditional Indigenous spirituality:

- "Cultural practitioners are a minority within the Indigenous populations, so let's say of ten people, seven of them will be of a Christian background, two of them will be of non-believing some sort, and then you'll have one traditional practitioner who goes to sweats, carries a pipe, sun dances, and so forth."

- "Culture and traditions are different for me, right—for me I am more comfortable in a Christian setting...I had to attend this [traditional] event....I was uneasy."

- "Some communities are more Christian than traditional so that's kind of a battle....There's like this splitting."

- "A lot of our agencies are within their community, so very church-based. I was warned, when I was heading to [community] to be very careful in terms of what you introduce."

The presence of supportive colleagues and leadership was the third theme identified as contributing to cultural safety. This sense of support emanated from both a shared identity and shared culture:

- "First off, working for an organization that identifies as Indigenous makes you feel safe right at the beginning. And, having other staff that look like you...reinforces that safety when you work within an organization of peers that are of like mind working towards the betterment of our people."

- "Supervisors who are aware when we're going through some hard stuff and they come and do a check-in. Do you need to debrief? What do you need?...I feel supported."

- "Whenever we're feeling stressed at work our cultural advisor's door is always open. We have a smudge room...if we need to go and smudge."

All colleagues did not share the same values. Co-researchers spoke about the tension they experienced with some colleagues that did not support a sense of cultural safety:

- "How can a social worker teach culture if they have no knowledge of it or have been tainted or biased due to residential teachings, colonization? How can they take a person to a sweat lodge when it's against their beliefs?"

- "You feel marginalized within your own group of people that you work with, because: 'Oh, X is an Indian, you know...so go ask them.'"

- "There were these paternalistic attitudes; workers seemed like they were disciplining clients; it felt like they were being judged."

Further, leadership is not homogenous in any community. Co-researchers spoke about the tension they felt with respect to leaders who did not support their sense of cultural safety:

- "You need leadership that practise it. They say we need culturally appropriate services but they don't even know how to advocate for what to bring in. How can they bring any cultural services if they don't know it?"
- "When you have to fight for things that you shouldn't have to, it disheartens you. When you have leadership that promotes....It strengthens the worker to provide better services and become more creative to think outside the box. When you have the leaders that don't see, don't practise, you feel unsafe that you're gonna get fired for doing the wrong thing. You feel not backed. You feel oppressed, suppressed."
- "That was a nail in my heart with leadership; nice brown person leading, but no belief in that system, in the culture....On the other hand, a white one encouraged ceremony. And that inspired me, to see a leader, thinking outside the box, role modelling. They knew what was needed that for the organization."

Leadership that created and interpreted policy for the benefit of its own community was also seen as contributing to cultural safety:

- "The policies, procedures, HR and so forth—management have the same understanding as you do and therefore can better provide services for the population that we're serving...so it makes you feel a little better. You also have that pride in working for an Indigenous organization."
- "From an organization and network or a government situation, I would say it would probably be practices, policies, procedures that were developed by communities to help strengthen us to express themselves so we can maintain and retain our own cultural belief systems."

Unsurprisingly, child welfare legislation created outside the community could be seen in the negative, as a structural cause for cultural unsafety:

- "Because we're still working according to the Child & Family Services Acts, the standards, all these things not developed by us, and...the Indian Act."

- "So it goes to show that the policies, procedures, regulations, and laws have done their job well, and now we as people are reinforcing those within ourselves."

Finally, leaders with unsupportive influence outside the agency could bring a political tension to bear on the worker:

- "It's not just legislation: when a worker is new, they go ask the supervisor about what to do. The supervisor has management to deal with. The executive director answers to others. There can be political pressure put on people. A worker can have a good plan approved by the supervisor but then the decision gets taken away—even though the worker knows that family."

- "This girl disclosed to me....It was a close community and there were a bunch of guys involved. Of course, I followed the procedures....I got a letter saying my job was discontinued."

The importance of social work education that decolonizes was a fourth theme, and one that cannot be overstated. Education to decolonize was frequently cited as critical to the workers' sense of cultural safety:

- "Exposure to true history through social work education; it gave me an understanding first of all and then it gave me a sense of positive identity....I was always ashamed of being Aboriginal growing up."

- "[My social work education] brought a happiness. It brought a joy.... There was no shame in being who I was anymore. I learned that I have a beautiful culture and I wanted that for my children."

- "I decided to go back to school as a mature student to help understand; I knew culture, but I didn't understand the systems at play that affected our people. I didn't have the ideology to how to put it into words to teach my people what we're going through. So education brought me to where I am today."

Put negatively, the lack of a decolonizing social work education for one's self and others detracted from the sense of cultural safety:

- "I was one of them: I didn't want to have a brown face. I didn't want to be Aboriginal."

- "Communities are very close in some ways but detached in other ways because you know everyone is fighting their own battles. It's hard to be supportive when you can't even look after yourself, so we need supports in there."

- "Most communities are not practising culture. Most of them are in trauma. There are addictions of all different types...residential schools...CFS involvement, fractured families."

Having access to culturally appropriate resources for family and staff was the fifth theme identified as adding to the sense of cultural safety. It was another avenue by which Indigenous culture could be affirmed:

- "Now as part of our assessment questions we ask about the residential school piece...first generation, second generation, third generation, how does that affect you in your daily life, and your parenting?...Is there abuse or domestic violence?"

- "We have a ton of resources, for every issue that there is, like domestic violence, like alcohol programs, and a program for sobriety and they use the 7 Teachings. I send a lot of referrals because families are interested in the cultural piece."

- "We had some parenting groups and youth groups that would help identify with their culture, educate them and give them pride for their own culture, 'cause there was a lot of shame, guilt...we did have Elders available at one time."

- "We have cultural camp and each worker is allowed to invite a family to come to [location] and we do all kinds of cultural stuff: smudging, medicine picking, fires and sweats and just learn about the culture."

Yet, culturally appropriate resources are often very vulnerable to being cut:

- "When I first started we had money for support workers but then it just disappeared."

- "There was a façade....We were an Indigenous agency but we conducted ourselves like the mainstream but without the funding."

- "Some of our families are asking for an Elder. Asking for a sweat lodge, asking for a sun dance, asking to go powwow....So a cultural position was created....They would lead ceremonies, and bring traditional foods like pickerel, deer meat, or moose meat, but there was no dedicated monies for it."

The five positive themes that emerged are connected; augmenting one theme strengthens the others. These themes are the ability to participate in cultural practices; resilience of the families worked with; supportive colleagues and leadership; social work education that was decolonizing; and access to culturally appropriate resources. A lack of support in one aspect, or theme, reduces support for the other aspects. This may explain an additional tension that surfaced with respect to expectations in the workplace. Even when the cultural recommendations of the TRC's calls to action were adopted by an agency, the expectation that Indigenous social workers could achieve those goals often felt unrealistic. These social workers expressed a sense of frustration that the good way forward was neither possible nor even visible:

- "I keep hearing we've got to do the work culturally—but what is that? What does that look like? No one has been able to tell me."

- "The cultural mission on paper? Who's that for? The people who read it, for the funders, for the province, for the communities to see that this is what they're doing, but in practice on a daily basis, I don't see it yet."

- "I question the resources we use—mostly it is non-Aboriginal foster families—are we following our mission statement?"

This study has clarified that colonization, like climate change, is an environment-wide problem. The burden of colonial traumas, like the incredible weight of carbon pervading the atmosphere, remains for generations. For example, though residential schools have been closed, their impact affects more than their survivors. Traumas experienced by Indigenous children in their most formative stages brought loss in personal confidence, relationship skills, and social trust that, if not healed, are transmitted to the next generation. Even when healed, persistent experiences of racism and inequality can trigger new releases of additional shame and grief:

- "I was raised in terms of not knowing about the residential school, so for me, it was an eye-opener. So when I hear, 'Why am I parenting the way I am now? Why am I struggling in certain areas?' If the opportunity arises I give a history of residential school and when were raised in situations where their great-grandmother, grandmother, mother went through the system and how that affects their parenting, how that affects the way they are now."

Reversing this trauma of experiencing a lack of cultural safety requires an ecological response. Dealing with colonization cannot be done piecemeal by individual training, offering a program, or hiring a great leader, just as one action cannot reverse climate change. As important as those positive themes are, the co-researchers noted, if one positive program is undercut, the problem quickly returns. As in the climate change metaphor, individual initiatives can hardly deal with the challenge of the whole.

Whether we recognize and address the problem or deny and perpetuate it, it seems that the best way forward is still being discerned. The development of decolonized, transformed relations in child welfare is not yet sufficient to show the shape of the future. Many questions remain:

- How can child welfare systems serve the purposes of child protection and family support?
- How does one deal with expectations of confidentiality when straddling the two worlds of settler-defined professionalism and traditional community methods? In Sharing Circles people share what they need to share and that is sacred and respectful.
- What does it look like in the field when the Indigenous social worker is successful and likes their job? What's the difference between that social worker and others?
- How can one be an appropriate ally to Indigenous colleagues when coming from a life experience shaped by entitlement and privilege?

Reversing an ecological threat is hard work. It requires commitment to respond broadly, bravely, deeply, and consistently. Not surprisingly, in their recommendations these co-researchers spoke about commitment.

Commitment to a Decolonizing Education Framework

First, we must commit to social work education that promotes decolonization of child welfare systems and legislation. It became clear that knowledge of Indigenous history, recognition of historical entitlements, and respect for the lived experience of Indigenous people contribute to Indigenous social workers' sense of cultural safety and give them strength to lead and help heal their communities:

- "Commit to understand and work toward decolonization of approaches that are built into mainstream child welfare systems."

- "There's individual stories but then there's all the systemic stuff and you can't separate all of that out, and so when you think about your history and every person has a history, right? With the racism, with those horrendous experiences, the walking in two worlds, the micro-aggressions, the macro-aggressions. So in terms of cultural safety, child welfare agencies, are, you know, they're microcosms of the larger world, right, and so there's still a lot of that trying to find balance within the agencies and do the work."

Second, we must continue and commit to support community building. Obviously, there is no one Indigenous experience. Each co-researcher spoke their unique experience and described their own values and interests. Every community in which they worked is different. What is accepted in one community may not be in another. Even within one tradition (say, Ojibway), each community may differ in its interests and efforts in decolonizing. Different circumstances will influence how to have an impact on the influence of colonial structures. However, there is a value in recognizing commonalities, in celebrating the resilience of the families with whom they work. Returning respect and appreciation for Indigenous community, however that identity is expressed, helps to replace what was lost to colonization:

- "Cultural safety can't be reliant on one person. It has to be deeper. It has to be, you know, more systemic; that if you have one leader who leads in a particular way that's holistic and inclusive, if they go away, the whole place can change...it has to be deeper than that. Or like when I left the agency and nobody's smudging, or if somebody leaves, that training doesn't go away. That's cultural safety."

Third, we must commit to infuse cultural safety into all levels of social work practice. Co-researchers urged ongoing efforts in agencies to develop culturally safe practices and work toward decolonization of mainstream child welfare systems:

- "I wish we could set up mandatory information programs to explain ceremonies, the medicines, how they can be used to help."

- "Training—looking at the impact of residential schools, intergenerational trauma, and Truth and Reconciliation [Commission] in a two-day training. How do you do that?"

- "The training offered? I do not think it was developed by First Nations people—it was the same old story of 'we got input.'"

Fourth, we must commit to the goal of creating cultural safety as a lifelong activity:

- "When we talk about vision and mandate, it has to mean something. It's something that needs to be focused all the time, upon hire, at meetings, in difficult situations where you're dealing with internally at the agency level."

- "It's got to be that organization and their philosophy and their practice and...cultural safety infuses into everything, it's not a checklist."

- "You have to be all in on it, each organization, each individual. It doesn't matter what role we play, whether you're the cleaner, whether you're the executive director....Walking this traditional way has not been easy. It is hard work but I wouldn't change the journey."

- "Nobody seems to be able to tell me what culturally appropriate means...it's not a title. It's not a name. It's a way of life. It's who we are. It's a spirit; it's not a manual."

Loxley and Puzyreva (2017) found that non-Indigenous child welfare agencies were more robustly funded by the province of Manitoba than Indigenous agencies. Fifth, then, provincial and federal governments must commit dedicated money to support Indigenous cultures to ensure availability of traditional cultural practices within mandated agencies and culturally appropriate resources for families and staff:

- "If we have a mission statement that says we practise in culturally safe ways then we need to stick to that—not keep reducing the cultural services we have."

- "More federal, provincial dollars allocated to support workers, to develop more cultural workers that can complement the social workers, implement more practices within social work, managers, directors, CEOs, to be able to have a greater understanding. HR practices need to have more culturally sensitive practices of hiring staff, not just because there's a vacant position, but find workers that have quality."

- "People talked about promoting culture but there was no dollars.... You have to have people that are gonna be dedicated and allocated to work cultural pieces and give the dollars. And if not, they're doing the same old business, old practices just with brown faces."

Though cultural programs tend to disappear when financial support is withdrawn, one co-researcher indicated that commitment need not end the drive toward healing:

- "Sometimes we think government money is needed to do work with our people and communities; we can do the work without that money—grassroots can also do what we need to do."

- "It is incumbent on us to not let that prevent cultural activities. We just kept at it; found funding."

Key Turning Points

Once again, we hope we are at a turning point in history. Awareness of the pernicious effects of colonization in Canada seems substantial. Responsibility for Indigenous child protection and family services, at least in Manitoba, has largely devolved to Indigenous child welfare authorities. Many organizations have instituted diversity in hiring committees to increase the opportunities for Indigenous and BIPOC candidates. The Faculty of Social Work at the University of Manitoba is revamping its BSW curriculum to more clearly highlight TRC responses. Many increasingly look to First Nations teachings to find healthy ways to live with nature. There is increased interest in "how to be an ally."

Recent events have amplified Canadians' awareness of and desire for reconciliatory action. As told by survivors but not previously believed, unmarked graves have been identified by Tk'emlúps te Secwépemc near residential schools (Paperny, 2021). There have been renewed calls to remove statues or rename facilities bearing names of the architects of residential schools ("Macdonald statue removed," 2021). There have been calls for the Pope to apologize for the role played by the Roman Catholic Church in running the majority of residential schools and to release relevant documents pertaining to that administration. In light of the toppling of statues and the burning of several Roman Catholic Churches, Sinclair's (2019) warning that violence may come if profound change is delayed seems prophetic.

Conclusion

Child welfare workers yearn for change because they labour where the ecological challenge of colonization hits home. They work with hurting families and see the destruction in communities, caused by racial inequality, poverty, injustice, and neglect. They know how hard it is to overcome the inertia of systems while the demands for change are urgent. Hope is fed by action. It may well take seven generations to erase the burden of colonization. Do Indigenous social workers feel "culturally safe enough" in their agencies to persevere even if support and direction are not always available? The Indigenous child welfare workers get the last word, because they are the ones walking courageously through the transformation of Manitoba's child welfare systems:

- "It feels weird saying: I feel culturally safe. I love my work. I feel like I've got a really supportive environment. I feel confident that I can really do good work with families and they'll be in a better space having been served by the system. I know I do really good work just from the feedback that I get and the working relations with my families."

- "It may be hard but we do it for the families."

Learning Questions

1. What do the terms "cultural safety" and "cultural humility" mean to you and how can you apply these in your practice?
2. What challenges might an Indigenous social worker find in a mandated child welfare system?
3. What are the core principles in Indigenous child welfare practice?
4. What role does social work education have in transforming child welfare practice to ensure cultural safety?
5. What changes can be made to reduce the overrepresentation of Indigenous children in child welfare care?

References

Bala, N., Zapf, M. K., Williams, R. J., Vogl, R., & Hornick, J. P. (Eds.). (2004). *Canadian child welfare law: Children, families and the state* (2nd ed.). Thompson Educational. http://dx.doi.org/10.11575/PRISM/32627

Blackstock, C. (2011). The Canadian Human Rights Tribunal on First Nations child welfare: Why if Canada wins, equality and justice lose. *Children and Youth Services Review 33*(1), 187–194. https://doi.org/10.1016/j.childyouth.2010.09.002

Blackstock, C., Brown. I., & Bennett, M. (2007). Reconciliation: Rebuilding the Canadian child welfare system to better serve Aboriginal children and youth. In I. Brown, F. Chaze, D. Fuchs, J. Lafrance, S. McKay, & S. Thomas-Prokop (Eds.), *Putting a human face on child welfare: Voices from the prairies* (pp. 59–87). Prairie Child Welfare Consortium/Centre of Excellence for Child Welfare.

Charmaz, K. (2014). *Constructing grounded theory: A practical guide through qualitative analysis* (2nd ed.). Sage Publishing.

Clare, K. (2013). It's the WEC way: Transformative social work education. In J. Silver (Ed.), *Moving forward, giving back: Transformative Aboriginal adult education* (pp. 61–74). Fernwood Publishing.

Fulcher, L. (1998). Acknowledging culture in child and youth practices. *Social Work Education, 17*(3), 321–338.

Gray, M., Coates, J., Yellow Bird, M., & Hetherington, T. (Eds.). (2016). *Decolonizing social work*. Routlegde.

Hughes, T. (2013). *The legacy of Phoenix Sinclair: Achieving the best for all our children* (Vol. 2). Commission of Inquiry into the Circumstances Surrounding the Death of Phoenix Sinclair. http://www.phoenixsinclairinquiry.ca/rulings/ps_volume2.pdf

Kinequon, D. (2009). Passion within the First Nations social work profession. In S. McKay, D. Fuchs, & I. Brown (Eds.), *Passion for action in child and family services: Voices from the prairies* (pp. 1–13). Canadian Plains Research Center.

Krugel, L. (2018, October 26). Child welfare system is the new residential school "monster," senator says. *Globe and Mail*. https://www.theglobeandmail.com/canada/article-residential-school-monster-now-lives-in-child-welfare-system-2/

Kufeldt, K., & McKenzie, B. (Eds.). (2011). *Child welfare: Connecting research, policy, and practice*. Wilfred Laurier University Press.

Loxley, J., & Puzyreva, M. (2017, October 27). *Development of a new federal-provincial funding model for First Nations child and family services in Manitoba*. Funding Model Group: A subcommittee of the Regional Advisory Committee. https://media.winnipegfreepress.com/documents/John%2BLoxley%2BCFS%2Bfunding%2Bmodel%2Breport%2Bcompressed.pdf

Macdonald statue removed from Kingston's City Park. (2021, June 18). *Whig-Standard* (Kingston, ON). https://www.thewhig.com/news/local-news/macdonald-statue-removed-from-kingstons-city-park

Milliken, E. (2008). *Toward cultural safety: An exploration of the concept for social work education with Canadian Aboriginal peoples* [Unpublished doctoral dissertation]. Memorial University.

Milliken, E. (2012). Cultural safety and child welfare systems. In D. Fuchs, S. McKay, & I. Brown (Eds.), *Awakening the spirit: Moving forward in child welfare* (pp. 93–116). Canadian Plains Research Center.

National Inquiry into Missing and Murdered Indigenous Women and Girls. (2019). *Reclaiming power and place: The final report of the national inquiry into missing and murdered Indigenous women and girls*. The National Inquiry. https://www.mmiwg-ffada.ca/final-report/

Paperny, A. M. (2021, May 28). Remains of 215 children found at former Indigenous school site in Canada. *Reuters*. https://www.reuters.com/world/americas/remains-215-children-found-former-Indigenous-school-site-canada-2021-05-28/

Polaschek, N. R. (1998). Cultural safety: A new concept in nursing people of different ethnicities. *Journal of Advanced Nursing, 27*(3), 452–457.

Sinclair, M. (2019, May 2). Murray Sinclair warns of violent rebellion if Indigenous rights continue to be oppressed. *Nation to Nation* [Interview]. APTN News. https://www.aptnnews.ca/national-news/murray-sinclair-warns-of-violent-rebellion-if-indigenous-rights-continue-to-be-oppressed/.

Sinclair, M., Bala, N., Lilles, H., & Blackstock, C. (2004). Aboriginal child welfare in Canada. In N. Bala, M. K. Zapf, R. J. Williams, R. Vogl, & J. P. Hornick (Eds.), *Canadian child welfare law: Children, families and the state* (2nd ed., pp. 199–204). Thompson Educational.

Tervalon, M., & Murray-García, J. (1998). Cultural humility versus cultural competence: A critical distinction in defining physician training outcomes in multicultural education. *Journal of Health Care for the Poor and Underserved, 9*(2), 117–125. https://doi.org/10.1353/hpu.2010.0233

Trocmé, N., Knoke, D., & Blackstock, C. (2004). Pathways to the overrepresentation of Aboriginal children in Canada's child welfare system. *Social Service Review, 78*(4), 577–600.

Trocmé, N., MacLaurin, B., Fallon, B., Daciuk, J., Billingsley, D., Tourigny, M., Mayer, M., Wright, J., Barter, K., Burford, G., Hornick, J., Sullivan, R., & McKenzie, B. (2001). *Canadian incidence study of reported child abuse and neglect*. Minister of Public Works and Government Services Canada.

Truth and Reconciliation Commission of Canada. (2015a). *Honouring the truth, reconciling for the future: Summary of the final report of the Truth and Reconciliation Commission of Canada*. McGill-Queen's University Press.

Truth and Reconciliation Commission of Canada. (2015b). *Truth and Reconciliation Commission of Canada: Calls to action*. https://www2.gov.bc.ca/assets/gov/british-columbians-our-governments/indigenous-people/aboriginal-peoples-documents/calls_to_action_english2.pdf

PART IV

Education

CHAPTER 9

The Heart of Allyship: Examining the Pursuit of Ally Relationships with Indigenous Peoples in Child Welfare and Social Work Education

Jennifer Hedges, Eveline Milliken, and Elder Mae Louise Campbell

In pursuit of truth and reconciliation, this chapter explores two questions. First, what does it mean to be an ally? Second, how does one prepare social work students for allyship work with Indigenous families in the field of child welfare? These questions are important in that the term "ally" can be merely the buzzword *du jour*. In common parlance the word connotes "supporter." It is easy to put on an orange shirt and imagine that one is an ally, a supporter of the Indigenous struggle for justice. When that happens without insight, commitment, or action commensurate with the need, the term "ally" falls into disrepute. Indigenous Peoples have learned to distrust "allies" who speak nice words but bring little helpful action to bear (McCoy, 2020). This chapter explores the ethical pursuit of ally relationships for non-Indigenous people teaching and working in the field of child

Suggested Citation: Hedges, J., Milliken, E., & Campbell, Elder M. L. (2022). The heart of allyship: Examining the pursuit of ally relationships with Indigenous Peoples in child welfare and social work education. In J. Albert, D. Badry, D. Fuchs, P. Choate, M. Bennett, & H. Montgomery (Eds.), *Walking together: The future of Indigenous child welfare on the prairies* (pp. 175–195). Regina, SK: University of Regina Press.

welfare. Guided by teachings from Elder Mae Louise Campbell, we present four requirements of allyship: heart, honesty, humility, and healing.

Child welfare and education are two main areas addressed by the Truth and Reconciliation Commission of Canada's calls to action (TRC, 2015). Significant social movements in child welfare have been led by Indigenous advocates; as Crowe et al. (2021) point out, "Our Elders, matriarchs, Knowledge Keepers and community leaders organized, advocated for and demanded the creation of Indigenous child welfare agencies for Indigenous child and family safety and well-being" (p. 1). However, Indigenous people cannot carry the responsibility of replacing the system they did not create; nor can they succeed in dismantling it alone. Allies are needed because the work is too big and the burden of reconciliation should not fall to those who have been oppressed.

We are all treaty people living on Turtle Island. Indigenous Peoples have been generous in sharing their experiences and knowledges to help us know how to move forward in a good way, a way that is relational, respecting Indigenous ways of knowing, and accepting accountability (Chewka, 2021; Van Patton, 2021). It is time for potential allies to take up calls for reconciliation in earnest. The systems of assimilation remain in place despite hundreds of years of trauma (Navia et al., 2018; Sinclair, 2016). Social workers are at the forefront of delivering child welfare services and have the potential to practise in ways that are more just and culturally relevant. Social work educators have a responsibility to help students understand these systems, critically examine our role in maintaining them, and develop the knowledges and skills to transform them (Hedges, 2018).

Authors' Allyship Journey

The topic for this chapter reflects a shared commitment by the authors to be actively engaged in allyship. Much of the content stems from themes emerging from Hedges's doctoral research. In that research she explored how social work education can be a platform for transformation in child welfare practice and policy. As settler educators, Hedges and Milliken sought to explore a journey deeper into allyship. Recognizing our positions of power and responsibilities, we reflected on our own social locations and our consequent ability/inability not only to model ally relationship building and behaviours but also to equip non-Indigenous students with the knowledge and skills to engage in these necessary relationships.

Hedges grew up on the beautiful island of Newfoundland, the ancestral homelands of the Mi'kmaq, Beothuk, and Innu. Working in the child welfare system and teaching social work courses, she began to confront her own settler privilege and complicity in oppressive structures. Reading and learning from Indigenous Peoples transformed her understanding of settler-Indigenous relations and Indigenous knowledges. Hedges is committed to listening for and learning ways she can "show up" and play an active role in reconciliation. In her role as educator at the University of Manitoba Inner City Social Work Program (ICSWP), in Treaty 1 territory, she helps prepare students for transforming the child welfare system.

Raised in Treaty 3 territory, Milliken was fortunate to sit with Anishinaabe Elders and was invited to participate in ceremony from the time she was a teenager. At that time, Elder Redsky and Abanaki leader Roger Obonsawin gave her the responsibility of being a genuine ally, saying that as Indigenous peoples they know what they need, so her job was to listen to Indigenous people and respond according to their needs. This responsibility has been her guide since her early career as a social worker, working for the University of Manitoba Ongomiizwin Health Services—in Norway House Cree Nation, Peguis First Nation, Fisher River (Ochekwi-Sipi) Cree First Nations, and Kinonjeoshtegon First Nation—through returning to her home community as director of adult mental health services, to the present in which, as long-time faculty at the University of Manitoba Faculty of Social Work ICSWP, she currently acts as director.

This chapter benefits from the guidance and teachings from Ojibwa, Métis, Ishkote Odeima Ikwe Campbell from Treaty 5 region now living in Treaty 1 territory. Among many associations, Campbell is co-founder of Grandmother Moon Lodge and Clan Mothers Healing Village and Knowledge Centre, and Knowledge Keeper of the Grandmothers Council of Manitoba and the First Nations Advisory Committee to Canada's prenatal nutritional program. She served as an Elder and advisor for the Canadian Women's Foundation on matters concerning the sexual exploitation and human trafficking of women and girls and was the recipient of a 2016 Indspire Award for Culture, Heritage, and Spirituality. Elder Campbell received a Red River College (RRC) honorary diploma in Indigenous social enterprise and the Lieutenant-Governor's Award for the Advancement of Interreligious Understanding (2012) for promoting Indigenous knowledge, values, heritage, spirituality, ceremonies, and ancient ways of being. Elder in Residence at RRC until 2020 and, since 2005, visiting Elder for the ICSWP, Elder Campbell is the embodiment of allyship. She generously sat with us and offered teachings about what is needed for allyship during this time of working together toward reconciliation and healing in child welfare.

Reflections from a Constructivist Grounded Theory Study

While Hedges's doctoral research sought to help social work education programs understand how to prepare students for working in child welfare, comments made by respondents within that study have led to this exploration of allyship (Hedges, 2021). Twenty-eight interviews were conducted with persons holding various roles within social work education and child welfare delivery systems, primarily across the Prairie provinces. Interview transcripts were analyzed using constructivist grounded theory (CGT) methods (Charmaz, 2008) to glean from participants' experiences insight into transformative ways of education for practice in child welfare.

CGT is useful for studies concerned about social justice and power inequity because it "locates the research process and product in historical, social and situational conditions" and requires ongoing reflexivity by the researcher (Charmaz, 2017, p. 34). Themes from the data suggest that maintaining commitments to social justice and advocacy can be challenging in child welfare because of bureaucratic influences and that some graduates feel unprepared for the reality of practice in child welfare. Throughout this chapter, the participants' experiences helped inform our understanding of the role of social work education in building ally relationships.

Defining Allyship in Social Work: Allyship is the Pursuit of Social Justice

Some may argue the term "ally" is not effective and call for more clearly defined language such as "accomplice" or "co-resistor" (Swiftwolfe, 2018). These words suggest a stronger stance of solidarity and action, but the root concern remains: that people in power claim to be allies without doing the work of allyship. Rather than discarding the language of allyship, we suggest embracing the critical feedback about how allyship has been misunderstood and, at worst, been used to mask continued harms by those with privilege and power. In doing so, one seeks a deeper understanding of what it means to act in relationships of allyship and the possibilities of accomplice and co-resistor as important roles on this journey.

The Anti-Oppression Network (n.d.) defines "allyship" as follows:

> *an active, consistent, and arduous practice of unlearning and re-evaluating, in which a person in a position of privilege and power seeks to operate in solidarity with a marginalized group...allyship is not an identity—it is a lifelong process of building relationships based on trust, consistency, and accountability with marginalized individuals and/or groups of people. Allyship is not self-defined—our work and our efforts must be recognized by the people we seek to ally ourselves with.*

Social workers are logical candidates for allyship. The new Canadian Association for Social Work Education (CASWE) standards for accreditation require students to "develop professional identities as practitioners whose goal is to advance social justice and facilitate the collective welfare and wellbeing of all people" (CASWE, 2021, p. 13). Despite social justice being a core social work value, defining social justice in social work practice has not always been clear, which impacts the way students are prepared for practice (Asakura et al., 2020; Bhuyan et al., 2017; CASW, 2005; Kiesel & Abdill, 2019).

Participants in Hedges's study highlighted the need to prepare students for the tensions that exist between social work values and work in a mandated field like child welfare. Allyship in child welfare has been described as "listening to and sharing power with communities oppressed by the system, as well as advocating for and allocating resources towards programs and services that support equity-seeking groups" (OACAS, n.d.). One participant explained that this is easier said than done: "How do you maintain that commitment to social justice and also make sure kids are safe? That's the struggle in child welfare."

In Hedges's study, participants shared their sense of frustration that even when they understood how Indigenous families are treated unfairly in the child welfare system, they felt powerless to impact any significant change. Part of what prevents settler child welfare workers from true solidarity with Indigenous service users is that allyship has been grounded in whiteness (Amponsah & Stephen, 2020). De Leeuw and Greenwood (2017) contend that social work's conceptualization of allyship requires decolonizing the white "saviour" perspective that has dominated the child welfare system. Experiential learning helps facilitate self-awareness and critical analysis skills, confronting notions of the social worker as expert and making space for sharing power, valuing service-user knowledge, and considering alternative ways for practice (Hedges, 2021).

Learning about Indigenous ways of knowing can help inform what allyship relationships require: respect, reciprocity, reflexivity, and resistance (Clarke et al., 2012). The First Nations Child and Family Caring Society (https://fncaringsociety.com) is an organization dedicated to the well-being of Indigenous families through policy and education initiatives. Its Touchstones of Hope movement offers opportunities and resources for reconciliation in child welfare that aligns with Indigenous ways of knowing. The movement promotes relationships that engage in truth telling, acknowledging, restoring, and relating and follows culturally relevant principles that respect self-determination, culture and language, holistic approaches, structural interventions, and non-discrimination (Blackstock et al., 2019). Accessing these resources online can help one to learn in depth how to implement these principles in practice, whether it be in education or in the field.

Teaching for Allyship

In a conversation about equity, Blackstock and Fallon called for an advocacy curriculum for social work students to prepare them with the skills for everyday practice (Caring Society, 2021). Advocacy as a skill set moves away from blaming individuals, accepts accountability, and promotes moral courage (Caring Society, 2021; Blackstock, 2011). Students enter university with various levels of knowledge about the impacts of colonization (Burke, 2019). One participant in Hedges's study explained that most social work students come with a social justice mindset; however, "understanding the history and how social work came to be a profession was eye-opening." This suggests that many students come into their education with good intentions but a limited awareness of the ways the profession and child welfare are intertwined with colonialism.

Education is an important platform for practising decolonization because critical social workers in academia have some freedom to critique government systems (Healy, 2001). Kennedy-Kish (Bell) et al. (2017) recommend "teaching various versions of progressive analysis and different pedagogies that disrupt systemic inequalities" (p. 83). Gibson (2014) extends the Ally Model of Social Justice to social work pedagogy to help students develop the knowledge and skills necessary for engaging in allyship. Through experiential learning activities, students learn about the characteristics of an ally and move through phases of awareness and knowledge, confronting attitudes, beliefs, and feelings, and developing action/skills. Craig et al. (2021) describe the Practicing Alliance curriculum, a similar approach to helping increase students' confidence for practising allyship. These learning experiences help to build a foundation and commitment for the continued learning and ongoing self-reflection that is required of allyship.

Allyship Requires Our Heart

Hedges, Milliken, and Campbell discussed our experiences of allyship, and together with the themes from Hedges's research, we have come to understand that true allyship is more than a good idea; it must be a matter of the heart. It is about relationships that lead to shared responsibility and action. Elder Campbell was clear: if we understand oppression and injustice just with our minds, but do not feel it in our hearts, we will not be able to engage truthfully and act as allies, accomplices, and co-resistors. In our journey to understand oppression in our hearts, we encourage the reader to join us and to move allyship to their heart and there explore a new sense of honesty, humility, and healing in action. These responsibilities of allyship needed for reconciliation in child welfare arise from the voices of Indigenous peoples. This journey is ongoing, and perspectives continue to be limited by the settler-colonial paradigms. It is important to realize that these aspects of allyship are in constant motion as we continue to learn, re-learn, and grow in our efforts to become allies in child welfare. One cannot claim oneself to be an ally.

Allyship Requires Our Honesty

Allyship is strengthened and deepened as we come to know a fuller, more accurate history that includes Indigenous wisdom and experience, as well as understanding about settler privilege and culpability. The TRC's calls to action require social workers to understand not only the history and impacts of residential schools but also Indigenous peoples' capacity and knowledges for providing care (TRC, 2015).

In considering this history, Elder Campbell shared teachings about truth and honesty. She explained that truth is external and comes from the intellect whereas honesty is within, adding that "we have to be honest with ourselves to heal what is not right." Honesty and heart make up the true spirit of who we are. We must learn Indigenous history, Indigenous ways of caring, and Indigenous worldviews about community, family, and children. Kennedy-Kish (Bell) et al. (2017) explain that to omit Indigenous history is to operate in a vacuum:

> *This vacuum, consciously or unconsciously, contributes to the colonial privilege that normalizes the social relations of subjugation, inequality, and mistreatment imposed on Indigenous populations. As social work students, educators, and practitioners, we have an ethical responsibility to uncover injustices that have been rendered invisible. Acting on this ethical responsibility can interrupt colonial subjugation and allow for a new relationship, based on mutual respect between mainstream Canadians and Indigenous nations, communities, families and individuals. That becomes a first step to correcting the wrongs of the past which continue into the present.* (p. 63)

The truth about the child welfare system is that it has been an "agent of colonialism" and continues relying on separation tactics to ensure the safety and well-being of children instead of focusing on prevention and interventions grounded in Indigenous ways of caring (Blackstock et al., 2006, p. 6). Most Indigenous families come to the attention of child welfare systems as a result of structural issues, such as poverty and substance abuse, that can be directly linked to trauma and intergenerational effects of residential schools and the Sixties Scoop (Bombay et al., 2020; Crowe et al., 2021). The most recent First Nations Ontario Incidence Study of Reported Child Abuse and Neglect confirms continued higher rates of involvement for Indigenous families across child welfare services (Crowe et al., 2021). The child welfare system, while seeking the best interests of the child, continues to have poor outcomes for kids in care (Alberton et al., 2020; Fallis & Nixon, 2020). Sinclair (2016) advises that we need to understand the history of the system as well as what sustains it as an "Indigenous child removal system" (p. 8).

Participants in Hedges's study expressed the importance of "owning" their role in history as child welfare workers and stated that by doing this they felt more comfortable having open conversations with families about their fears. In the voice of one participant, "It's pretty normal that families would distrust us, hate us, see us as all-powerful, fear we're gonna take away their kids for no reason." Participants described the importance of social work education connecting history to the present: "now let's talk about what that might look like on the front lines." Students should read the Canadian Association of Social Workers (CASW) (2019) statement of apology and commitment to reconciliation acknowledging social work's role in supporting systemic injustice toward Indigenous families. A student's developing social work knowledge and skill should be grounded in this awareness and accountability (Gibson, 2014). One exercise to help establish this connection could be inviting students to write their own statements of apology and commitments to reconciliation.

True allyship is often misunderstood or pursued half-heartedly within the child welfare system (Gaumond, 2020). Participants in Hedges's study experienced frustration when they were able to identify and witness injustice but felt they lacked the "how to" to change the child welfare system. One participant explained, "we talk a lot about the history of colonization...and why we have kids in care. But then how do you change that? How do you change that more at a mezzo and micro level?" Bhuyan et al. (2017) studied perspectives on social justice in social work education and found that when critical approaches are minimized, social justice rhetoric can become performative, and students learn that "social justice theories do not translate well to 'skills' and thus are not useful in everyday social work practice" (p. 386). Educators need to help students imagine what allyship can look like in the field.

In Hedges's study, participants witnessing the impacts of injustice in their day-to-day work explained that knowing history helps them complete meaningful assessments. One participant explained the importance of "drawing the connections between the history of the family, the history within generations as well, and what that means currently." Another participant cautioned that workers still need to do the work to understand families and their specific circumstances: "There's no single way really to categorize Indigenous people or any family who's having troubles that's leading them to contact with the child welfare system." McLaughlin et al. (2017) found that child welfare workers who considered social justice central to their practice were more often experienced workers who understood the nature of the child welfare system: "They also tended to think structurally about the causes of child abuse and neglect, to be reflective about their own use of power, and prefer a collaborative approach to practice" (p. 573). Newer workers were seen as focused more on "learning the job, managing their delegated authority, developing confidence, and proving themselves" (p. 573). It is important for new workers to feel prepared by their education to enter the child welfare field and to have a support network when getting started.

Allyship Requires Our Humility

To grow in our allyship requires a willingness to become more self-aware, to admit what we don't know and can't understand, to let go of control and to listen for guidance from the people, to make connection with others and be willing to be touched by some of the pain others feel due to colonization (Absolon & Absolon-Winchester, 2016).

Elder Campbell noted that we need to humble ourselves; allies need to admit what they don't know and seek knowledge about what has happened to Indigenous peoples beyond a superficial level. We must genuinely want to learn more about each other, to get to know each other and hear each other's stories. Gehl (n.d.), an Algonquin Anishinaabe-kwe, created an "Ally Bill of Responsibilities," which begins, "do not act out of guilt, but rather a genuine interest in challenging the larger oppressive power structures."

In Hedges's study, participants identified learning critical self-reflection and developing self-awareness as necessary for understanding how child protection services reinforce oppression. One participant explained that social work education has the responsibility of "opening up that critical dialogue...the ways in which the social work student is going to have to confront their own values and be able to face what that means for front-line practice."

Diane Roussin of Skownan First Nation, project director at the Winnipeg Boldness Project, described learning from Indigenous youth that not all spaces will be safe, so there needs also to be "brave spaces" (personal communication, September 1, 2017). Roussin advised that humility, courage, and bravery are required to confront the ongoing injustice in the child welfare system, by "turning the light on yourself" and asking, "What I can do to be helpful and good?" Roussin explained that her most important learning in practice comes from the relationships with the people she serves and that sharing power acknowledges service-user wisdom. It is necessary in social work to move beyond cultural competencies to engage in critical consciousness and address power in relationships (Asakura et al., 2020). Arao and Clemens (2013) describe a brave-space framework for educators, "to help students better understand—and rise to—the challenges of genuine dialogue on diversity and social justice issues" (p. 136). Recognizing that this type of learning entails risk and discomfort, they advise educators to balance confrontation with encouragement and support for new learning. They offer suggestions for creating ground rules with students to help facilitate this process.

Cultural humility includes an intersectionality perspective that promotes self-awareness and understanding of power dynamics between worker and service user (Ortega & Faller, 2011; Tervalon & Murray-García, 1998). Rather than claim cultural expertise, workers demonstrate an openness, engaging from a "learning mode as opposed to maintaining power, control, and authority in the working relationship" (Ortega & Faller, 2011). Shifting to a framework of cultural humility and cultural safety is a change of perspective that attends to the directions of the more vulnerable population. Within a child welfare perspective, one would ask, "Does this family, child, community consider me safe/an ally?" The shift from cultural competence to cultural safety (Milliken, 2012) moves awareness and control from the dominant-culture service provider to the vulnerable service user. De Leeuw and Greenwood (2017) recognize cultural safety as a means for decolonizing child welfare and creating space for new relationships.

It is not surprising that participants in Hedges's study described relationships as integral to child welfare practice. As one participant explained, it's "not your technique, not your 'am I using this model or that model of counseling'...can you form a relationship in spite of what's going on, genuine relationship like human to human." Thomas and Green (2015) state,

> *mainstream social work education and training stresses the importance of being objective: we assess, we recommend, and we implement—then we move onto our next 'casefile.' However, the 'heart' in our practice teaches us and encourages us to practice differently because we as people, as social workers, are responsible for the relations we make.* (p. 38)

Indigenous youth have described how information about them can be "weaponized" by social service systems, requiring the need to use silence or withdrawal as resistance (Navia et al., 2018). In child welfare systems, signs of resistance are often misunderstood and documented as individual bad behaviours. A participant in Hedges's study explained the importance of "recognizing that anger is often the only mechanism that disadvantaged or disempowered populations have in reaction to child welfare." Using a cultural safety approach would help workers to recognize silence as a necessary coping strategy when service users feel culturally unsafe (Milliken, 2013).

Fairbairn and Strega (2015) describe "socially just assessments" for developing collaborative and respectful relationships in child welfare practice (p. 163). They explain, "It is through relationship and engagement that workers might come to understand how a family's troubles are aggravated by political and social conditions such as colonialism, poverty, racism, stigma, lack of resources and other social injustices" (p. 168). Carrière and Strega (2015) call for child welfare practitioners to "see double," understanding structural factors and being able to practice ethically in the moment (p. 3). Opportunities for allyship and collaboration need to be considered in all forms of communication. Instead of just documenting that the "mom has substandard housing" it is noted in Hedges' study that it is critical from an ally's perspective to look more deeply at the situation and ask clarifying questions about the mother's problem with housing such as:

> *Well, why? What has she done to try, how many barriers has she faced to try and get decent housing that are out of her control,*

right? And making sure that's in the notes and then sharing your notes with your client and making it more of a collaborative process instead of I'm the expert, you're not.

Gaumond (2020) explored settler social worker allyship and Indigenous social justice, highlighting the importance of locating the good in families. Regarding relationships in child welfare, a participant in Hedges's study explained, "I have never met a parent who said 'I don't love my kids'...it's like this parent is doing the best they can. It may not be good and so we need to act. I mean our job is important. We need to push on, but we need to do it so that people aren't humiliated by us, they're not scared of us." Another participant noted the importance "that we really embody that Indigenous knowledge, you know, how can we come to that as an ally....I think encompassing that knowledge and that understanding, developing that lens I think is really crucial." Gaumond (2020) echoes this need for understanding and valuing Indigenous ways of helping and relating: "it is crucial for social work pedagogy to be Indigenized and to properly train staff prior to frontline work, it is the social worker's responsibility to continue learning, thinking critically, and to self-care in order to uphold allyship standards of practice" (p. 44).

From its inception in 1982, the ICSWP has tried to practice allyship, listening to Indigenous students, communities, and Elders and seeking closeness with the community. Milliken notes that faculty, counsellors, Elders, and staff are dedicated to helping students feel safe within, around, and throughout (Bruning et al., 2006).

Allyship Requires Our Healing

Many settler social workers may think we are not in need of any healing related to Indigenous experience. To the extent that we see Indigenous suffering as "their problem," tipping our hat or donning an orange shirt is all that is needed, we are disconnected from our relations, our responsibilities, and our self. Part of what would make us whole is missing. To be an ally and share hope is to heal our dissociation and move to action:

To the [Truth and Reconciliation] Commission, "reconciliation" is about establishing and maintaining a mutually respectful relationship between Aboriginal and non-Aboriginal peoples in this

> *country. For that to happen, there has to be awareness of the past, acknowledgement of the harm that has been inflicted, atonement for the causes, and action to change behaviour. We are not there yet.* (TRC, 2015, vol. 6, p. 3)

Empty efforts toward reconciliation have contributed to an understandable lack of trust by Indigenous communities toward those in power. We earn trust through our actions (Healy, 2015). Navia et al. (2018) collaborated with Indigenous youth to explore how the current child welfare system continues the assimilation process of the residential school system, in that "systems that further distance kin, that displace youth from home communities, and disrupt cultural continuity are not built around care, but rather grounded in a history of racism, institutionalized assimilation, and ultimately erasure of that which does not suit capital accumulation" (p. 160).

Rev. Stan McKay explained we have all been harmed by the lack of truth around Indigenous sovereignty and settler complicity: "The perpetrators are wounded and marked by history in ways that are different from the victims, but both groups require healing" (quoted in TRC, 2015, vol. 6, p. 5). Allies might imagine how they would have stood up to the residential school system if they had had the chance. Educators can remind students that these are not problems without answers (Caring Society, 2021). The final reports of the TRC and the National Inquiry into Missing and Murdered Indigenous Women and Girls (MMIWG) are comprehensive documents that honour Indigenous voices and provide specific calls to action (TRC, 2015; National Inquiry into Missing and Murdered Indigenous Women and Girls, 2019). The job of an ally is to listen and to understand what our responsibilities and roles can be in the effort (Gehl, n.d.).

As outlined throughout this chapter, knowing is only one part of allyship. The action required of allyship requires courage. One must avoid performative and uninformed allyship that ignores the work that oppressed groups have done and centres the knowledge and experience of the ally (Amponsah & Stephen, 2020). True solidarity requires "relentless persistence" and does not come naturally, which may be surprising to students who have good intentions (Amponsah & Stephen, 2020, p. 12). Oliver et al. (2017) found that curriculum to support moral courage is necessary for students to learn and practise how to have difficult conversations.

Using experiential learning opportunities that promote both safety and discomfort can help students "move from knowing the right thing to say, to saying the thing they know to be right" (Oliver et al., 2017, p. 712). A participant in Hedges's research required her students to read Cindy Blackstock's 2009 article "The Occasional Evil of Angels" and complete a project linking social justice issues to child welfare; "instead of focusing on the problem, they were supposed to do something that would change the issue or help promote change in their area." Although not a requirement, some students carried out their project in the field, demonstrating the potential that curriculum choices can have on direct practice and service delivery (Craig et al., 2021). Below is a list of activities that educators could consider for helping students build allyship skills in social work courses. These activities help to move learning and awareness into action:

- attend rallies and marches together as a class
- write advocacy letters related to assignment topics, to practise advocacy skills
- present justice issues to your peers and engage them in an action
- make advocacy posters together as a class
- invite social justice activists to come and share their experiences
- plan a social justice event, such as a rally for murdered and missing Indigenous girls and women
- share community events for educators and students to attend together.

Conclusion

There are many promising changes happening in the child welfare system that provide opportunities for engagement by students and educators. These include the first national Indigenous child welfare legislation (*An Act respecting First Nations, Inuit and Métis children, youth and families*, 2019), the full implementation of Jordan's Principle, elimination of birth alert practices, education scholarships for youth in care, and service-user advocacy groups like FearlessR2W (https://www.fearlessr2w.ca). In addition, the 2021 agreement between Cowessess First Nation, the Province of Saskatchewan, and the Government of Canada enabling the First Nation to retake control of its own child welfare system is historic and suggests others will follow.

The global COVID-19 pandemic has taught us not only to appreciate and recognize front-line responders but also to see how disproportionately Indigenous and racialized people are impacted (McCracken, 2021; Wright, 2021). Joyce Echaquan's unnecessary death, allowed by abusive, racist healthcare workers (Shingler, 2021), highlights the danger that helping systems still pose. The overrepresentation of Indigenous families in the child welfare system is a national crisis. Child welfare workers are part of the front-line response to this injustice, and they require the knowledge, resources, and skills to respond in a good way (Wilson, 2021). Social work education needs to implement pedagogies for allyship to increase student commitment and capacity to transform child welfare practice (Caring Society, 2021). Child welfare agencies and government institutions can create supportive environments that allow for emerging social workers to be allies.

The pursuit of allyship is continuous and ongoing; it is not finished. The Honourable Murray Sinclair (CBC News, 2021) stated recently that seven generations of children went to residential schools, and it will take seven generations for reconciliation to occur. The recovery of 215 buried children at a residential school site in Tk'emlúps te Secwépemc First Nation, and the hundreds that have followed at other sites, "hurt the hearts of all Canadians" (Wab Kinew, quoted in Sanders, 2021). The requirement for allyship has never been more crucial, and non-Indigenous people must do better. We encourage you to explore in your own context what allyship might look like and what the needs of the community and people you are serving are. The pursuit of allyship requires heart, honesty, humility, and healing.

Learning Questions

1. How would you describe being an ally in the child welfare system?
2. Create your own bill of responsibilities as an ally.
3. List three actions you can take in the pursuit of allyship.
4. What barriers prevent people with good intentions from being allies?
5. Describe how you relate to one of the "four Hs": heart, honesty, humility, or healing.

Online Resources to Support Your Allyship Journey

Dr. Lynn Gehl's Ally Bill of Responsibilities: https://www.lynngehl.com/ally-bill-of-responsibilities.html

First Nations Child & Family Caring Society—7 Free Ways to Make a Difference: https://fncaringsociety.com/7-free-ways-make-difference

OACAS Library Equity and Anti-oppression in Child Welfare: https://oacas.libguides.com/equity-AOP/allyship

CASW Reconciliation Hub: https://www.casw-acts.ca/en/resources/casw-reconciliation-hub

Brave Spaces Toolkit: Brave_Spaces_Toolkit_FILLABLE_5411f6fef7.pdf

References

Absolon, K., & Absolon-Winchester, A. E. (2016). Exploring pathways to reconciliation. *Consensus 37*(1), Article 2. https://scholars.wlu.ca/consensus/vol37/iss1/2

Alberton, A. M., Angell, G. B., Gorey, K. M., & Grenier, S. (2020). Homelessness among Indigenous peoples in Canada: The impacts of child welfare involvement and educational achievement. *Children and Youth Services Review, 111*, Article 104846. https://doi.org/10.1016/j.childyouth.2020.104846

Amponsah, P., & Stephen, J. (2020). Developing a practice of African-centred solidarity in child and youth care. *International Journal of Child, Youth & Family Studies, 11*(2), 6–24. https://doi.org/10.18357/ijcyfs112202019516

An Act respecting First Nations, Inuit and Métis children, youth and families, SC 2019, c C-24. https://laws.justice.gc.ca/eng/acts/F-11.73/page-1.html

Anti-Oppression Network. (n.d.). *Allyship*. Retrieved June 6, 2021, from https://theantioppressionnetwork.com/allyship/

Arao, B., & Clemens, K. (2013). From safe spaces to brave spaces: A new way to frame dialogue around diversity and social justice. In L. M. Landreman (Ed.), *The art of effective facilitation: Reflections from social justice educators* (pp. 135–150). Stylus Publishing.

Asakura, K., Strumm, B., Todd, S., & Varghese, R. (2020). What does social justice look like when sitting with clients? A qualitative study of teaching clinical social work from a social justice perspective. *Journal of Social Work Education, 56*(3), 442–455. https://doi.org/10.1080/10437797.2019.1656588

Bhuyan, R., Bejan, R., & Jeyapal, D. (2017). Social workers' perspectives on social justice in social work education: When mainstreaming social justice masks structural inequalities. *Social Work Education, 36*(4), 373–390. https://doi.org/10.1080/02615479.2017.1298741

Blackstock, C. (2009). The occasional evil of angels: Learning from the experiences of Aboriginal peoples and social work. *First Peoples Child & Family Review, 4*(1), 28–37. https://doi.org/10.7202/1069347ar

Blackstock, C. (2011). Wanted: Moral courage in Canadian child welfare. *First Peoples Child & Family Review, 6*(2), 35–46. https://doi.org/10.7202/1068875ar

Blackstock, C., Cross, T., George, J., Brown, I, & Formsma, J. (2006, republished 2019). *Reconciliation in child welfare: Touchstones of Hope for Indigenous children, youth, and families*. First Nations Child & Family Caring Society of Canada.

Bombay, A., McQuaid, R. J., Young, J., Sinha, V., Currie, V., Anisman, H., & Matheson, K. (2020). Familial attendance at Indian Residential School and subsequent involvement in the child welfare system among Indigenous adults born during the Sixties Scoop era. *First Peoples Child & Family Review, 15*(1), 62–79. https://fpcfr.com/index.php/FPCFR/article/view/401

Bruning, N. S., McCaughey, D., & Milliken, E. (2006). The "mosaic" in practice: An examination of multi-cultural diversity within Canadian universities. In G. Vedder (Ed.), *Managing equity and diversity at universities* (pp. 49–71). Rainer Hampp Verlag.

Burke, S. (2019). Teaching the history of colonization in the postsecondary classroom. *Journal of Social Work Education, 55*(4), 658–668. https://doi.org/10.1080/10437797.2019.1611510

Canadian Association for Social Work Education. (2021). *Education policies and accreditation standards for Canadian social work education*. https://caswe-acfts.ca/wp-content/uploads/2021/08/EPAS-2021.pdf

Canadian Association of Social Workers. (2005). *Code of ethics*. https://www.casw-acts.ca/files/attachements/casw_code_of_ethics.pdf

Canadian Association of Social Workers. (2019). *Statement of apology and commitment to reconciliation*. https://www.casw-acts.ca/files/attachements/Statement_of_Apology_and_Reconciliation_FINAL_2021.pdf

Carrière, J., & Strega, S. (Eds.). (2015). *Walking this path together: Anti-racist and anti-oppressive child welfare practice* (2nd ed.). Fernwood Publishing.

CBC News—The National. (2021, June 22). *Murray Sinclair on moving reconciliation forward in Canada*. YouTube. https://www.youtube.com/watch?v=42yzZ1WuxFo

Charmaz, K. (2008). Constructionism and the grounded theory. In J. A. Holstein & J. F. Gubrium (Eds.), *Handbook of constructionist research* (pp. 397–412). Guilford Press.

Charmaz, K. (2017). The power of constructivist grounded theory for critical inquiry. *Qualitative Inquiry, 23*(1), 34–45, https://doi.org/10.1177/1077800416657105

Chewka, D., with Hesjedal, C. (2021). Worlds colliding or merging? Sharing relational knowledge that transformed my practice in working with Indigenous children, youth, parents, families, communities, and nations. In K. Kufeldt, B. Fallon, & B. McKenzie (Eds.), *Protecting children: Theoretical and practical aspects* (pp. 211–228). Canadian Scholars.

Clarke, J., Aiello, O., Chau, K., Zakiya, A., Rashidi, M., & Amaral, S. (2012). Uprooting social work education. *LEARNing Landscapes, 6*(1), 81–105.

Craig, S. L., Gardiner, T., Eaton, A. D., Pang, N., & Kourgiantakis, T. (2021). Practicing alliance: An experiential model of teaching diversity and inclusion for social work practice and education. *Social Work Education*, 1–19. https://doi.org/10.1080/02615479.2021.1892054

Crowe, A., Schiffer, J., with Fallon, B., Houston, E., Black, T., Lefebvre, R., Filippelli, J., Joh-Carnella, N., and Trocmé, N. (2021) *Mashkiwenmi-daa Noojimowin: Let's have strong minds for the healing* (First Nations Ontario Incidence Study of Reported Child Abuse and Neglect—2018). Child Welfare Research Portal. https://cwrp.ca/publications/mashkiwenmi-daa-noojimowin-lets-have-strong-minds-healing-first-nations-ontario

de Leeuw, S., & Greenwood, M. (2017). Turning a new page: Cultural safety, critical creative literary interventions, truth and reconciliation, and the crisis of child welfare. *AlterNative: An International Journal of Indigenous Peoples*, *13*(3), 142–151. https://doi.org/10.1177/1177180117714155

Fairbairn, M., & Strega, S. (2015). Anti-oppressive approaches to child protection: Assessment and file recording. In J. Carrière & S. Strega (Eds.), *Walking this path together: Anti-racist and anti-oppressive child welfare practice* (2nd ed., pp. 157–175). Fernwood Publishing.

Fallis, J., & Nixon, K. (2020). From protection to expulsion: A critical examination of aging out of care. In H. Berman, C. Richardson, K. Elliot, & E. Canas (Eds.), *Everyday violence in the lives of youth: Speaking out and pushing back* (pp. 37–56). Fernwood Publishing.

First Nations Child & Family Caring Society (2021). *A conversation about equity with Dr. Cindy Blackstock and Dr. Barbara Fallon* [Video]. YouTube. https://www.youtube.com/watch?v=oHqopurJ-Sc

Gaumond, G. (2020). *Bridging the gaps between settler social worker allyship and Indigenous social justice* [Unpublished master's thesis]. University of Ottawa. http://hdl.handle.net/10393/41142

Gehl, L. (n.d.). *Ally bill of responsibilities*. https://www.lynngehl.com/ally-bill-of-responsibilities.html

Gibson, P. A. (2014). Extending the ally model of social justice to social work pedagogy. *Journal of Teaching in Social Work*, *34*(2), 199–214. https://doi.org/10.1080/08841233.2014.890691

Healy, K. (2001). Reinventing critical social work: Challenges from practice, context and postmodernism. *Critical Social Work*, *2*(1).

Healy, K. (2015). Becoming a trustworthy profession: Doing better than doing good. *Australian Social Work*, *70*, 7–16. https://doi.org/10.1080/0312407X.2014.973550

Hedges, J. (2018). Transforming the classroom: Supporting critical change in social work education in the spirit of reconciliation for child welfare. In D. Badry, H. Montgomery, D. Kikulwe, M. Bennett, & D. Fuchs (Eds.), *Imagining child welfare in the spirit of reconciliation* (pp. 249–267). University of Regina Press.

Hedges, J. (2021). [Unpublished raw data on social work education and child welfare]. University of Manitoba.

Kennedy-Kish (Bell), B., Sinclair. R., Carniol, B., & Baines, D. (2017). *Case critical: Social services and social justice in Canada* (7th ed.). Between the Lines.

Kiesel, L. R., & Abdill, L. R. (2019). "Mapping social justice": Integrating policy practice across the curriculum. *Journal of Social Work Education, 55*(4), 695–709. https://doi.org/10.1080/10437797.2018.1491360

McCoy, H. (2020, November 9). Indigenous researcher puts allyship under the microscope. *UCalgary News*. https://ucalgary.ca/news/indigenous-researcher-puts-allyship-under-microscope

McCracken, M. (2021). *Manitoba's covid recovery must be feminist.* Canadian Centre for Policy Alternatives.

McLaughlin, A. M., Gray, E., & Wilson, M. G. (2017). From tenuous to tenacious: Social justice practice in child welfare. *Journal of Public Child Welfare, 11*(4/5), 568–585. https://doi.org/10.1080/15548732.2017.1279997

Milliken, E. (2012). Cultural safety and child welfare systems. In D. Fuchs, S. McKay, & I. Brown (Eds.), *Awakening the spirit: Moving forward in child welfare* (pp. 93–116). Canadian Plains Research Center.

Milliken, E. (2013). You have the right to remain silent...but I'm your lawyer! You are supposed to talk to me! Working toward creating culturally safe working relationships. *Manitoba Law Journal, 37*(1), 403–414.

National Inquiry into Missing and Murdered Indigenous Women and Girls. (2019). *Reclaiming power and place: The final report of the national inquiry into missing and murdered Indigenous women and girls*. The National Inquiry. https://www.mmiwg-ffada.ca/final-report/

Navia, D., Henderson, R. I., & First Charger, L. (2018). Uncovering colonial legacies: Voices of Indigenous youth on child welfare (dis)placements. *Anthropology & Education Quarterly, 49*(2), 146–164. https://doi.org/10.1111/aeq.12245

Oliver, C., Jones, E., Rayner, A., Penner, J., & Jamieson, A. (2017). Teaching social work students to speak up. *Social Work Education, 36*(6), 702–714. https://doi.org/10.1080/02615479.2017.1305348

Ontario Association of Children's Aid Societies. (n.d.). *Equity and anti-oppression in child welfare*. Retrieved June 6, 2021, from https://oacas.libguides.com/equity-AOP/allyship

Ortega, R. M., & Faller, K. C. (2011). Training child welfare workers from an intersectional cultural humility perspective: A paradigm shift. *Child Welfare, 90*(5), 27.

Sanders, C. (2021, July 6). Justice minister appeals for calm after queen's statues toppled. *Winnipeg Free Press*. https://www.winnipegfreepress.com/local/justice-minister-appeals-for-calm-after-queens-statues-toppled-574771442.html

Shingler, B. (2021, May 29). Joyce Echaquan's death lays bare, once again, problems in Quebec's health-care system. *CBC News*. https://www.cbc.ca/amp/1.6044631

Sinclair, R. (2016). The Indigenous child welfare removal system in Canada: An examination of legal decision-making and racial bias. *First Peoples Child*

& Family Review, 11(2), 8–18. https://fpcfr.com/index.php/FPCFR/article/view/310

Swiftwolfe, D. (2018) *Indigenous ally toolkit*. Montreal Urban Aboriginal Community Strategy Network.

Tervalon, M., & Murray-García, J. (1998). Cultural humility versus cultural competence: A critical distinction in defining physician training outcomes in multicultural education. *Journal of Health Care for the Poor and Underserved, 9*(2), 117–125. https://doi.org/10.1353/hpu.2010.0233

Thomas, R., & Green, J. (2015). Indigenous perspectives on anti-oppressive child welfare practice. In J. Carrière & S. Strega (Eds.), *Walking this path together: Anti-racist and anti-oppressive child welfare practice* (2nd ed., pp. 157–175). Fernwood Publishing.

Truth and Reconciliation Commission of Canada. (2015a). *Truth and Reconciliation Commission of Canada: Calls to action*. https://ehprnh2mwo3.exactdn.com/wp-content/uploads/2021/01/Calls_to_Action_English2.pdf

Truth and Reconciliation Commission of Canada. (2015b). *Canada's residential schools: Reconciliation. The final report of the Truth and Reconciliation Commission of Canada*, (Vol. 6). McGill-Queen's University Press.

Van Patton, K. (2021, May 14). Team sees Indigenous research as heart work, not hard work. *UCalgary News*. https://ucalgary.ca/news/team-sees-indigenous-research-heart-work-not-hard-work

Wilson, T. (2021, June 1) *"Passing on" critical social work* [Conference session]. Canadian Association for Social Work Education Conference.

Wright, T. (2021, March 24). Indigenous communities facing "dual pandemic" due to the impact of COVID-19 on mental illness and addiction, report says. *Globe and Mail*. https://www.theglobeandmail.com/canada/article-indigenous-communities-facing-dual-pandemic-due-to-the-impact-of-covid/

CHAPTER 10

Post-Secondary Indigenous Education as It Relates to Indigenous Child Welfare

Jason Albert and Susannah Walker

Indigenous people have always had their own ways of caring for their children and community. They have relied on methods passed on from generation to generation that follow traditional practices of their culture. For Indigenous communities, "traditional systems of care shared basic characteristics, including an emphasis on extended families and a worldview which prized children as gifts from the creator" (Sinha et al., 2011, p. 5). With Bill C-92 coming into effect in Canada, allowing Indigenous communities to create their own child welfare systems and services (Hyslop, 2021), the process of traditional practice, as it relates to child welfare, is coming full circle. Cowessess First Nation in Saskatchewan made history by signing an agreement with provincial and federal governments for funding to control its local child welfare system (Atter, 2021). As a result of Bill C-92, Cowessess First Nation created the *Miyo Pimâtisiwin Act*, which exercises jurisdiction over child and family services and focuses on prevention

Suggested Citation: Albert, J., & Walker, S. (2022). Post-secondary Indigenous education as it relates to Indigenous child welfare. In J. Albert, D. Badry, D. Fuchs, P. Choate, M. Bennett, & H. Montgomery (Eds.), *Walking together: The future of Indigenous child welfare on the prairies* (pp. 197–217). Regina, SK: University of Regina Press.

and making sure families have the resources to decolonize their homes and cope with the impact of intergenerational trauma (Solomon, 2021). Indigenous communities are reverting to their traditional methods of child welfare. Indigenous people feel it is about time that they can utilize their methods and practices and not have the non-Indigenous way encompassing their way of life.

Indigenous children are overrepresented in the Canadian child welfare system, and the current system is not working for Indigenous children and families (Mandell et al., 2003). If the system's current approach was working, there would not be overwhelming numbers of Indigenous children in care, nor would there be "family cycles of poverty, addictions, unemployment, and violence" (Tait et al., 2013, p. 47). It has been proven that the broken bond that is experienced when children are separated from their families has generational consequences (Mosher & Hewitt, 2018). For example, the landmark Canadian Human Rights Tribunal case on Indigenous child welfare found that the Canadian government had "discriminated against First Nations children by under-funding on-reserve child welfare services" (Barrera, 2019) and was required to compensate for this mistreatment; this fight continues in court. Landertinger (2021) suggests that the continued practice of fighting Indigenous people reinforces the colonizer's annihilative and accumulative instincts and the process of disconnecting Indigenous peoples from their land and community.

Indigenous child welfare is fraught with issues that are historical and can be attributed to an unbalanced approach to Indigenous issues. The government of Canada has remained in control of Indigenous people for generations, and as this colonial control continues, governments have failed in upholding their obligations to the treaties (McMillan, 2021). As this is currently the case, Indigenous people have a hard time believing in the child welfare system and, as the dysfunction continues, will maintain this perspective. Non-Indigenous people who see the overrepresentation of Indigenous children in the child welfare system may draw conclusions "that Indigenous peoples are 'morally' or 'socially' failing at a most basic human level, that of being able to raise and provide for their own children" (Tait et al., 2013, p. 45). Through an educational lens, Indigenous people can learn to acknowledge the process of child welfare through their own principles, approach, and perspective and create a process that reflects their own worldview.

Understanding Indigenous child welfare is a complex but necessary process, so it is important that students comprehend and recognize both the historical aspect and the negative strategies that are involved. The involvement of Indigenous children with child welfare systems is often driven by reports and investigations related to neglect. In Canada, cases involving child neglect are a primary driver of the overrepresentation of Indigenous children and are linked to factors including poverty, poor housing, domestic violence, and substance use (Sinha et al., 2021; Sinha & Kozlowski, 2013; Sinha et al., 2011). It is critical for social workers to "consider the broader contexts in which these [child welfare] interactions take place. Indeed, research since the 1980s has increasingly embraced a perspective in which child maltreatment occurs when multiple individuals, family, community and societal level risk factors outweigh protective factors" (Sinha et al., 2011, p. 4). Child welfare has affected Indigenous individuals and communities in different ways.

To clearly understand Indigenous child welfare issues, those issues must be placed in the structural context of colonization. For example, the impact of residential schools on Indigenous families has been well documented. The dysfunction that arose from the schools is still evident in the high rates of family breakdown, addiction issues, and emotional disconnection present in Indigenous communities today. According to Miller (1996), the first known residential school for Indigenous children in Canada was established in 1620. Europeans perceived Indigenous people as incapable of surviving in a European-based society. Barman et al. (1986) describe a misconception among European colonists that for Indigenous people to survive, they needed to be assimilated into the European social order. To achieve this social order, Europeans believed, education was the key to successful assimilation. The trauma that resulted from the residential schools still affects how Indigenous people experience life. According to the Assembly of First Nations (1994), "the outcome of ongoing discussion is an awareness that residential schooling wounded First Nations individually and communally in various ways: spiritually, mentally, emotionally and physically" (p. 2). Indigenous children encountered various forms of abuse, including physical, mental, and sexual, which had devastating effects on the victims. Miller (1996) mentions that Indigenous children were not permitted to speak their mother tongue or practise their traditional culture, and their appearance was altered to reflect the

European vision of civilization. They were unable to voice their concerns or take appropriate steps necessary to solve their problems, and they were expected to conform and not express any dissension toward authority, or they would be punished. The resulting impacts on families included "the inability to express love or nurturance, a loss of communication, emotional abuse and traumatic bonding, and having children taken into foster care" (Muir & Bohr, 2019, p. 69). For Indigenous youth in care, the cycle continues; once they grow up and have their own children, those children are often taken into care as the parents "were deemed unfit often as a result of trauma faced in their own lives through growing up in the system" (Navia et al., 2018, p. 155). Abusive actions and policies in the schools and child welfare system increased the colonial authority over Indigenous children.

Indigenous child welfare needs to be explored and examined within the classroom by students in Indigenous and non-Indigenous social work programs. Students need to learn about child protection, abuse, and systemic and institutional barriers, as well as how the child protection system defines neglect. Students must be prepared for working with Indigenous people involved with the child welfare system and understand the relevant principles and policies. This can be accomplished through in-depth examination of child welfare, with a historical focus that describes how a colonial approach to child welfare has affected Indigenous people through multiple generations.

The profession of social work, which led the child welfare practice, has not been kind to Indigenous people in Canada. Sinclair (2009) mentions that Indigenous people were introduced to the social work profession as wards of the federal government through the Department of Indian Affairs. This introduction has manifested in a distrust of the social work profession. The term "social worker" has always had a negative connotation for Indigenous people. In the 1960s, child welfare workers began entering Indigenous communities and apprehending children from their families (Heinonen & Spearman, 2001). This resulted in ambivalence among those communities and families, as Indigenous people view social workers as oppressors and agents of social control sent by an agency that does not represent the Indigenous communities' interest (Heinonen & Spearman, 2001). Hart (2002) mentions that colonialism still exists in the social work profession. In trying to put an end to the colonialist approach to social work practice, Indigenous people stood up and demanded a different approach to social work that took into consideration the needs of Indigenous people. The social work profession is rooted in professional imperialism, and social work has imposed Eurocentric theories and techniques, without considering Indigenous cultures and development issues (Midgley, 1981; Yunong & Xiong, 2008). Sinclair (2004) notes that the profession and social work education have not been free from colonial influence. As a result of this unbalanced and dysfunctional approach to social work education, the curriculum within Indigenous social work education (ISWE) focuses on an approach that reflects the Indigenous worldview, practice, and protocol rather than the colonial method that continues to exist.

Indigenous Social Work Education

Indigenous social work education (ISWE) emerged out of a need to educate Indigenous and non-Indigenous social workers on the needs of Indigenous people. According to Sinclair (2004), ISWE is not just about content; it is also about pedagogy. ISWE uses a "pedagogy that is framed within colonial history and the Indigenous worldview and is premised upon the traditional sacred epistemology of Indigenous people" (p. 49). It brings knowledge about Indigenous cultures and traditions to the forefront of education. Being disconnected from culture has been shown to produce negative mental health impacts, including "experiences of 'othering' [and] emotional struggles of feeling lost, detached, and isolated," as well as rejecting and questioning Indigenous identity (Auger, 2016, p. 14). It is important for Indigenous students to incorporate their cultures and traditions in their social work education, as these programs appear to be essential for student success (Baskin, 2005; Bruyere, 2009; Sinclair, 2004).

ISWE incorporates Indigenous history, values, and responsibilities that evolve from the Indigenous worldview, includes a decolonization framework, and uses the concept of *mino-pimatisiwin* (the good life) (Hart, 2002; Sinclair, 2004). It contrasts with a view that knowledge generated from the western Eurocentric standpoint is superior and legitimate—a view conferred to students in the educational system (Smith, 1999). Sinclair (2004) argues that the current model of education has limited applicability to Indigenous people because it does not reflect the epistemology, ontology, and worldview of Indigenous people. As a result, students of Indigenous social work (ISW) are learning about social work through a non-Indigenous view. Baikie (2009) and Hart (2002) state that social work is concerned with the individual, their environment, and the way the two intersect. ISWE is an alternative approach to social work education, one that is particularly accommodating to Indigenous people and that trains them on a platform that incorporates epistemological, axiological, and cosmological methods, within a historical Indigenous context (Sinclair, 2004).

ISWE is a culturally specific approach to social work education. Indigenous students are coming into ISWE with the expectation that they will learn from an Indigenous perspective and have their ways of knowing validated (Bruyere, 2009). Similarly, B. Harris (2006) notes that ISWE must reflect the cultural diversity of First Nations, as differences exist. Ives et al. (2007) point out that Indigenous people need to be teaching Indigenous content in this area, as students expect to see Indigenous instructors teaching Indigenous issues from a cultural perspective. Buker (2014) states that as an Indigenous professor, she brings an Indigenous perspective into her teachings, along with a commitment to Indigenous epistemologies, cultural worldviews, and community partnerships. There is a critical need for Indigenous people to be educated in ISW so their communities can heal and continue the reconciliation process.

School of Indigenous Social Work Kiskinowatacikewin—Hawk

The School of Indigenous Social Work (SISW) at First Nations University of Canada (FNUniv) uses the symbol of the hawk to represent its program. The hawk is seen as a symbol of power, a strong connection and messenger to the spirit world, and, importantly, the hawk has the power of observation and the ability to focus on the task at hand (E. Harris, n.d.). The hawk is an important animal in Indigenous culture and, for the SISW, the hawk symbolizes a need to start looking forward, envisioning an educational path, and preparing for and expanding the vision of education (Innes, 2018). The sixteen black upper feathers represent all the Indigenous social work classes that each student will take in the SISW program. The

Figure 10.1. Hawk. Source: Clipart-Library.com.

bottom four tail feathers represent the four sacred colours—Red, White, Blue, and Yellow—along with the four directions, North, East, West, and South. The middle portion of the body represents the faculty of the SISW program, and the tail represents the Elders who are an important part of the program. The head oversees everyone in the program and makes sure that everything is good and that everyone has a clear vision of their responsibilities and cares for one another.

One of the core classes of the SISW curriculum is the Indigenous child welfare course. This course "examines the history of Indigenous child welfare, with a critical examination on child protection, abuse, neglect, and support systems for Indigenous families. Indigenous child welfare agencies are also examined, along with jurisdictional issues" (FNUniv, 2021). This course was originally an elective course offered once a year, but the faculty believed the topic was so important that it should be a core class offered twice a year and be part of their program. The faculty have extensive experience in child welfare and collaborate to provide a knowledgeable and effective course. Use of the faculty's knowledge and an Indigenous approach to learning and teaching are what define the success of the course.

Indigenous people often describe themselves as holistic and visual learners and tend to learn through observation and imitation rather than verbal instruction (Rasmussen et al., 2004; S. Harris, 1980; Hughes, 1997). There is a strong link between an Indigenous cultural setting and learning style (Cooper, 1980; Swisher & Deyhle, 1989). Indigenous students learn in a circle format in SISW. According to Lewis (2003), a circle format is student centred and includes five aspects:

1. Students and the teacher are the learners, and everyone is equal.
2. All participants bear responsibility for the circle.
3. The circle encourages storytelling.
4. The centre of the circle is sacred.
5. A talking piece such as a rock or feather is passed around to facilitate sharing.

Indigenous learning addresses the whole person, encompassing the mental, physical, spiritual, and emotional capabilities of that person in relation to all living things (Dragonfly Consulting Services Canada, 2012). Indigenous students are more likely to develop a positive self-concept in a classroom where their cultures are valued and their individual gifts are recognized than in one where they are not (Alberta Education, 2005). Indigenous students have been shown to benefit from the presence of culture in their lives through ceremony.

Indigenous culture is part of the SISW program as culture is sacred and an important part of Indigenous society. Indigenous culture includes Indigenous epistemology, ontology, and axiology. Wilson (2001) states that ontology is your way of being, your belief in the world; epistemology is how you think of reality; and axiology is a set of ethics or morals. These components comprise the philosophical underpinnings of Indigenous culture because spirituality and reciprocity are elements of ontology, storytelling is an integral aspect of epistemology, and respect is shown in axiology (Hart, 2010).

Indigenous Child Welfare Curriculum

The curriculum is centred around four Cree principles: nisitohtamowin—understanding, manitowakêýimowin—believing, kiskinwahamâtowin—learning, and kiskêýihtamowin—knowledge. The curriculum is set up to represent each area, covering specific topics. For example, in nisitohtamowin, students learn how and why Indigenous people are involved in the child welfare process. It is important to understand the intergenerational trauma and issues affecting Indigenous people because students may have these issues in their past, and they will be working and interacting with individuals with these experiences. When students discuss their experiences of intergenerational trauma and education, they often disclose histories of poverty, family dysfunction, child welfare involvement, and addiction (Gaywish & Mordoch, 2018). These disclosures need to be handled effectively in the classroom, and Indigenous students need to feel empowered to assist their future clients with overcoming those issues.

nisitohtamowin (Understanding)

nisitohtamowin is the action of understanding, so applying it to child welfare makes sense because Indigenous child welfare is a multifaceted process. Several aspects of the educational curriculum need to be understood. For example, students need to understand how Indian Child and

Family Services (ICFS) operates within Indigenous communities. Also, the curriculum explores how ICFS is different from the mainstream and how this agency is servicing the needs of Indigenous people. There is a distinction between mainstream and Indigenous child welfare agencies, and this must be conveyed to students. For example, Kanaweyimik Child & Family Services in North Battleford, Saskatchewan, takes an Indigenous approach by utilizing Indigenous culture, belief, and traditional practices to empower Indigenous families to sustain a healthy environment (Kanaweyimik Child & Family Services, n.d.).

Incorporating an Indigenous perspective is an important aspect of this process because this educational paradigm will be presented from this perspective. An Indigenous perspective centres on the Indigenous worldview, a central feature of which is the relationship between Indigenous people and nature. It provides the foundation for Indigenous people's relationships with one another and to the spiritual being that inhabits the universe (Martin & Mirraboopa, 2003). Sinclair (2004) identifies two key concepts in an Indigenous worldview: "all my relations" and the sacred. These concepts remind us of who we are as Indigenous people and of our interrelatedness and interconnectedness to all human relations, both living and unborn. The notion of "sacred" is viewed as a supreme law in an Indigenous worldview, as it is the thread of interconnectedness between dreaming, humans, and the natural world, while "all my relations" is a reminder of who we are as Indigenous people and the relationship we have with our family and relatives (Sinclair, 2004; Grieves, 2008). Traditional religion usually views the sacred in the context of another world, such as "heaven" or "paradise," where there is a disconnection between this world and that one (Grieves, 2008). Although students will learn from this perspective, many will be of Indigenous ancestry, and thus may understand the approach and the principles such as culture, practice, and protocol and will be comfortable in this environment. However, it is important to note that some Indigenous individuals may not hold a strong connection to the culture and traditions, even though they bring an Indigenous perspective.

kiskinwahamâtowin (Learning)

kiskinwahamâtowin represents a philosophy of teaching one another. In Indigenous pedagogy especially, the transmission of cultural knowledge is critical and relies on the teachings of the Elders. Capturing the teachings of the Elders is central to cultural preservation because Elders possess formal knowledge and expertise. Through orality, Elders provide lessons on how to go about living the good life, and they impart knowledge, values, and traditions (Burns, 1998). McDowall (2021) infers that universities are grappling with how best to incorporate Indigenous content and frameworks to work effectively in Indigenous communities. Although this is the case with most universities, it is not an issue within the SISW, as the program's pedagogical approach is based on the Indigenous principles, practice, and philosophy and reflects the different Nations that are represented. Creaser (2020) suggests that the most important opinions related to Indigenous educational curriculum are those of Indigenous people themselves. The SISW has an advantage because all of the faculty are of Indigenous ancestry and represent First Nations and Métis communities in Canada and the United States.

A strong focus on Indigenous culture, worldviews, and historical trauma is essential in supporting students to learn and understand not only how to work with Indigenous people in child welfare because of Bill C-92 but also how to work and in an Indigenous organization. For example, the Lac La Ronge ICFS (n.d.) is responsible for the delivery of child and family services to the band members of the six Indigenous communities that make up the Lac La Ronge Indian Band in Saskatchewan. Learning about this agency, along with how Indigenous child welfare organizations work, is necessary for students studying Indigenous child welfare in social work programs. Also, having Indigenous workers from the ICFS agencies come into the classroom and talk about their experiences and knowledge of Indigenous child welfare is necessary because an Indigenous pedagogical approach must include Indigenous culture, language, and worldviews (Toulouse, 2008).

In terms of Indigenous child welfare, it is important to learn about intergenerational trauma and its impact on Indigenous people and communities. Historical colonial government policies such as residential schools and the Sixties Scoop resulted in a lack of connection between children and parents that has traumatized many Indigenous communities and continues to plague Indigenous people. "Many of the problems facing Native American people today—such as alcoholism, child abuse, suicide, and domestic violence—have become part of the [Indigenous heritage] due to the long decades of forced assimilation and genocidal practices implemented by the federal government" (Duran & Duran, 1995, p. 35). The lasting problems need attention and ways in which to heal. For example, Greer (2021) presents a trauma-responsive care model based on research in Aotearoa New Zealand. Having a model that is based on Indigenous research and perspective is important since Western approaches often marginalize Indigenous peoples, presenting them through a Western lens. Menzies (2010) suggests that individual indicators of intergenerational trauma include low self-esteem, mental health issues, addictions, and difficulty with personal relationships, to name a few. An examination of these indicators, along with family and community indicators, can make students aware of the negative aspects of intergenerational trauma and have them understand that trauma is not only a major cause of dysfunction in the lives of Indigenous people but also directly connected to negative outcomes in child welfare.

manitowakêŷimowin (Believing)

manitowakêŷimowin represents a person's own belief as well as others believing in them, along with acknowledging the ancestors who believed in them. Believing in Indigenous child welfare can be a difficult process because of historical experiences such as the Sixties Scoop, the Adopt Indian Métis (AIM) program, and the residential schools, to name a few, and their effect on Indigenous people. Although the historical aspect is negative and continues to plague Indigenous communities, the implementation of Bill C-92 puts the control of the welfare process in the hands of the community; however, it is important to note that the structure of child welfare remains under Bill C-92 and the power to change continues to rest in the hands of the colonizers. So, this practice is going to take time and effort among the community and those involved, and it is the responsibility of the Indigenous individuals, families, and communities to begin a new journey that considers the perspective of Indigenous people.

Among Indigenous peoples, there is mistrust and resentment of the government of Canada and its policies (Thibodeau & North Peigan, 2007; Proulx & Perrault, 2000; LaRocque, 1993). This historical process needs examination and discussion so students understand how this process created trauma and resulted in loss of trust, caring, and emotions and limited the ability to be open and to share thoughts and feelings (Thibodeau & North Peigan, 2007; Thibodeau, 2003). Burge (2021) cites research that shows Indigenous children in care who do not experience a strong sense of family, community connection, and belonging will likely have poor outcomes in their lives. Indigenous children continue to be involved in child welfare because of poverty and substance abuse, but a resilient Indigenous community is the best hope for these children to have a safe and healthy environment (Blackstock & Trocmé, 2005).

It is unfathomable that Indigenous people can and will believe in a system that has negatively affected their lives for many generations. The previous approach to child welfare sustains the annihilative and greedy impulses of the present and continuous disposal of the lands and sovereignty of Indigenous people; therefore, with Bill C-92, a new approach is being established to reflect the needs of Indigenous people (Landertinger, 2021). A belief system is important but can only be accomplished with the direction of Indigenous people. It is necessary to believe in and take pride in who they are and what they represent because growing up in child welfare can strip away one's identity and create a need to reconnect to the traditional system (Fiedeldey-Van Dijk et al., 2017).

kiskêýihtamowin (Knowledge)

kiskêýihtamowin is viewed as knowledge, learning, and experience. Indigenous child welfare is a complex process because of the different jurisdictions and parties involved, so it is necessary to learn and gain knowledge about it. Indigenous children in Canada are served by multifaceted systems, spearheaded by provincial, territorial, federal, and Indigenous governments, through 300 child welfare agencies in Canada (Aboriginal Children in Care Working Group, 2015; McMillan, 2021). The timeline of formalized Indigenous child welfare services begins in the late 1960s, when Aboriginal Affairs and Northern Development Canada (later Indigenous and Northern Affairs Canada) began to set up child welfare agreements with bands and tribal councils. In the 1980s, a transfer of responsibilities to First Nation communities took place, and by 2008, 125 Indigenous child and family service agencies existed (Sinha et al., 2011, p. 9). First Nation agencies tend to involve more prevention and preservation, cultural programming, and community-based principles than mainstream government agencies. When First Nation communities oversee their own services, including child welfare, there is a psychological benefit (Sinha et al., 2011, p. 9). Understanding and gaining comprehensive knowledge about the system can be a difficult process. Examining the different jurisdictional issues, leadership issues, and the different Indigenous communities that are involved is just the beginning of the knowledge process. With Bill C-92 providing Indigenous communities with a process through which to exercise their inherent jurisdiction over the care of their own children and families according to their traditional laws and values (Faille & Christoff, 2020), the time is right to generate the knowledge necessary so that Indigenous communities know, understand, and can be effective in their own delivery of child welfare. It is important to note that Bill C-92 has a few flaws, such as no guaranteed funding and judication issues between the provincial and federal governments (Faille & Christoff, 2020), and legislation and standards issues are only the first step toward equitable child welfare and the very least that can be asked of provinces, territories, and the federal government. For progress to occur, Indigenous families and communities also require "effective implementation" (Sinha et al., 2011, p. 13). Necessary knowledge includes cultural teachings and protocol, history of child welfare, jurisdictional issues, provincial and federal laws, funding agreements, and administrative capacity building.

Within ISWE, Indigenous students become knowledgeable about the child welfare agency in their Indigenous community and the policies that govern it. Education and training prepare Indigenous child welfare professionals to deliver and design services in their community (Tracy & Pine, 2000). Students need knowledge not only of the child welfare agency in their community but also of the programs and jurisdictional and funding issues, along with how to best serve the community in a leadership position. Additionally, there are challenging areas for Indigenous agencies in child welfare, which include "program planning, applied research, and evidence-based policy development affected by local factors such as agency remoteness, technological limitations, and cultural and linguistic variability" (Thomas Prokop et al., 2018, p. 52).

Education and child welfare systems contain structural inequalities and relationships (Milne & Wotherspoon, 2020). A number of issues are critical to understanding child welfare within the Indigenous community, including the destructive unhealthy legacy of residential schools and the Sixties Scoop. Therefore, educational institutions must provide safe and culturally competent spaces and incorporate Indigenous knowledge and culture (Nelson et al., 2019). The topic of Indigenous child welfare needs to be at the forefront of the educational milieu. It is time for Indigenous issues related to child welfare to be a required course for all social work students in Canada. This method is present in SISW, which provides Indigenous social work knowledge that is founded upon Indigenous cultures, values, and philosophies (SISW, 2021). Research has shown that Indigenous and non-Indigenous post-secondary students are a highly stressed population (Wo et al., 2019). Thus, it is important that an educational environment reflect Indigenous philosophies, ideologies, knowledge systems, and methodologies, as these provide a strong foundation for a commitment to respect, research, reconciliation, and self-determination for Indigenous people (SISW, 2021).

Conclusion

Indigenous people have lost their identity, been involved in child welfare, and experienced abuses because of internalized oppression and colonization (Baskin, 2006). Indigenous child welfare education is taking a more prominent role as a result of Bill C-92—specifically because there is a need to know, understand, believe, and learn everything that it encompasses in order to drastically transform the system and the experiences of Indigenous children and families who continue to be overrepresented within it. The SISW program effectively addresses the historical, cultural, and societal needs of Indigenous people by providing an educational foundation for those students returning to their communities or choosing to work in Indigenous child welfare agencies. Indigenous people are recruited after obtaining a social work degree because there is a need for trained social workers to fulfill important child welfare positions within the community. With the inclusion of Bill C-92 in Indigenous child welfare, now is the time for Indigenous students to be working in their communities. As change occurs, Indigenous students will be at the forefront and will be transforming the system from a Western approach to child welfare to an Indigenous one. By having the Indigenous child welfare course as one of its required courses, SISW is taking the initiative to train students on all aspects of Indigenous child welfare and have them become effective workers in their communities.

The course is centred on four principles—nisitohtamowin, manitowakêýimowin, kiskinwahamâtowin, and kiskêýihtamowin—that explore Indigenous child welfare in a way conducive to an Indigenous approach to learning. Within the course, students share their experiences, thoughts, and knowledge on child welfare, and this process contributes to everyone's education throughout their time in the course and the program. Indigenous communities need individuals with strong child welfare knowledge and experience to serve their people on a communal and national level, and this is happening at the post-secondary level, especially in the SISW program, which has been educating students on Indigenous social work for over forty-five years and continues to be an important part of the Indigenous community.

Learning Questions

1. What is the connection between colonization and the current overrepresentation of Indigenous children in the child welfare system?
2. What are some ways that social workers could address the stigma around the profession of social work in Indigenous communities?
3. How is the pedagogy of Indigenous social work education (ISWE) different from that of mainstream social work education? What are the justifications for these differences?
4. What is the main aim of Bill C-92? What opportunities and challenges are involved?
5. Why is it important to learn Indigenous child welfare and how is this approach different from a Western approach to child welfare?

References

Aboriginal Children in Care Working Group. (2015). *Aboriginal children in care: Report to Canada's premiers*. Council of the Federation Secretariat. https://fncaringsociety.com/sites/default/files/Aboriginal%20Children%20in%20Care%20Report%20%28July%202015%29.pdf

Alberta Education. (2005). *Our words, our ways: Teaching First Nations, Métis and Inuit learners.* Aboriginal Services Branch and Learning and Teaching Resources Branch. https://education.alberta.ca/media/3615876/our-words-our-ways.pdf

Atter, H. (2021, July 7). Cowessess First Nation signs historic agreement to control local child welfare system. *CBC News.* https://www.cbc.ca/news/canada/saskatchewan/cowessess-first-nation-in-photos-1.6092800

Assembly of First Nations. (1994). *Breaking the silence: An interpretive study of residential school impact and healing as illustrated by the stories of First Nations individuals.* Assembly of First Nations.

Auger, M. (2016). Cultural continuity as a determinant of Indigenous peoples' health: A metasynthesis of qualitative research in Canada and the United States. *International Indigenous Policy Journal, 7*(4). https://doi.org/10.18584/iipj.2016.7.4.3

Baikie, G. (2009). Indigenous-centered social work: Theorizing a social work way-of-being. In R. Sinclair, M. Hart, & G. Bruyere (Eds.), *Wícihitowin: Aboriginal social work in Canada* (pp. 42–64). Fernwood Publishing.

Barman, J., Hébert, Y., & McCaskill, D. (1986). The legacy of the past: An overview. In J. Barman, Y. Hébert, & D. McCaskill (Eds.), *Indian education in Canada* (Vol. 1, pp. 1–22). UBC Press.

Barrera, J. (2019, December 11). House passes motion calling on Ottawa to pay First Nations child welfare compensation ordered by tribunal. *CBC News.* https://www.cbc.ca/news/indigenous/child-welfare-compensation-motion-ndp-1.5393231

Baskin, C. (2005). Centring Aboriginal worldviews in social work education. *Australian Journal of Indigenous Education, 34*, 96–106. https://doi.org/10.1017/S1326011100004014

Baskin, C. (2006). Aboriginal worldviews as challenges and possibilities in social work education. *Critical Social Work, 7*(2). https://doi.org/10.22329/csw.v7i2.5726

Blackstock, C., & Trocmé, N. (2005). Community-based child welfare for Aboriginal children: Supporting resilience through structural change. In M. Ungar (Ed.), *Handbook for working with children and youth: Pathways to resilience across cultures and contexts* (pp. 105–120). Sage Publishing. https://doi.org/10.4135/9781412976312.n7

Bruyere, G. (2008). Picking up what was left by the trail: The emerging spirit of Aboriginal education in Canada. In M. Gray, J. Coates, & M. Yellow Bird (Eds.), *Indigenous social work around the world: Towards a culturally relevant education and practice* (pp. 231–244). Ashgate Publishing.

Buker, I. (2014, October). Taking the long view of Indigenous teacher education. *Academic Matters.* https://academicmatters.ca/taking-the-long-view-of-indigenous-teacher-education/

Burge, P. (2021, February 5). Indigenous child welfare is grounded in community and children's needs. *Queen's Gazette.* https://www.queensu.ca/gazette/stories/indigenous-child-welfare-grounded-community-and-children-s-needs

Burns, G. (1998). *Toward a redefinition of formal and informal learning: Education and the Aboriginal people* [Conference presentation]. Joint session of New Approaches to Lifelong Learning (NALL) Conference and Canadian Association for the Study of Adult Education (CASAE), University of Ottawa. http://www.oise.utoronto.ca/depts/sese/csew/nall/res/28towardaredef.htm

Cooper, G. (1980). Different ways of thinking. *Minority of Education, 2*(5), 1–4.

Creaser, J. (2020). *Representation of Indigenous education in primary classrooms* [Unpublished master's portfolio]. Lakehead University.

Dragonfly Consulting Services Canada. (2012). *Aboriginal worldviews*. http://dragonflycanada.ca/resources/aboriginal-worldviews/ [site inactive]

Duran, E., & Duran, B. (1995). *Native American postcolonial psychology*. State University of New York Press.

Faille, M., & Christoff, A. (2020, October 20). Bill C-92: Towards restoring Indigenous jurisdiction over child and family services. *Gowling WLG*. https://gowlingwlg.com/en/insights-resources/articles/2020/bill-c92-indigenous-jurisdiction-child-and-family

First Nations University of Canada. (2020). *School of Indigenous Social Work*. https://www.fnuniv.ca/academic/undergraduate-programs/indigenous-social-work/

Fiedeldey-Van Dijk, C., Rowan, M., Dell, C., Mushquash, C., Hopkins, C., Fornssler, B., Hall, L., Mykota, D., Farag, M., & Shea, B. (2017). Honoring Indigenous culture-as-intervention: Development and validity of the Native Wellness Assessment. *Journal of Ethnicity in Substance Abuse, 16*(2). https://doi.org/10.1080/15332640.2015.1119774

Gaywish, R., & Mordoch, E. (2018). Situating intergenerational trauma in the educational journey. *IN Education, 24*(2), 3–23. https://doi.org/10.37119/ojs2018.v24i2.386

Green, J. (2009). The complexity of Indigenous identity formation and politics in Canada: Self-determination and decolonisation. *International Journal of Critical Indigenous Studies, 2*(2), 36–46. https://ijcis.qut.edu.au/article/view/29/29

Greer, A. (2021). Trauma responsive care model: An Aotearoa New Zealand research informed practice model for residential group homes. *Aotearoa New Zealand Social Work, 33*(1), 81–93. https://doi.org/10.11157/anzswj-vol33iss1id825

Grieves, V. (2008). Aboriginal spirituality: A baseline for Indigenous knowledges development in Australia. *Canadian Journal of Native Studies, 28*(2), 363–398.

Hart, M. A. (2002). *Seeking mino-pimatisiwin: An Aboriginal approach to helping*. Fernwood Publishing.

Hart, M. A. (2010). Indigenous worldviews, knowledge, and research: The development of an Indigenous research paradigm. *Journal of Indigenous Voices in Social Work, 1*(1), 1–16. http://hdl.handle.net/10125/15117

Harris, B. (2006). A First Nations' perspective on social justice in social work education: Are we there yet? (A post-colonial debate). *Canadian Journal of Native Studies, 26*(2), 229–263.

Harris, E. (n.d.). *Hawk spirit animal.* Spirit Animal. Retrieved January 15, 2022, from https://www.spiritanimal.info/hawk-spirit-animal/

Harris, S. (1980). *Culture and learning: Traditions and education in Northeast Arnhem Land.* Professional Services Branch, Northern Territory Department of Education.

Heinonen, T., & Spearman, L. (2001). *Social work practice: Problem solving and beyond.* Irwin.

Hughes, P. (1997). *A compact of Aboriginal Education* [Unpublished paper]. Adelaide.

Hyslop, K. (2021, March 23). How to create an Indigenous child welfare system. *The Tyee.* https://thetyee.ca/News/2021/03/23/How-To-Create-Indigenous-Child-Welfare-System/

Innes, L. J. (2018, January 16). *The meaning of a hawk sighting.* California Psychics. https://www.californiapsychics.com/blog/animal-sightings-symbolism/meaning-hawk-sighting.html

Ives, N., Aitken, O., Loft, M., & Phillips, M. (2007). Rethinking social work education for Indigenous students: Creating space for multiple ways of knowing and learning. *First Peoples Child & Family Review, 3*(4), 13–20. https://fpcfr.com/index.php/FPCFR/article/view/55

Kanaweyimik Child & Family Services. (n.d.). *Vision statement.* Retrieved February 22, 2022, from https://www.kanaweyimik.com/

Lac La Ronge Indian Child & Family Services. (n.d.). *Our history.* Lac La Ronge Indian Band. Retrieved February 22, 2022, from http://www.icfs.ca/about-icfs/

Landertinger, L. (2021). Settler colonialism and the Canadian child welfare system. In C. Schields & D. Herzog (Eds.), *The Routledge companion to sexuality and colonialism* (1st ed., pp. 136–144). Routledge. https://doi.org/10.4324/9780429505447

LaRocque, E. D. (1993). *The path to healing.* Canada Communication Group Publishing.

Lewis, G. (2003). Teaching and learning in a circle. *Conflict Management in Higher Education Report, 3*(2). https://www.creducation.net/resources/cmher_vol_3_2_lewis.pdf

Mandell, D., Clouston Carlson, J., Fine, M., & Blackstock, C. (2003). *Aboriginal child welfare* (Partnerships for Children and Families Project, Reports and Papers, Rep., 1–64). Wilfrid Laurier University.

Martin, K., & Mirraboopa, B. (2003). Ways of knowing, being and doing: A theoretical framework and methods for Indigenous and indigenist re-search. *Journal of Australian Studies, 27* (76), 203–214. https://doi.org/10.1080/14443050309387838

McDowall, A. (2021). Layered spaces: A pedagogy of uncomfortable reflexivity in Indigenous education. *Higher Education Research & Development, 40*(2), 341–355. https://doi.org/10.1080/07294360.2020.1756751

McMillan, L. J. (2021). Unsettling standards: Indigenous peoples and child welfare. In J. Graham, C. Holmes, F. McDonald, & R. Darnell (Eds.), *The social life of standards: Ethnographic methods for local engagement* (pp. 179–198). UBC Press.

Menzies, P. (2010). Intergenerational trauma from a mental health perspective. *Native Social Work Journal, 7*, 63–85. https://www.collectionscanada.gc.ca/obj/thesescanada/vol2/OSUL/TC-OSUL-384.PDF

Midgley, J. (1981). *Professional imperialism: Social work in the third world.* Heinemann.

Miller, J. (1996). *Shingwauk's vision: A history of Native residential schools.* University of Toronto Press.

Milne, E., & Wotherspoon, T. (2020). Schools as "really dangerous places" for Indigenous children and youth: Schools, child welfare, and contemporary challenges to reconciliation. *Canadian Review of Sociology, 57*(1), 34–52. https://doi.org/10.1111/cars.12267

Mosher, J., & Hewitt, J. (2018). Reimagining child welfare systems in Canada. *Journal of Law and Social Policy 28*(1), 1–9. https://digitalcommons.osgoode.yorku.ca/jlsp/vol28/iss1/1

Muir, N., & Bohr, Y. (2019). Contemporary practice of traditional Aboriginal child rearing: A review. *First Peoples Child & Family Review, 14*(1), 153–165.

Navia, D., Henderson, R. I., & First Charger, L. (2018). Uncovering colonial legacies: Voices of Indigenous youth on child welfare (dis)placements. *Anthropology & Education Quarterly, 49*(2), 146–164. https://doi.org/10.1111/aeq.12245

Nelson, H., Cox-White, T., & Ziefflie, B. (2019). Indigenous students: Barriers and success strategies—A review of existing literature. *Journal of Nursing Education and Practice, 9*(3), 70–77. https://doi.org/10.5430/jnep.v9n3p70

Proulx, J., & Perrault, S. (2000). *No place for violence: Canadian Aboriginal alternatives*. Fernwood Publishing.

Rae, J. (2019, June). *A roadmap to C-92, the federal child welfare law*. Olthuis Kleer Townshend LLP. https://www.oktlaw.com/a-roadmap-to-c-92-the-federal-child-welfare-law/

Rasmussen, C., Baydala, L., & Sherman, J. (2004). Learning patterns and education of Aboriginal children: A review of the literature. *Canadian Journal of Native Studies, 24*(2), 317–342. http://www3.brandonu.ca/cjns/24.2/cjnsv24no2_pg317-342.pdf

Sinclair, R. (2004). Aboriginal social work education in Canada: Decolonizing pedagogy for the seventh generation. *First Nations Child & Family Review, 1*(1), 49–62. https://fpcfr.com/index.php/FPCFR/article/view/10

Sinclair, R. (2009). Bridging the past and the future: An introduction to ISW issues. In R. Sinclair, M. Hart, & G. Bruyere (Eds.), *Wícihitowin: Aboriginal social work in Canada* (pp. 19–24). Fernwood Publishing.

Sinha, V., Caldwell, J., Paul, L., & Fumaneri, P. (2021). A review of literature of the involvement of children from Indigenous communities in Anglo child welfare systems: 1973–2018. *International Indigenous Policy Journal, 12*(1). https://doi.org/10.18584/iipj.2021.12.1.10818

Sinha, V., & Kozlowski, A. (2013). The structure of Aboriginal child welfare in Canada. *International Indigenous Policy Journal, 4*(2). https://doi.org/10.18584/iipj.2013.4.2.2

Sinha, V., Trocmé, N., Fallon, B., MacLaurin, B., Fast, E., Prokop, S. T., & Richard, K. (2011). *Kiskisik awasisak: Remember the children. Understanding the overrepresentation of First Nations children in the child welfare system.* Assembly of First Nations. https://cwrp.ca/sites/default/files/publications/en/FNCIS-2008_March2012_RevisedFinal.pdf

Smith, L. T. (1999). *Decolonizing methodologies: Research and Indigenous peoples.* Zed Books.

Solomon, M. (2021, July 6). Sask. First Nation transferred control over children in care under federal law. *CTV News.* https://regina.ctvnews.ca/sask-first-nation-transferred-control-over-children-in-care-under-federal-law-1.5498229

Swisher, K., & Deyhle, D. (1989, August). The styles of learning are different, but the teaching is just the same: Suggestions for teachers of American Indian youth. *Journal of American Indian Education*, special issue, 1–14. https://www.jstor.org/stable/44466403

Tait, C. L., Henry, R., & Walker, R. L. (2013). Child welfare: A social determinant of health for Canadian First Nations and Métis children. *Pimatisiwin: A Journal for Aboriginal and Indigenous Community Health, 11*(1), 39–53.

Thibodeau, S. (2003). *Study of the problematics of implementing initiatives that prevent violence against women in Aboriginal communities* [Unpublished doctoral thesis]. University of Manchester.

Thibodeau, S., & North Peigan, F. (2007). Loss of trust among First Nations people: Implications when implementing child protection treatment initiatives. *First Peoples Child & Family Review, 3*(4), 50–58. https://doi.org/10.7202/1069374ar

Thomas Prokop, S., Hicks, L., & Melymick, R. (2018). Working with First Nations child welfare to build professionalism. In D. Badry, H. Montgomery, D. Kikulwe, M. Bennett, & D. Fuchs (Eds.), *Imagining child welfare in the spirit of reconciliation* (pp. 27–42). University of Regina Press.

Toulouse, P. R. (2008, March). Integrating Aboriginal teaching and values into the classroom. *What works? Research into Practice.* Literacy and Numeracy Secretariate, Ontario. https://www.oise.utoronto.ca/deepeningknowledge/UserFiles/File/FNMI_-_Research_Monograph_11_-_Aboriginal_Perspectives_Toulouse.pdf

Tracy, E., & Pine, B. (2000). Child welfare education and training: Future trends and influences. *Child Welfare, 79*(1), 93–113.

Wilson, S. (2001). What is Indigenous research methodology? *Canadian Journal of Native Education, 25*(2), 175–179.

Wo, N., Anderson, K., Wylie, L., & MacDougall, A. (2019). The prevalence of distress, depression, anxiety, and substance use issues among Indigenous post-secondary students in Canada. *Transcultural Psychiatry, 57*(2), 263–274. https://doi.org/10.1177/1363461519861824

Yunong, H., & Xiong, Z. (2008). A reflection on the indigenization discourse in social work. *International Social Work, 51*(5), 611–622. https://doi.org/10.1177/0020872808093340

Epilogue

Peter Choate

In academia, we are often advised to write in the third person. In this instance, I cannot do that. This book is about the personal. It is about the ways in which individual lives are impacted by the ongoing "old mindset" that Mathews, King, and Blackstock identify in Chapter 1. The various chapters have shown that Indigenous Peoples in Canada have been and are subject to systems that continue to separate, isolate, and dominate.

Trauma has been at the heart of the relationship between child protection and Indigenous peoples as an extension of colonialism. The Truth and Reconciliation Commission of Canada (TRC) (2015) called for change. Yet, many voices before the TRC did too. I think of the Royal Commission on Aboriginal Peoples (1996). I also think of the more recent report of the National Inquiry into Missing and Murdered Indigenous Women and Girls (2019). There are numerous reports from child and youth advocates from across Canada that echo the words of Graff and Eaton-Erickson in this volume (Chapter 6). There are so many reports and far too little change.

There remains resistance in Canada. Let's be very clear about that. The government of Canada has steadfastly resisted implementing the orders of the Canadian Human Rights Tribunal, as noted by Mathews, King, and Blackstock. It seems that Canada feels resistance is better than substantive change. Yet, there are glimmers of hope. Friedland and Lightning-Earle write in Chapter 2 about the new federal child welfare legislation regarding First Nations, Inuit, and Métis children, youth and families. This law has created a possible pathway for greater control by Indigenous peoples over the protection of their own children. The Cowessess First Nation in

Saskatchewan has boldly been the first to implement its own legislation with its own child welfare agency. Others may soon follow. We must now see if the courts will uphold the spirit and intent of this opportunity. I fear this will be a challenging journey, with uneven acceptance of the new law ultimately requiring the Supreme Court of Canada to settle the position of it relative to provincial and territorial statutes.

This is not a benign worry. Despite the commissions and inquiries noted above, 52.2 per cent of children in care in Canada are Indigenous, while Indigenous children make up only 7.7 per cent of the Canadian population (Statistics Canada, 2016). In the Prairie provinces, the location of the Prairie Child Welfare Consortium (PCWC), the numbers are far more challenging, ranging from 70 to 90 per cent of children in care. Some might want to argue that we are in a post-colonial period. We are not, as evident by the ongoing overrepresentation. In 2018, I was a member of a child intervention review panel in Alberta. During a year of listening to social workers, professionals, academics, and, most importantly, the people impacted by child welfare, we heard repeatedly about the how the system continues to fracture rather than to sustain. At one of the public meetings, a senior manager stated, “We are an Indigenous serving agency.” That quote has stayed with me. How badly we serve.

This volume demands of us better outcomes by doing the work of child protection differently. That will not be easy. It means that we, as a profession, must be willing to look at our role in colonization and cultural genocide, as my colleague Gabrielle Lindstrom and I suggest (Chapter 4). Assessment, data gathering, and understanding Indigenous ways of parenting should be the focal point, as opposed to the comfortable pattern of using Eurocentric approaches, definitions, and case planning. Milliken and Dano-Chartrand (Chapter 8) reach deeply into practice done in a culturally meaningful and appropriate way. It is hard work that requires intent as well as dedicated resources to allow for building relationships, gathering data, supporting cultural solutions, and being willing to travel the pathway. Yet, as so often happens, doing it differently is not matched by the funding, supports, or staffing needed to be successful. Their work really lets us know that success is occurring despite the inadequacy of government supports. But why should it be that way? The sad answer is the unwillingness of power systems to give up the structural control, believing, it would seem, that they know better.

Provost and Tortorelli (Chapter 5) tell us that, even within a provincial structure, the intention to use Indigenous ways of knowing can result in better connections for children and youth. They speak of the kind of connections that allow Indigenous youth to know who they are, to be grounded in their own ways of knowing and have a place where they belong. That really is a "mighty" theme of this book: Indigenous children knowing themselves as part of their own legacy and having systems that make it not just possible but in fact necessary. Iahtail (Chapter 7) adds to the theme, telling us that families need to be at the root of the work.

Colonial threads run through this volume. Fetal Alcohol Spectrum Disorder (FASD) is a critical topic that impacts many children and families involved with the child welfare system, and a more concerted effort is required to disseminate knowledge and training among child welfare staff. I was deeply moved by many of the stories, but for me, one stood out—that of Maaja Man (Chapter 3), and in particular, this line: "The only protection Maaja ever experienced came from his extended Aboriginal family and community." They cared.

The chapters in this book are intended to assist our profession of social work in meeting the calls to action by the TRC, the first five of which are specific to child welfare. Central to them is the need to keep Indigenous families together, which is something that Canada has not done—indeed, is something Canada specifically sought not to do. Child protection picked up the legacy of the Indian residential schools to continue the degradation of Indigenous communities, families, and caregiving systems through ongoing removal of children from their families and communities. The TRC said, "Enough." The Indigenous authors who led each chapter of this book are also saying, "Enough."

Social work is a profession that intersects with multiple others in health, justice, and education. The TRC (2015) also called on those professions to change what they do with Indigenous families. Those other professions, too, support the legacies of child welfare, given how Indigenous peoples are dealt with in their systems and how that leads to increased placements of children into care. Consider that Indigenous peoples are also overrepresented in the justice systems and jails, meaning further community fragmentation. For example, in 2016–17, Indigenous youth aged twelve to eighteen represented about 8 per cent of all youth in Canada but 46 per cent of youth in the justice system. They are also more likely than non-Indigenous youth to be incarcerated (Clark, 2019). Consider that Indigenous peoples are denied access to the social determinants of health at a rate far higher than that of other Canadians. These denials of the elements that provide for sufficient resources to lead a vibrant life are structurally denied (Greenwood et al., 2018).

In terms of health, Professor Mary Ellen Turpel-Lafond (2021) points out that "addressing systemic racism requires coherent, systematic action. Uprooting Indigenous-specific racism in health care requires shifts in governance, leadership, legislation and policy, education, and practice" (p. 2). Structural racism was visibly evident in the death in Québec of Joyce Echaquan, who was subjected to racial taunts as she died. She live-streamed the verbal abuse against her in the hospital moments before she died. Her story is not an isolated one. The point is that social work cannot assume it can work alone in changing the landscape of child protection. It must advocate for change both within its own profession and across intersecting professions that can join us in reconciliation.

The PCWC was founded in 1999 and to date has published seven books with a unique focus on child welfare on the Prairies. The tri-provincial partnership between Alberta, Saskatchewan, and Manitoba has kept the focus on the distinct issues relevant to First Nations and Métis engagement with child welfare. The PCWC is embarking on a vision of renewal in 2022 with the launch of this book and with the goals of continuing (post-pandemic) to offer biennial conferences and to find meeting places on the Prairies where we can gather together to talk about child welfare issues. In light of Bill C-92, it is anticipated that Indigenous governance of child welfare will continue to grow, which will spark new and important conversations. We are also committed to supporting new and emerging scholars researching and writing on Indigenous child welfare concerns and plan to support and promote such scholarship. The work of the PCWC is about bringing forth the voices of Indigenous and non-Indigenous scholars working collaboratively in this space to continue to challenge old discourses and old mindsets, as so well articulated in Chapter 1 by Mathews, King, and Blackstock. It is time for new narratives and new discourses in child welfare on the Prairies and in Canada, and the PCWC remains committed to advancing scholarship and mobilizing knowledge.

As researchers and academics, we need to interrogate the content of our work with students in classrooms and in field education as well as in our writing. It cannot be otherwise. This volume joins other voices in identifying how change can occur. Will our profession take the action?

References

Clark, S. (2019). *Overrepresentation of Indigenous people in the Canadian criminal justice system: Causes and responses*. Department of Justice Canada. https://www.justice.gc.ca/eng/rp-pr/jr/oip-cjs/oip-cjs-en.pdf

Dussault, R., & Erasmus, G. (1996). *Report of the Royal Commission on Aboriginal Peoples*. Ottawa, ON: Commission.

Greenwood, M., de Leeuw, S., & Lindsay, N. M. (Eds.). (2018). *Determinants of Indigenous peoples' health: Beyond the social* (2nd ed.). Canadian Scholars.

Statistics Canada. (2016). *Reducing the number of Indigenous children in care (2016)* [Infographic]. https://www.sac-isc.gc.ca/eng/1541187352297/1541187392851

Truth and Reconciliation Commission of Canada. (2015). *Honouring the truth, reconciling for the future: Summary of the final report of the Truth and Reconciliation Commission of Canada*. McGill-Queen's University Press.

Turpel-Lafond, M. E. (2021). *In plain sight: Addressing Indigenous-specific racism and discrimination in BC health care*. Addressing Racism Review, Victoria, BC. https://engage.gov.bc.ca/app/uploads/sites/613/2020/11/In-Plain-Sight-Full-Report.pdf

Abstracts

Chapter 1. **Canada's "Old Mindset" and the Struggle to Fully Honour Jordan's Principle**
by Brittany Mathews, Jennifer King, and Cindy Blackstock

Equity for First Nations children in Canada is hindered by a mindset of colonialism that privileges the best interests of government over the needs and interests of children. In a landmark 2016 decision, the Canadian Human Rights Tribunal found Canada to be discriminating against First Nations children by failing to properly implement Jordan's Principle, a child-first principle named in memory of Jordan River Anderson to ensure that First Nations children get the help they need, when they need it. The Tribunal ordered that Canada's implementation of Jordan's Principle must be based on the principles of substantive equality and the best interests of the child, must be needs based, and must account for distinct community circumstances. The Tribunal has cited Canada's "old mindset" as a barrier to government compliance, describing Canada's continued discrimination as "willful and reckless." Canada's "old mindset" refers to ways of thinking and doing that have been found to be discriminatory yet continue to inform government practices and behaviours concerning Jordan's Principle in ways that have real-life and harmful implications for First Nations children and families.

Chapter 2. **Bill C-92: The Restoration of Indigenous Jurisdiction and Right Relations in Canada**
by Hadley Friedland and Koren Lightning-Earle

Bill C-92, or *An Act respecting First Nations, Inuit and Métis children, youth and families*, became federal law in Canada on June 21, 2019, and came into force on January 1, 2020. The new Act is the first federal law relating to Indigenous children, youth, and families. The preamble sets out pressing issues and lofty aspirations. The legislation itself states that its express goals are to (1) recognize Indigenous jurisdiction relating to child and family services, (2) establish national standards for Indigenous child and family service delivery, and (3) contribute to the implementation of the United Nations Declaration on the Rights of Indigenous Peoples (UNDRIP) in Canada. There is no doubt that law has played, and continues to play, a significant role in the current abysmal status quo for Indigenous children and youth in care. Can the new federal law create the necessary changes to move beyond it? This chapter sets out the basics of the new Act, the hopes and possibilities that it opens up, and some of the existing and emerging barriers to achieving its goals and aspirations.

Chapter 3. **Colonial Threads of Fetal Alcohol Spectrum Disorder in Canada and Australia: Parallel Stories**

by Robyn Williams, Dorothy Badry, Don Fuchs, Yahya El-Lahib, Michael Doyle, Bernadette Iahtail, and Peter Choate

The focus of this chapter is on the shared colonial experiences, parallels, and threads related to the impact of colonization on Indigenous people in Canada and Australia and the subsequent relationship to Fetal Alcohol Spectrum Disorder (FASD). Through a critical disability lens, FASD is viewed as a consequence of a colonial agenda to subdue and coerce Indigenous peoples through the introduction of alcohol by settlers in both countries. The need exists to decolonize FASD and to recognize that it is connected to inherited disparity, a significant aspect of the colonial agenda in both Canada and Australia. Through focused narrative conversations with several Indigenous Elders, scholars, and allies, we draw out the parallels between Canada and Australia, while focusing on existing literature on and insight into the colonial threads of FASD informed by an Indigenous, culturally based lens.

Chapter 4. **Indigenous Social Work: Colonial Systems Can't Change What They Don't See as Wrong**

by Gabrielle Lindstrom, Tsapinaki, and Peter Choate

Indigenous children continue to be oversurveyed and overrepresented as children in care in the child intervention systems of the Canadian prairies. Numerous inquiries, reviews, and legislative adjustments have been made without any significant change in the rates. The real changes needed have not been made, including addressing the authority and control over child intervention; the racially biased investigation, assessment, and case management approaches; and legislation that fails to address the underlying problems, such as the social determinants of health and the underfunding of prevention programming. Further, the state does not see that solutions lie within the Indigenous peoples and not within provincial control systems. In this chapter, we identify ten practices that are impeding progress and then propose five steps that are essential to recognizing that if the colonial provincial systems either knew how or had the motivation to achieve change, it would have occurred.

Chapter 5. **Making Connections for Our Children: Indigenous Youth Transitioning out of Care**

by Kelly Provost—Miah'nistik'anah'soyii (Sparks in a Fire) and Christina Tortorelli

The history of residential schools, the Sixties Scoop, and the ongoing overrepresentation of Indigenous infants, children, and youth in the care of child welfare set the backdrop for this chapter. Situated on the Blackfoot Territory of Treaty 7 in Alberta, Canada, we are guided by niitaa koo kah poo taa kiimaa (Blackfoot), or "Making connections for our children." We delve deeper into the lived experiences of children in care, most specifically their transition into adulthood. The authors explore key challenges and failures, including specific unmet recommendations made by the Truth and Reconciliation Commission of Canada (2015) and the Office of the Child and Youth Advocate Alberta (2019, 2018, 2016). Community is central to Indigenous ways of being, and Indigenous ways of knowing, informed through generations of oral stories rich in connection to the spirit, land, and people, reinforce connection as critical to achieving positive change. Through this written exploration, the authors uncover opportunities, celebrate successes, and challenge all of us to step into the space of connection. The path forward for Indigenous youth transitioning from care begins with a sense of belonging—the opportunity to know their clan, their story, and their traditions and to pass along their proud connections to future generations.

Chapter 6. **Child Advocacy Work in Alberta: The Importance of Children's Voices on Critical Issues**

by Del Graff and Arlene Eaton-Erickson

The Office of the Child and Youth Advocate (OCYA) is an independent office of the Legislative Assembly of Alberta. The OCYA is mandated to work with vulnerable young people involved with the child welfare and youth justice systems through key legislation: the *Child and Youth Advocate Act*. The OCYA advocates on behalf of children and youth by ensuring that their rights, interests, and viewpoints are acknowledged and acted upon. Its core work also includes research related to improving designated services, investigations into systemic issues arising from the serious injury or death of a child or youth receiving designated services, and public education. The OCYA, which works in rural, remote, and Indigenous communities across Alberta, has raised two critical concerns: that Indigenous children are overrepresented in care and that the majority of children and youth served in advocacy work are Indigenous. The OCYA highlights the need to approach work with children and youth from a holistic perspective and to this end has taken up critical questions around balancing individual and collective rights of children and youth. The work of the OCYA is child centred and the rights of children and youth are the primary focus of advocacy work in Alberta.

Chapter 7. **Grassroots of Child Welfare Advocacy for Indigenous Children in Alberta: The Creating Hope Society**
by Bernadette Iahtail

Grassroots child welfare advocacy for Indigenous children involved in the child welfare system in Alberta is a growing movement that will not be silenced. The Creating Hope Society (CHS) began in 2006 with a bold vision: "An Aboriginal Home for Every Aboriginal Child by 2025." When the CHS began, 2025 seemed far away—now it is just around the corner. Certainly, systems would have evolved over the past decade that would support this vision. As a non-profit society, the CHS was established to recognize the 1960s and 1970s child welfare scoop of Indigenous children as a continuation of the residential school era. The growing number of Indigenous children in care has been described as the Millennium Scoop, and in fact the number of children in out-of-home care has surpassed that of the Sixties Scoop. The voice of survivors is at the heart of the CHS, and key principles guiding the journey of this organization include building on the resiliency of survivors, remembering the past while moving forward into the future, and learning from and acknowledging the past while continuing to forge ahead. The CHS is a learning and educational organization that is deeply involved in the community and provides hope and supports to children and families through various cultural events.

Chapter 8. **Walking Courageously: The Voices of Indigenous Child Welfare Workers in Manitoba**
by Eveline Milliken and Linda Dano-Chartrand

This chapter is based on research that explored the sense of cultural safety felt by Indigenous child welfare workers who work in mandated Manitoba child welfare systems. Workers from the four Manitoba authorities participated. Contributors shared examples of experiences of feeling culturally safe and examples of feeling culturally unsafe within child welfare work. They identified whether a sense of cultural safety influenced their decision to remain working in a mandated child welfare agency. Transforming child welfare depends on supporting Indigenous child welfare workers who work in mandated agencies. Given that the Truth and Reconciliation Commission of Canada's *Calls to Action* document begins with five recommendations for child welfare, it is imperative to canvass Indigenous child welfare workers in Manitoba to gain their insights about working within child welfare systems. Recommendations that contribute to increased cultural safety for Indigenous child welfare workers in Manitoba's mandated child welfare agencies include (1) access to traditional cultural practices; (2) the resilience and commitment of the families with whom they work; (3) supportive colleagues and leadership; (4) access to culturally appropriate resources; and (5) ongoing decolonizing education.

Chapter 9. **The Heart of Allyship: Examining the Pursuit of Ally Relationships with Indigenous Peoples in Child Welfare and Social Work Education**
by Jennifer Hedges, Eveline Milliken, and Elder Mae Louise Campbell

This chapter explores teaching solidarity in social work education. There is an urgent need for transformation in child welfare, and educators and students are looking for resources to help inform their meaningful engagement with social justice movements. In a recent conversation about equity, child welfare scholars Dr. Cindy Blackstock and Dr. Barbara Fallon called for an advocacy curriculum in social work to prepare students for leading social justice movements. Advocacy is a fundamental responsibility that impacts all levels of practice in child welfare. This chapter discusses the language of allyship in today's social context and reviews the literature on best practices related to teaching advocacy. Drawing from constructs such as cultural safety, moral courage, and experiential learning models, the authors consider what an advocacy curriculum could look like for social work. Consideration will be given to understanding barriers that prevent advocacy or make it difficult in child welfare. To illustrate, the authors draw on their own experiences of co-teaching a child welfare course. This chapter is a valuable resource for anyone interested in teaching and learning advocacy skills in preparation for addressing systemic issues and practising in child welfare.

Chapter 10. **Post-Secondary Indigenous Education as It Relates to Indigenous Child Welfare**
by Jason Albert and Susannah Walker

The implementation of Bill C-92 in Indigenous communities across Canada has many implications for Indigenous families and communities. To fully understand the importance of this legislation, there needs to be an examination of the involvement of child welfare in the lives of Indigenous people and the different aspects that are being contrived. To achieve this, a focus on child welfare is required in Indigenous education. Indigenous students need to learn, share their experiences, and exchange information on child welfare within the classroom. The School of Indigenous Social Work at the First Nations University of Canada is an Indigenous social work program with a mission to enhance the strengths of Indigenous individuals, families, groups, and communities and to support self-determination. This chapter also demonstrates the principles of knowledge, understanding, learning, and believing within Indigenous child welfare and how these are translated into the context of Indigenous post-secondary education, specifically, Indigenous social work. The curriculum of Indigenous child welfare is centred around four principles, represented in the Cree context: nisitohtamowin (understanding), manitowakêýimowin (believing), kiskinwahamâtowin (learning), and kiskêýihtamowin (knowledge). The chapter also discusses how learning about Indigenous child welfare is important to the Indigenous communities, along with how Indigenous people are taking their education back to their communities, with the intention of making change in Indigenous child welfare and its operation.

Contributors

Jason Albert, PhD, MSW, is associate professor with the School of Indigenous Social Work at First Nations University of Canada in Saskatoon, Saskatchewan. Jason serves as the program chair and graduate program coordinator of the Indigenous social work program and is actively engaged in both teaching and research. Jason has been an active member of the Prairie Child Welfare Consortium for sixteen years and continues to promote child welfare education across the Prairie universities (the universities of Calgary, Manitoba, and Regina and FNUniv). His research interests include Indigenous leadership, management, and administration in social work. Jason has experience in social work administration and Indigenous community development.

Dorothy Badry, PhD, MSW, RSW, is a professor in the Faculty of Social Work, University of Calgary, and worked for sixteen years in the child welfare system in Alberta. Her primary research focuses on Fetal Alcohol Spectrum Disorder, its impact on child welfare, disability, and youth suicide, as well as ways to advance knowledge and prevention through education. She is also interested in loss and grief issues. Dorothy is the child welfare research lead for the Canada FASD Research Network and has received research grants from multiple provincial and national funders. She has been working with Dr. Robyn Williams on collaborative research between Canada and Australia on FASD and continues to advocate for inclusion of individuals with FASD in disability services. In 2020 she served as co-editor of the book *Youth in Care Chronicles*, which received the Canadian Association of Social Workers Distinguished Service Award in 2021. Dorothy is a co-author of the recently published Australian book *Decolonising Justice for Aboriginal Youth with Foetal Alcohol Spectrum Disorders* (2020). A critical disability scholar, she continues to advocate for children and families living with FASD.

Leonard Bastien is a member of the Piikani First Nation with the Blackfoot Confederacy. He has provided Elder services to the Indigenous Services office of

Children's Services in Calgary, Alberta. Leonard has provided advocacy and support to countless children through his work. He has offered ceremony for children, youth, families, and workers involved with the child welfare system. Leonard was a contributor to the Indigenous Cultural Understanding Framework published in 2019 that guides practice in children's services in Calgary, Alberta. Leonard has been a consultant/Traditional Cultural Support for Region 3, Child and Family Services, for the past two decades. He is a Blackfoot Traditional Knowledge Keeper and Support for Blackfoot Confederacy (Piikani Nation, Siksika Nation, Blood Tribe, Blackfeet Nation of Montana) and former Head Chief of the Piikani Nation. He is married to Audrey Weasel Traveller, and together they have four beautiful daughters and five wonderful grandchildren.

Marlyn Bennett, PhD, is a member of the Sandy Bay Ojibway First Nation in Manitoba and commences a new position at the University of Calgary, Faculty of Social Work, on July 1, 2022. She holds expertise in Aboriginal child welfare, with a special interest in qualitative and photovoice research including narrative—digital storytelling among First Nations youth who have transitioned out of care toward adulthood. Marlyn has received many awards in recognition of her achievements in policy and research and has published extensively on matters related to First Nations child welfare. She is an advisory member of the First Nations Canadian Incidence Study (CIS) Advisory Committee and has served on the Manitoba College of Social Workers board of directors as a public representative. She is a mother to one daughter and resides in Winnipeg with her life partner, Mike.

Cindy Blackstock is executive director of the First Nations Child & Family Caring Society of Canada, a member of the Gitxsan First Nation, and a professor at McGill University's School of Social Work. She has over thirty years of experience working in child welfare and Indigenous children's rights and has published more than seventy-five articles on topics relating to reconciliation, Indigenous theory, First Nations child welfare, and human rights. Cindy was honoured to work with First Nations colleagues on a successful human rights challenge to Canada's inequitable provision of child and family services and failure to implement Jordan's Principle. This hard-fought litigation has resulted in hundreds of thousands of services being provided to First Nations children, youth, and families. She recently served on the Pan American Health Organization's Commission on Equity and Health Inequalities in the Americas and fundamentally believes that culturally based equity is fundamental to meaningful reconciliation. Cindy is frequently sighted in the company of the Caring Society's reconciliation Am*bear*rister, Spirit Bear, engaging children in meaningful actions to implement the TRC's calls to action.

Elder Mae Louise Campbell has been the Elder in Residence at the Inner City Social Work program at the University of Manitoba, Faculty of Social Work, and at Red River College (RRC). Ojibwa, Métis, Ishkote Odeima Ikwe Campbell, Elder

Mae Louise is co-founder of Grandmother Moon Lodge and Knowledge Keeper of the Grandmothers Council of Manitoba and the First Nations Advisory Committee to Canada's prenatal nutritional program. She served as an Elder and advisor for the Canadian Women's Foundation on matters concerning the sexual exploitation and human trafficking of women and girls. Elder Mae Louise offers workshops on healing, leads ceremony, and has taught countless students. She continues to support healing in the area of intergenerational trauma in the community and was a founder of the Clan Mothers Healing Village Project, a land-based healing project that in 2021 received a $250,000 grant from the Advancing Indigenous Gender Equity through Innovation and Social Entrepreneurship program in Winnipeg.

Linda Dano-Chartrand, MSW, RSW, Keeshic Anung Ikkwe, Pissew Dodem, "Daystar" from the Lynx Clan, is a former director of regional programs for West Region Child and Family Services in Manitoba and is now a Knowledge Keeper with the University of Manitoba, Faculty of Social Work, Inner City Social Work Program.

Peter Choate is professor of social work at Mount Royal University. He is an expert witness in the area of parenting capacity (including risk, domestic violence, and addictions). He has been qualified on over 150 occasions in the Provincial Court of Alberta and the Court of Queen's Bench in Calgary and Medicine Hat. Peter's areas of research include assessment of parents within child protection systems, practice errors in child protection linked to serious injury and death, Fetal Alcohol Spectrum Disorder, stigma and implications for front-line practice, and implementation of the TRC's calls to action within the practice of social work. He was a member of the Ministerial Panel on Child Intervention (Alberta), joining three other experts on this all-party committee of the legislature. His teaching focuses on assessment issues in social work, including families, as well as child and adolescent mental health. He has published extensively in the field of assessment and child protection and spoken nationally and internationally in this area to social workers, lawyers, the judiciary, and other mental health practitioners. He has also been a member of expert panels reviewing child protection errors with the Office of the Child and Youth Advocate in Alberta.

Michael F. Doyle is a Bardi Aboriginal man from the Kimberley region of Western Australia and a senior research fellow at the University of Sydney. He began his career as a trainee Aboriginal health worker in his remote home community of Djarindjin. After ten years working predominantly in Aboriginal community-controlled health services he moved into research in 2008. Michael has completed three degrees: a graduate diploma of Indigenous health promotion (2009), a master of public health (2013), and a PhD (2018), in which he investigated how to improve alcohol and other drug (AoD) treatment programs to better meet the needs of Aboriginal and Torres Strait Islander men in prison. As a post-doctoral researcher, Michael became interested in Fetal Alcohol Spectrum Disorder in 2020, as it is likely that FASD is highly prevalent among Aboriginal men in the Australian prison system. Michael continues to work closely with Aboriginal community-controlled organizations and is the co-chair of the Aboriginal Health and Medical Research Council of New South Wales's Human Research Ethics Committee.

Arlene Eaton-Erickson, MSW, RSW, has been a social worker for twenty-five years and is currently the manager of Intake, Outreach, and Systemic Advocacy with the Office of the Child and Youth Advocate Alberta (OCYA). She has been with the OCYA for sixteen years in a number of different roles, including individual advocacy, community engagement, youth engagement, quality assurance, and leadership. Prior to this she was with Child and Family Services (Human Services) as a front-line worker and supervisor from 1996 to 2004. Arlene's formal education includes a master's degree in social work from Dalhousie University and a bachelor's degree in social work from the University of Regina. She is committed to social work and building capacity in others and thus feels really fortunate to be a sessional instructor at both the University of Calgary and MacEwan University.

Yahya El-Lahib, PhD, MSW, RSW, is an associate professor in the Faculty of Social Work at the University of Calgary, Canada. A critical disability scholar, he has conducted research nationally and internationally on immigration and disability issues. Yahya is closely associated with the disability movement in Lebanon and Canada; he works from a grassroots social justice perspective, valuing equity and diversity in his community work, teaching, and research. Critical topics in his work include issues related to education, employment, poverty, and political and civic engagement, as well as the impacts of war.

Hadley Friedland is an associate professor at the University of Alberta Faculty of Law and research director of the Wahkohtowin Law and Governance Lodge. Her research and teaching focus on Indigenous law, Aboriginal law, family law and child welfare law, criminal justice, and therapeutic jurisprudence. Hadley was co-founder and first research director of the Indigenous Law Research Unit (ILRU) at the University of Victoria Faculty of Law. Prior to law school she obtained a child and youth care diploma from MacEwan University and worked in the child and youth care field for a decade. She has published numerous articles and collaborated to produce accessible Indigenous legal resources for Indigenous communities, legal professionals, and the general public. She is the author of *The Wetiko [Windigo] Legal Principles: Cree and Anishinabek Responses to Violence and Victimization* (2018).

Don Fuchs, PhD, is professor and dean emeritus in the Faculty of Social Work at the University of Manitoba. He is a trailblazing scholar on disability issues and child welfare, notably Fetal Alcohol Spectrum Disorder, where his contributions to knowledge are recognized locally, nationally, and internationally. He has creatively integrated the roles of academic administrator and scholar in expanding the knowledge base of social work education. Don has authored or co-authored six books and sixty refereed articles or chapters. A founding member of the Prairie Child Welfare Consortium, he has co-edited all six books emerging from the biennial conferences held in Alberta, Saskatchewan, and Manitoba. His current program of research focuses on establishing the prevalence of children with disabilities in care and examining the determinants that result in children with disabilities (particularly FASD) coming into care and their experiences while in care.

Del Graff was the child and youth advocate for Alberta for the past ten years. He has worked in the social services field for over thirty-five years and has developed and implemented a wide range of social programs to improve the circumstances for vulnerable people in both urban and rural settings. Del has demonstrated leadership in moving organizational development initiatives forward to improve service results for children, youth, and families. His formal education includes a master's degree in social work from the University of Calgary and a bachelor's degree in social work from the University of Victoria. Del is a member of the Métis Nation of Alberta. He is married to Veronica, who is also Métis, originally from Paddle Prairie, Alberta. Together they have raised three children and now have two wonderful grandchildren.

Jennifer Hedges is a PhD candidate at the University of Manitoba (UM) Faculty of Social Work. Her thesis explores social work education for the critical transformation of child welfare policy and practice. She completed her MSW at the State University of New York at Buffalo with a concentration in mental health, health, and disability. Jennifer worked in the child welfare field in Ontario for nine years prior to joining the School of Social Work at Booth University College as assistant professor in 2012. She is currently a full-time faculty member at the UM Inner City Social Work Program.

Bernadette Iahtail was born in Attawapiskat First Nation and is Muskeg Cree from Treaty 9. She is a registered social worker, advocate, researcher, writer, film producer, entrepreneur, wife, mother, and grandmother. She is executive director and co-founder of the Creating Hope Society, an organization dedicated to providing a safe, supportive community for people to make changes and new life choices and to be successful in mainstream society. Bernadette has been part of the leadership team of the Edmonton COVID-19 Rapid Response Collaborative and the Government of Alberta's Anti-Racism Advisory Council. She also serves on the board of the Alberta Hate Crimes Committee and the Alberta Human Rights Commission's Indigenous Advisory Circle. Bernadette is committed to bringing awareness about the importance of addressing and preventing systemic discrimination and advancing a fair and inclusive society where everyone is valued and treated with equal dignity and respect. She also wants to increase awareness of the high percentage of Indigenous children and youth in care of child welfare, Indigenous education, missing and murdered Indigenous women and girls+, and incarcerated Indigenous women and men. Lastly, she wants to work with others to create an environment where political, economic, social, and cultural issues in Indigenous communities are brought to the forefront to advance a vision of human rights that reflects Indigenous perspectives, worldviews, and issues.

Jennifer King is Anishinaabe of mixed descent with family ties to the Wasauksing First Nation. She has been working in areas of research, policy, and public engagement in support of First Nations families for over fifteen years. Jennifer has a master of social work degree, with a focus on Indigenous methodologies and Indigenous perspectives on policy and practice. She is passionate about the role of critical education and research in promoting justice, equity, and meaningful reconciliation in Canada. An experienced presenter and facilitator, Jennifer has authored or co-authored several publications on Indigenous issues and has also worked as a sessional instructor in the School of Social Work, University of Victoria.

Gabrielle Lindstrom, Tsapinaki, PhD, is a member of the Kainaiwa Nation, which is a part of the Blackfoot Confederacy. As educational development consultant for Indigenous ways of knowing, Gabrielle works closely with the Taylor Institute and vice-provosts of teaching and learning and Indigenous engagement to advance Indigenous ways of knowing in campus teaching and learning communities, cultures, and practices. Her teaching background includes instructing in topics related to First Nations, Métis, and Inuit history and current issues, Indigenous studies (Canadian and international perspectives), Indigenous cross-cultural approaches, and Indigenous research methods and ethics. Her dissertation research focused on the interplay between trauma and resilience in the post-secondary experiences of Indigenous adult learners. Other research interests include meaningful assessment in higher education, Indigenous homelessness, intercultural parallels in teaching and learning research, Indigenous lived experience of resilience, Indigenous community-based research, parenting assessment tools reform in child welfare, anti-colonial theory, and anti-racist pedagogy.

Koren Lightning-Earle, LLB, LLM, Blue Thunderbird Woman, is Cree from Samson Cree Nation. She is legal director and a lawyer with Wahkohtowin Law and Governance Lodge. She is vice-president of Kasohkowew Child Wellness Society, board member for the First Nations Child and Family Caring Society, and acting commissioner for the Alberta Utilities Commission. She was also the Indigenous Initiatives liaison at the Law Society of Alberta and, for six years, president of the Indigenous Bar Association. Koren graduated from law school in 2007 at the University of Alberta, and was called to the bar in February 2009, where she had the honour of having her bar call on her reserve of Samson Cree Nation. She was called by Chief Justice Wachowich and Federal Court Justice Mandamin. In addition to her bachelor of laws, she holds a bachelor of arts (Special) degree and a BA in recreation and leisure studies. Koren received her master of laws from Osgoode Hall Law School, York University; her concentration was alternative dispute resolution. Awarded the "Tomorrow's Leader" award from Women in Law Leadership Awards and the Alumni Horizon Award (2017) from the University of Alberta, Koren is an alumna of the Governor General's Canadian Leadership Conference and co-founder of Hub, a community mobilization program to help reduce crime. She was an elected council member for Samson Cree Nation from 2011 to 2014 and co-chair of the First Nations Women's Economic Security Council. She is also a sessional instructor at Maskwacis Cultural College, a post-secondary school within the Four Nations of Maskwacis, Alberta, and at the University of Alberta Faculty of Law. Koren is married, has two daughters, and is a sole practitioner at Thunderbird Law in her home community.

Brittany Mathews is Michif and a member of the Métis Nation of Alberta. Her family more recently comes from St. Paul, Alberta, with ancestry from St. François Xavier, Manitoba. She has an honours BA with a major in Indigenous studies and a minor in conflict studies and human rights. Brittany is passionate about the role that human rights, especially the rights of Indigenous children and youth, plays in achieving justice and ensuring an ethical standard of relations between generations of Indigenous and non-Indigenous peoples. She is honoured to have worked alongside Indigenous youth to research and write reports on ethical research requirements and accountability mechanisms. In addition, Brittany is dedicated to elevating the collective vitality of Indigenous peoples through community organizing and creative outlets.

Eveline Milliken, PhD, MSW, RSW, is associate professor, Faculty of Social Work, University of Manitoba (UM), and currently acting as director of the Inner City Social Work Program. Eveline was born and raised in northwestern Ontario's Treaty 3 Anishinaabeg Territory. She has served on community and labour boards, on university committees including the UM Centre for Human Rights Research, and on the Advisory Board for the UM Master of Human Rights program, and currently is co-chair of UM's Gaa Wii Ji'i diyaang. Eveline has worked as a social worker with Ongomiizwin Medical Unit, as director of a community mental health program, in a family therapy clinic, and in child welfare and justice systems.

H. Monty Montgomery is of Irish Canadian and Mi'kmaq ancestry from the Eastern Shore of Nova Scotia. Over the past twenty-five years, he has worked with provincial and First Nations governments and non-profit Aboriginal organizations, and he is an associate professor at the University of British Columbia, School of Social Work. His extensive professional experience spans child welfare practice and social welfare policy development for Indigenous and provincial governments and the planning, development, and administration of First Nations social development, post-secondary education, and child welfare programs. Monty's major areas of scholarly interest include social science research with Indigenous peoples, distance education and First Nations, and child welfare research.

Kelly Provost—Miah'nistik'anah'soyii (Sparks in a Fire) is a proud member of the Piikani First Nation and executive director of Piikani Child and Family Services. He has been serving families, children, and his community for twenty years with Piikani CFS. It has been said that when dealing with matters that pertain to children, Kelly is always accessible, open, and interested in the viewpoint of the child and will seek to do what is fair and right. He is a strong proponent of maintaining cultural connections and the Blackfoot language. Genuine, compassionate work has been the hallmark of his career.

Christina Tortorelli is assistant professor in the Department of Child Studies and Social Work at Mount Royal University. She has extensive experience in child welfare, working with children, families, and communities, with experience in family violence, disabilities, child development, child abuse, mental health, trauma, and resiliency. Chris is a doctoral student in the Faculty of Social Work at the University of Calgary pursuing research in the area of resiliency.

Susannah Walker is an enrolled citizen of the Waganakising Odawa from northern Michigan, and her grandmother was from the Santee Sioux (Dakota) Nation of Nebraska. Susannah is a faculty member at the First Nations University of Canada in the School of Indigenous Social Work. Her BA is from the University of Wisconsin-Madison; she worked as a teacher in Texas and Medellín, Colombia, and completed her MSW at the University of North Carolina at Chapel Hill. Susannah's background is in community work, with non-profit experience in North Central Regina and as a part of the Regina Homelessness Community Advisory Board. She is currently a PhD student at the Johnson Shoyama Graduate School of Public Policy focusing on research on culture, mental health, and Indigenous youth. Susannah is a lecturer with the School of Indigenous Social Work at First Nations University of Canada, Regina, Saskatchewan.

Robyn Williams, PhD, is a Noongar woman from Western Australia and a senior research fellow at Curtin Medical School, Faculty of Health Sciences, Curtin University in Perth. Robyn has a research agenda focused on Fetal Alcohol Spectrum Disorder and its impact on children, youth, families, and caregivers and has been engaged with many Aboriginal research projects in Washington State including the WA Next Generation and Million Minds projects, playing a key role in community-engaged research. Robyn has worked in an advocacy role supporting families caring for children with FASD and delivered training in many communities. She is a co-author of the book *Decolonising Justice for Aboriginal Youth with Foetal Alcohol Spectrum Disorders* (2020). Robyn completed her PhD on FASD in the southwest region of Western Australia. Her professional roles have included working at various health agencies, among them Derbarl Yerrigan Health Service, Aboriginal Alcohol and Drug Service, Edith Cowan University, and the Office of Aboriginal Health (WA). Robyn remains committed to two-way learning and capacity building in the Aboriginal community, including Aboriginal-led solutions.

Subject Index

A

Aboriginal and Torres Strait Islander people (Australia): and Fetal Alcohol Spectrum Disorder (FASD), 48; overrepresented in out-of-home care, 55. *See also* Australia

Aboriginal and Treaty Rights in Canada: Essays on Law, Equity, and Respect for Difference, 88

Aboriginal fathers: and child access, 14, 142; discriminated against in child welfare, 143; and homelessness, 142. *See also* Indigenous parenting

Aboriginal Fathers Love Their Children Too! (documentary), 143

Aboriginal Fathers Love Their Children Too! program, 136, 143

Aboriginal History: A Reader, 88

Aboriginal Mothers Advocacy Program (AMAP), 136, 141–42, 144, 146

Aborigines Protection Act (Australia), 57–58

Acadia First Nation, 94

addiction: assumed for all Indigenous people, 144; effect of colonial practices, 138, 162, 198–99, 204; healing opportunities for, 139–40

Addressing Indigenous-specific Racism and Discrimination in BC Health Care, 223

Adopt Indian Métis (AIM) program, 207

adoptions, 33–34, 62, 86. *See also* child welfare placements

Advanced Social Work Practice in Trauma, 110

advocacy: for children in child welfare practice, xxiii–xxiv, 121, 178; education for, 180; shared understanding of, 131; as systemic, 125

Advocacy Practice Framework (OCYA), 115–17, 132

Advocacy Services: Policy and Procedure Manual (OCYA), 132

Alberta FASD Service Networks, 63

Alberta Support and Financial Assistance Program, 96

alcohol/alcoholism: as effect of colonial practices, 138; harmful levels of use, 48, 206; prohibition of, 58, 60; use during pregnancy, 49, 52–53, 60–61. *See also* Fetal Alcohol Spectrum Disorder (FASD)

Ally Bill of Responsibilities, 184, 191

Ally Model of Social Justice, 181

allyship: activities of, 189; in child welfare, xxiv, 179, 190; collaborative approach to, 186; importance of listening to Indigenous needs, 177; as locating the good in families, 187; by non-Indigenous people, 165, 175, 180; requirements for, 176, 182–84; role/responsibilities of, 144, 181, 188;

allyship *(continued)*: supported through natural teaching on the land, 108
Anderson, Jordan River, xxii, 3, 5–6, 18, 56
Anishinabek Nation, 36; Draft Child Well-Being Law, 37
Anitopisi creation story, 107
Annual Report: 2019–2020. 30th Anniversary Edition (OCYA), 132
Anti-Oppression Network, 179
Aotearoa (New Zealand): and cultural safety, 153; trauma-response care model, 207
The Art of Effective Facilitation: Reflections from Social Justice Educators, 191
Assembly of First Nations (AFN): agreement over Bill C-92, 78; filing human rights complaints, 4, 7
assimilation: apology for, 58; based on Eurocentric views, 79, 97; cause of trauma and other harms, 176, 207; not to be enabled in CFS delivery, 29, 35–36; policy encapsulated in treaties, 76; through residential schools, 57, 199. *See also* Eurocentrism; residential school system
Australia: Aboriginal control over decisions affecting their children, 55; definition of Aboriginal health, 56; effects of colonialism in, 57, 64, 73; Indigenous child welfare in, 47–48, 54–55, 57–60, 63; Indigenous youth in justice system, 47, 55; youth with FASD, 49, 51–53
Awakening the Spirit: Moving Forward in Child Welfare, 170, 194
Axis Rule in Occupied Europe: Laws of Occupation, Analysis of Government, Proposals for Redress, 90

B

Badry, Dorothy, 140
Bastien, Leonard (Weasel Traveller) (Elder), 100, 103, 109
Beadle, Maurina, 18
Bear Chief, Clement, 106, 108
Bear Chief, Roy (Big Coyote) (Elder), 104, 106–9
Bill C-15–*An Act respecting the United Nations Declaration on the Rights of Indigenous Peoples*, 16, 48
Bill C-92–*An Act respecting First Nations, Inuit and Métis children, youth and families*: aim of, 189, 211; applying to both in-reserve and off-reserve children, 38; and best interests of Indigenous children, 26, 28–32, 35, 78; court interpretations of, 40, 78–79, 84; and cultural continuity, 29–30, 35–36; full implementation of, 78, 84, 207; impact of, xxii, 131; inherent right of Indigenous Peoples to care for their children, xxii, 25–26, 78, 127, 219; jurisdictional provisions of, 26–27, 34, 36, 197, 206–10, 222; national standards for CFS, 27–28, 30–32, 35–37, 39–40, 42, 85
birth alerts, 31, 189
Blackfoot Confederacy, 93
Blackfoot Ways of Knowing: The Worldview of the Siksikaitsitapi, 88
Blackstock, Dr. Cindy, 39, 180, 189, 219, 222
Blanket Remembrance, 146
brave-space framework: for dialogue on social justice issues, 185
Brave Spaces Toolkit, 191
Bringing Them Home: Report of the National Inquiry into the Separation of Aboriginal and Torres Strait Islander Children from Their Families, 58, 65

Broken Hearts: For Families (documentary), 138, 140–41
Broken Hearts: Rights for Aboriginal Families with Children in Care (video), 148
Brown v Canada, 33
Bryce, Dr. Peter Henderson, 17–18, 76

C

Campbell, Mae Louise (Elder), 177, 181–82, 184; teachings on allyship, 176, 178
Canada: application of Jordan's Principle, 4–6, 9–10, 15, 18–19, 198; colonial approach to First Nations, 3, 5, 8, 19–20, 74, 82, 126, 198, 207; failure to honour treaties, 75; maintaining control over child care funding and decision-making, 10–12, 14–15, 207; non-compliance with CHRT decisions, 4, 7, 10, 17, 219
Canada's Residential Schools: Reconciliation. The Final Report of the Truth and Reconciliation Commission of Canada (Vol. 6), 45, 195
Canada's Residential Schools: The History, Part 1: Origins to 1939, 24
Canadian Association for Social Work Education (CASWE): standards for accreditation, 179
Canadian Association of Social Workers (CASW): apology and commitment to reconciliation, 183
Canadian Child Welfare Law: Children, Families and the State, 170–71
Canadian Council of Child and Youth Advocates: Declaration of Reconciliation, 130
Canadian Human Rights Tribunal (CHRT): Canada's discrimination of FN children, 198, 219; and Jordan's Principle challenges, 4, 85
Canadian Incidence Study on Reported Child Abuse and Neglect, 171
Canadian Women's Foundation, 177
Case Critical: Social Services and Social Justice in Canada, 194
Child, Youth and Family Enhancement Act (Alberta), 97, 113, 132
The Child and Family Services Act (Man., Sask.), 97
Child and Youth Advocate Act (Alberta), 113–14, 132
child intervention system: destruction of Indigenous families, 77; dismantling Eurocentric practices in, 87; diverse approaches to care and placements, 82; and trauma-informed care, 81. *See also* child welfare practice; poverty
child protection/child removal: assessment methods rooted in Eurocentric paradigm, 79; and child safety, 33, 97; control by Indigenous communities, 78; and disregard for Indigenous parenting, 200; and intergenerational trauma, 98, 198, 219; legacy of colonialism, 54–55, 57–59, 63, 73, 222; made according to legislation and policy, 85, 97; oppressing Indigenous families, 59, 62, 82, 184, 220–21; significant consequences to, 127. *See also* child welfare practice; Indigenous parenting
children's graves, unmarked, xxii, 5, 25, 160, 168, 190
children's rights, 114, 116–17, 122, 131
Child Welfare: Connecting Research, Policy, and Practice, 68, 170
Child Welfare Department (Australia), 58
child welfare legislation: contributing to cultural unsafety, 161; decolonizing of, 165. *See also* Bill C-92

child welfare placements: for children with disabilities, 62; as culturally appropriate, 152; with family, kin, 30, 40, 82; in non-Indigenous homes, 85; priorities in, 31–32, 85. *See also* foster care system

child welfare practice: and advocacy for Indigenous children, 135; allyship in, 190; child apprehension and removal, 55, 183, 200; and child attachment disorders, 62, 139; collaborative approach to, 184; as continuing assimilation process of residential schools, 188; control by Indigenous communities, 102, 222; culturally appropriate resources for cultural safety, 61, 154, 156, 162–63, 167, 169; effects of colonial approach on Indigenous Peoples, 198, 200; experiences of immigrant children, 140; informed by governmental legislation, 97; inherent biases in assessment and decision-making, 98, 184–85; overrepresentation of Indigenous children in, 77, 114, 118–21, 125–27, 131, 190, 198–99, 210, 220; paternalistic and genocidal policies of, 75; and power dynamic, 185; rooted in Eurocentric paradigm, 75, 97, 180–81; social justice issues in, 189; as state control over Indigenous communities, 60, 200; supporting child protection, 165; systemic racism in, 87, 143–44; transformative change needed in, xxiv–xxv, 124, 127, 130, 165–66, 176, 180, 190, 210; trauma caused by, 138–39; and trauma-informed care, 81. *See also* Indigenous child and family services; Indigenous social workers/child welfare workers

Christianity/Catholicism: and apologies for residential schools, 168; call for changes to, 169; and Indigenous spirituality, 158

Citizens Plus: Aboriginal Peoples and the Canadian State, 89

Clan Mothers Healing Village and Knowledge Centre, 177

collective rights, 115–16, 122, 128–29

colonialism/colonization: effects on child welfare system, 148, 169, 210–11, 220; effects on Indigenous Peoples, 48, 51, 57, 77, 164, 180, 186; existing in social work profession, 200; and genocidal practices, 51, 74; intergenerational trauma from, 84, 164, 219; legacy of, 53–54, 61, 63, 118; and link to missing and murdered Indigenous women and girls, 78; perpetuating institutional racism, 20–21, 126, 128; policies and practices of, 8; reflected in funding regimes for child welfare, 98; and relationship to Christian churches, 158; understanding of treaties, 75

Constitution Act, 27

Constructing Grounded Theory: A Practical Guide Through Qualitative Analysis, 170

constructivist grounded theory (CGT), 155, 178

Courtoreille, Colleen, 140

COVID-19 pandemic, 10, 19, 144, 146, 190

Cowessess First Nation Miyo Pimâtisiwin Act: coordination agreement, xxii, 25–26, 37–39, 189–90, 197, 220

Coyle, Senator Mary, 38

Creating Hope Society (CHS): advocacy and education role of, 144, 146–47; assistance to Aboriginal fathers, 142; vision,

initiatives, and programs of, xxiv, 135–41, 143, 145
Cree People: belly button ritual, 30; considering disabilities as special gifts, 56; traditional territory of, 153
critical empowerment: and Indigenous autonomy, 84
cultural competence, 80, 87, 185
cultural connections: giving sense of belonging and pride, 95, 119, 123; importance of maintaining it, 33–34, 62, 86, 103–4; limited for youth leaving care, 99; lost through colonial practices of child welfare, 206, 208; mentors to assist caregivers, 108; provided by Indigenous family/community, 97, 102–3, 123, 128, 221; through shared beliefs, values, language, 95, 99–100. *See also* family/community relationships; Indigenous Elders
cultural humility, 80, 154, 169, 185
cultural safety: agreement to maintain cultural connections, 34; communal aspect of, 154; culturally appropriate resources for, 61, 156, 162–63, 167; descriptions, conditions of, 153, 155–57, 159–62, 169; for Indigenous children in care, 103, 186; in Indigenous social work practice, 165–67; lack of as causing trauma, 164; as a means to decolonize child welfare, 185

D

Dakota People, 153
Dano-Chartrand, Linda, 152–53, 155, 220
Declaration on the Rights of Indigenous Peoples, 58
Decolonising Justice for Aboriginal Youth with Fetal Alcohol Spectrum Disorders, 69
Decolonizing Education: Nourishing the Learning Spirit, 88
Decolonizing Methodologies: Research and Indigenous Peoples, 216
Decolonizing Social Work, 170
delegated First Nations agencies (DFNAS), 38, 120–21
Delorme, Chief Cadmus, 25
Dene People, 153
Determinants of Indigenous Peoples' Health: Beyond the Social, 223
Development of a New Federal-Provincial Funding Model for First Nations Child and Family Services in Manitoba, 170
disabilities: non-Indigenous medical model of, 56. *See also* Fetal Alcohol Spectrum Disorder (FASD)

E

Eaton-Erickson, Arlene, 129
Echaquan, Joyce, 190, 222
education, post-secondary: reinforcing imperialism and negative view of Indigenous culture, 87
Effective Advocacy in Social Work Practice, 132
Eurocentrism: approaches to parenting, 79, 220; in child welfare practice, 75, 97, 180–81; destruction of Indigenous nations, 87; perspectives in social work, 73, 80, 87–88, 201; responsible for Indigenous oppression, 73–74, 79, 88, 97
Everyday Violence in the Lives of Youth: Speaking Out and Pushing Back, 193

F

Fallon, Dr. Barbara, 180
family/community relationships: in best interests of children, 28–30; and diverse approaches to care, 82;

family/community relationships (*continued*): important in Indigenous culture, 59, 101, 106; lost during separation and foster care, 146; promotion of in child placements, 32, 147; and right of child to access, 86; ways to maintain connections, 62, 106–7. *See also* cultural connections; Indigenous Elders
family group conferencing, 138
Family Matters Report, 55
FearlessR2W, 189
Fetal Alcohol Spectrum Disorder (FASD): as complex disability in child welfare populations, 47–49, 51–52, 221; consequence of colonialism, xxiii, 48–49, 51, 64; medicalized approaches to, 57; need to decolonize, xxiii, 54, 64; prevention and intervention services, 53, 60–61, 63; screening and diagnosis, 49, 53, 63; supports and services for, 63–64
Financial Administration Act (FAA), 15
First Nations and Inuit Health Branch (Canada), 56
First Nations CFS coordinators: at front line of Canada's non-compliance, 10, 12–14. *See also* Jordan's Principle
First Nations Child & Family Caring Society of Canada (Caring Society), xxii, 11, 18–19, 28, 57, 78, 191; filing of human rights complaints, 4, 7, 84; Touchstones of Hope movement, 180
First Nations Child & Family Caring Society of Canada et al. v Attorney General of Canada, 23
First Nations children. *See* Indigenous children and youth
First Nations Health Consortium (FNHC), 11, 13
First Nations Ontario Incidence Study of Reported Child Abuse and Neglect, 183
First Nations peoples. *See* Indigenous Peoples
First Nations University of Canada (FNUniv), 202–3
Fisher River Cree First Nation, 177
foster care system, 147, 200; challenges for children with disabilities, 56; as replacing residential schools, 138; supports for foster homes, 62. *See also* child welfare placements
Friedland, Hadley, 219

G

Gehl, Dr. Lynn, 191
A Generation Removed: The Fostering and Adoption of Indigenous Children in the Postwar World, 67
genocide, cultural, xxii, 8, 20, 54, 59, 74, 220; and Eurocentric approaches to child welfare, 73; through colonial practices, 207; through residential schools, 76. *See also* assimilation; residential school system
Gold, Steve, 140
Gord Downie & Chanie Wenjack Fund, 59, 67
Graff, Del, 98, 130
Grandmother Moon Lodge, 177
grandmothers: role of and benefits provided by, 101–2, 137, 139
Grandmothers Council of Manitoba, 177

H

Hancock, David, 143
Handbook for Working with Children and Youth: Pathways to Resilience Across Cultures and Contexts, 212
Handbook of Constructionist Research, 192

Hedges, Jennifer, 177; research study of, 176, 178, 181, 183, 185–87, 189
Homeward Trust Edmonton, 142
Honouring the Truth, Reconciling for the Future: Summary of the Final Report of the Truth and Reconciliation Commission of Canada, 24, 91, 112, 171, 223
How to Be an Antiracist, 90
Human Rights Education and Multiculturalism Fund (Alberta), 14

I

Iahtail, Bernadette, 52, 136, 141, 221
Imagining Child Welfare in the Spirit of Reconciliation, 193, 216
Indian Acts: establishing residential school system, 57; paternalistic and genocidal policies of, 75; prohibiting alcohol sales to First Nations, 58; setting provincial/territorial control over Indigenous child welfare, 77; and status, 13, 19
Indian Child Welfare Act (U.S.), 31
Indian Education in Canada, 212
Indian residential school system. *See* residential school system
Indigenous child and family services: as complex jurisdictional process, 208; coordination agreement, 36–37; dispute resolution mechanisms, 36–37; and evidence of compliance with Bill C-92, 40; grounded in Indigenous ways of caring, 81, 182; Indigenous jurisdiction over, 39; to maintain cultural, family connections, 29, 40; and provincial statutes, 28, 36; to reflect human rights framework, xxi; reliable funding for, 39; and strength-based intervention approaches, 73; threads of colonialism, 54; understood and delivered in cultural context, 199–200, 205
Indigenous children and youth: abuse suffered in residential schools, 80, 199; best interests of, in Bill C-92, 26, 28, 30, 32, 35, 78, 84; best interests of, in Jordan's Principle, 7, 10, 13, 16, 19; in child welfare care, 63, 96, 146, 186, 188, 200, 208; with disabilities, FASD, 48, 52–53, 56–57, 61–62, 117; FN families to decide best interests of children, 13, 41, 79; overrepresented in child welfare system, xxii–xxiii, 55, 61, 77, 97, 114, 117–21, 125, 169, 190, 198–99, 210–11; right to access culture, language, community, 86, 97, 101–3, 147. *See also* Indigenous youth, leaving care
Indigenous cultures: as collectivistic and communal, 79, 100; conceptualized as negatives in Western society, xxi, 83; formed by shared beliefs, values, routines, 107; incorporated into SISW, 206; as not homogeneous, 80; place of in Indigenous parenting, 82; rich history of storytelling, 95; right of child, youth to access, 86, 101, 104. *See also* cultural connections
Indigenous Elders: engaged in decision-making for Indigenous children, 86, 125, 176; engaged in teachings, storytelling, 95, 107, 145, 182, 206; integrated into wellness and social work education programs, 61, 139, 203; perspective on children's cultural connections, 33, 100, 104, 108, 124, 163; role in allyship, 181–82, 184, 187. *See also* allyship; storytelling
Indigenous epistemology: contributing to allyship, 180; and cultural knowledge, 96, 205; five aspects of learning style, 203;

Indigenous epistemology *(continued)*: incorporated into Indigenous social work education, 201–2, 210; knowledge transfer through storytelling, 49, 96; and relational ways of knowing, 176–78, 204
Indigenous identity: belief and pride in, 208; to be maintained while in care, 119; importance of cultural connections, 123, 201, 221; shared between CFS workers and families, 158
Indigenous lands: dispossession of, xxi, 54, 57–58, 74, 77, 198, 208
Indigenous parenting: and communal caregiving systems, 82–83, 197, 220; and preventative prenatal care, 30–31; and socially just assessments, 186; and social workers as allies, 187; stereotyping of, 83; and unresolved trauma, 138–39. *See also* Aboriginal fathers
Indigenous Peoples: capacity and knowledge for providing care, 182; control over Indigenous child care, 41, 62, 85, 127, 222; disempowered by colonialism, 51, 54, 84, 210; experiencing institutional racism, 126; and future of child welfare, 129; inherent jurisdiction over their children, 26, 35, 40, 130–31, 208–9; mistrust of Canadian government, 207; negative stereotype of, 31; overrepresented in justice system, 221–22; relationship with child welfare system, xxi, 55, 118, 151; and sacred laws underlying treaties, 75; self-determination for, 127, 180, 210; sovereignty of, 188, 208; understanding of treaty agreements, 76; world view of, 82, 128, 182, 197–98, 201–2, 205–6
Indigenous Services Canada (ISC): communication over Jordan's Principle requests, 11–13; funding calendar as unworkable in school settings, 15; interpretation of Bill C-92, 38; needing transformation to treat FN children fairly, 8–10, 20; relationship with Indigenous Peoples, 5
Indigenous Social Work Around the World: Towards a Culturally Relevant Education and Practice, 212
Indigenous social work education (ISWE): decolonized approach to social work education, 201–2; four principles of the curriculum, xxiv; knowledge of community child welfare agency, 209; as needed to fulfill Bill C-92, 210; pedagogy of, 202, 211. *See also* Indigenous epistemology; School of Indigenous Social Work (SISW) (FNUniv)
Indigenous social workers/child welfare workers: challenges faced by, 154; cultural safety for, xxiv, 156, 165, 169; experiences in child welfare systems, 152; sharing experiences and knowledge in SISW, 206. *See also* cultural safety; First Nations CFS coordinators
Indigenous ways of knowing. *See* Indigenous epistemology
Indigenous youth, leaving care: challenges faced by, 95–97, 125; and critical tasks of adulthood, 99; needs and concerns of, 100–103
Indspire Awards, 177
Industrial Schools Act (Western Australia), 57
Inner City Social Work Program (ICSWP), 153, 177, 187
Inuit people: and child welfare services, xxi, 129; control over Indigenous child care, 85, 127; cultures of, 80; and Fetal Alcohol Spectrum Disorder (FASD), 48;

funding supports for children with disabilities, 57; government's colonial approach to, 5, 8, 126; inherent right to raise their children, 130–31
Îyâxe Nakoda Nation, 93

J

Jordan's Principle: and best interests of children, 7, 10, 13, 16, 19; eligibility and requests for assistance, 10, 13–14, 16, 19; funding arrangements and infrastructure needs, 9, 14–16, 39; jurisdictional disputes and denials, 6, 11–12; medicalized approach to, 56–57; needing full implementation, xxii, 4, 21, 78, 84, 189; and substantive equality, 3, 7, 9, 13–14, 16, 19–20, 29. *See also* Canada
"Jumping Through Hoops": A Manitoba Study Examining the Experiences and Reflections of Aboriginal Mothers Involved with Child Welfare and Legal Systems Respecting Child Protection Matters, 148
justice system, 52; and Indigenous youth, 47, 55, 113, 125; overrepresentation of Indigenous youth in, 118, 126, 221

K

Kainai Nation, 93
Kamloops Residential School, 5. *See also* children's graves, unmarked
Kanaweyimik Child & Family Services (North Battleford), 205
Kellet, April, 143
Kelly, Brian, 141
Kinew, Wab, 190
King, Jennifer, 219, 222
Kinonjeoshtegon First Nation, 177
kinship systems. *See* child welfare placements; family/community relationships; Indigenous parenting
kiskêýihtamowin (knowledge), xxiv, 208, 211
kiskinwahamâtowin (learning), xxiv, 211; relies on teaching of Elders, 206
Knowing Your Rights (booklet), 140–41, 143–44
Knowing Your Rights: Understanding Child Welfare program, 136, 148

L

Labrador, Chief Charles, 94
Lac La Ronge ICFS, 206
Lafrance, Jean, 140
language, traditional: destruction of as genocidal, 74–75; integral part of identity, well-being, 28–30, 35–36, 42, 86, 95, 100–101, 103, 106–7, 180; loss of in child welfare system, 138; part of ISW curriculum, 206; right to know, speak, 121–23, 155
Laurier, Prime Minister Wilfrid, 18
A Legal History of Adoption in Ontario, 33, 43
LGBTQ2S+ young people: in child welfare and youth justice systems, 125
Lieutenant-Governor's Award for the Advancement of Interreligious Understanding, 178
Lightning-Earle, Koren, 219
Lindstrom, Gabrielle, 220
Little Bear, Dr. Leroy, 109
Littlechild, Wilton, 141
Louis, Kathy (Elder), 95

M

Maaja Man, 64, 221; and undiagnosed FASD, 49–51, 53

Macdonald, Prime Minister Sir John A., 41, 76
Managing Equity and Diversity at Universities, 192
manitowakêýimowin (believing), xxiv, 207, 211
Māori People, 81
Marshall, Albert, 94
Marten Falls Reserve, 59
Mathews, Brittany, 219, 222
McKay, Rev. Stan, 188
Métis Nation of Alberta, 93
Métis Peoples: and child welfare services, xxi, 118, 129; and Fetal Alcohol Spectrum Disorder (FASD), 48; funding supports for children with disabilities, 57; government control over, 5, 8, 85, 126–27; inherent right to raise their children, 130–31; traditional territories and culture, 80, 153
Métis Settlements FASD Network, 63, 70
Millennium Scoop, 77, 136, 228
Miller, Marc, 5
Milliken, Eveline, 152, 176–77, 181, 187, 220
Ministry of Children's Services (Alberta), 141, 145, 147
mino-pimatisiwin (the good life), 201
Moe, Premier Scott, 25
Moral Development in a Global World: Research from a Cultural Development Perspective, 111
Moving Forward, Giving Back: Transformative Aboriginal Adult Education, 170
Multicultural Health Brokers, 140

N

naming ceremonies: to convey traditional practices and place in family, 104
NAPI and the Rock, 107, 110
National Aboriginal Community Controlled Health Organisation (NACCHO), 56, 70
National Centre for Truth and Reconciliation, 59
National Indigenous Peoples Day, 58
National Inquiry into Missing and Murdered Indigenous Women and Girls (MMIWG), 188, 219; report of, 78, 99, 151
National Inquiry into the Separation of Aboriginal and Torres Strait Island Children from Their Families (Australia), 54, 65
Native American Postcolonial Psychology, 213
Native Children and the Child Welfare System, 111
Natives (Citizenship Rights) Act (Australia), 58
Nishnawbe Aski Nation, 78
nisitohtamowin (understanding), xxiv, 204, 211
Nistawatsimin: Exploring First Nations Parenting, 90
Noongar people (Western Australia), 49
No Place for Violence: Canadian Aboriginal Alternatives, 215
North Peigan, Harriet (Curly Haired Woman), 97, 109
Norway House Cree Nation, 5–6, 177
Nunatsiavut Government: control of its child welfare, 79

O

Obonsawin, Roger, 177
Office of the Child and Youth Advocate Alberta (OCYA), xxiii, 51, 53, 100, 108, 113, 118, 127; advocacy work of, 114–15, 121–22, 124–26, 129; mission and vision of, 115; strategic priorities, 122, 128; supporting Indigenous identity, 123

ohpikinawasowin/Growing a Child: Implementing Indigenous Ways of Knowing with Indigenous Families, 131–32
Ojibway/Oji-Cree People, 153
Ongomiizwin Health Services, 177
On Violence, 22
oral traditions, 95; not captured in treaties, 76
Overrepresentation of Indigenous People in the Canadian Criminal Justice System: Causes and Responses, 223

P

Passion for Action in Child and Family Services: Voices from the Prairies, 170
Patenaude, Carol Anne, 141
The Path to Healing, 214
Peguis First Nation, 177
Piikani Nation, 93–94; Blackfoot App (to support culture), 107
Piikani Nation Child and Family Services, 94, 105
Piikani Nation Child Protection Services, 94, 103
Pinaymootang First Nation, 17
Pipe Ceremony, 146
Plain Eagle, Mary (Longtime Meek Woman), 103, 109
poverty: causes and history of, 54, 60, 204; as cycle, 81, 198; oppressing children in care, 62; rationale for child welfare intervention, 98, 139, 151, 169, 182, 186, 199, 204, 208
Practicing Alliance curriculum: for practising allyship, 181. *See also* allyship
Prairie Child Welfare Consortium (PCWC), xxi, xxv, 220, 222
Pro Bono Canada, 143
Professional Imperialism: Social Work in the Third World, 215
Protecting Children: Theoretical and Practical Aspects, 192
Protection of Sexually Exploited Children Act (Alberta), 113
Provost, Kelly (Miah'nistik'anah'soyii), 94, 221
Psychosocial Resilience and Risk in the Perinatal Period: Implications and Guidance for Professionals, 67
Putting a Human Face on Child Welfare: Voices from the Prairies, 170

Q

Quebec Court of Appeal: jurisdictional challenge to Bill C-92, 79

R

Rabbit-Proof Fence (film), 58, 68
Racine v Woods, 32, 41, 78, 85
racism/racial discrimination: and colonial view of Indigenous culture, 53–54, 62, 83, 186, 188; inherent in settler-colonial definitions of parenting, 87; in not implementing Jordan's Principle, 4; placing Indigenous children at risk, 61; as systemic and structural, 88, 126, 222; triggering trauma and lack of cultural safety, 164–65, 169
Reclaiming Power and Place: The Final Report of the National Inquiry into Missing and Murdered Indigenous Women and Girls, 91, 111, 171, 194
reconciliation: burden to be shared by all, 176–77; in child welfare practice, 60, 188, 202, 210, 222; government commitment to, 5; requiring respectful relationships, 187
Reconciliation in Child Welfare: Touchstones of Hope for Indigenous Children, Youth, and Families, 192
Red River College (RRC), 177
Redsky (Elder), 177

relational accountability: and the teaching of wise practices, 49, 82
Report of the Royal Commission on Aboriginal Peoples, 91, 219, 223
Research is Ceremony: Indigenous Research Methods, 69
residential school system: apology to survivors of, 58; colonial practice to assimilate Indigenous children, 3, 8, 19, 57, 75–76, 188; contributing to intergenerational trauma, xxi, 55, 64, 98, 136, 199; death rates in, 17; disrupting/destroying Indigenous families, 96, 118, 141, 152, 164, 166, 182, 199–200, 206–7, 210, 221; effect on Indigenous parenting, 80–81; influence on child welfare, 151; loss of cultural connections, 32, 41; and relationship to churches, 158
resilience: of colonization survivors, 136; of families in social work practice, 156–57, 163, 166; as hope for safe environment in care, 208
resistance: of Indigenous youth when feeling unsafe, 186; to removal of children, 58, 60; to state control over Indigenous communities, 60
Revitalizing Culture and Healing: Indigenous Approaches to FASD Prevention: Revitalizing Culture and Healing, 61
right relations: restoration with Indigenous communities, 25–26, 40, 42
Roussin, Diane, 185
The Routledge Companion to Sexuality and Colonialism, 214
Royal Proclamation of 1763, 57, 74
Rudd, Prime Minister Kevin (Australia), 58

S

School of Indigenous Social Work (SISW) (FNUniv): curriculum and pedagogical approach of, 203, 205–6, 211; four Cree principles of, 204; incorporating Indigenous perspective, culture, 204–5; providing foundation for working in Indigenous communities, 210; symbol of the hawk, 202
Scott, Duncan Campbell, 18
Secret Path, 59, 70
Seeking mino-pimatisiwin: An Aboriginal Approach to Helping, 213
7 Sacred Ways of Healing Trauma through Mind, Body and Spirit, 153, 162
Shingwauk's Vision: A History of Native Residential Schools, 215
sibling relationships. *See* family/community relationships
Siksika Nation, 93
Sinclair, Dr. Raven, 140
Sinclair, Senator Murray, 58, 190
Six Steps to Successful Child Advocacy: Changing the World for Children, 132
Sixties Scoop: addiction and alcoholism of survivors, 138; disruption to Indigenous families, 96, 146; impact on child welfare, social work, 54, 148, 154, 169; impacts on Indigenous Peoples, 118, 141, 207; and intergenerational trauma, 64, 182; loss of Indigenous identity, 33, 210; as means of assimilation, 19, 77, 79, 206
Skownan First Nation, 185
social determinants of health, xxiii, 57, 61, 77, 222
social justice: and allyship, 178; and brave spaces for dialogue, 185; in child welfare practice, xxiv, 179, 184, 189; importance of locating the good in families, 187; in social work education, 183

The Social Life of Standards: Ethnographic Methods for Local Engagement, 90, 214
social work education: and culturally safe practice, 154, 169; decolonization of, 156, 161–63; Eurocentric perspectives in, 80, 87, 201; to incorporate Indigenous history, traditions, 182–83, 187, 201, 210; for Indigenous students, 153; role of allyship in, 176, 178, 190; as transforming child welfare practice, 176; and values in practice, 185. *See also* Indigenous social work education (ISWE); School of Indigenous Social Work (SISW) (FNUniv)
Social Work Practice: Problem Solving and Beyond, 214
social work profession/practice: embedding Indigenous cultural practices in, 156–57, 162–63, 166–67; and Eurocentric systems of thought, 73, 88, 201; importance of leadership in, 156, 159–61, 163; importance of listening to Indigenous storytellers, 129; need to decolonize, 80, 87, 165, 220, 222; social justice as core value, 179; stigma around it, 211; viewed as powerful, oppressive, 185, 200–201. *See also* Indigenous social workers/child welfare workers
Sorry Day (Australia), 58
South Island Wellness Society (SIWS) (Australia), 34, 45
Spirit Bear Plan (Caring Society), 21
Stamped from the Beginning: The Definitive History of Racist Ideas in America, 90
sterilization, forced: of Indigenous women and girls, 77
stigma: as aggravating family difficulties, 186, 211; of alcohol use during pregnancy, 60; of having a disability, FASD, 53, 57, 61; as oppressive, 62; of social work profession, 211
Stolen From Our Embrace: The Abduction of First Nations Children and the Restoration of Aboriginal Communities, 33, 44, 135, 148
Stolen Generations (Australia), 55, 58, 64
The Story of a National Crime: Being an Appeal for Justice to the Indians of Canada, 88
storytelling: in circle format, 203; digital methods of, 107; important part of epistemology, pedagogy, 139, 204; responsibility emanating from it, 129; transmitting knowledge and traditional teachings, 95–96. *See also* Indigenous epistemology

T

tipis (teepees): as symbol of family connection, 106
Tk'emlúps te Secwépemc Nation, 5, 190. *See also* children's graves, unmarked
Tortorelli, Christina, 94–95, 221
trauma, intergenerational: and addictions, 162; behavioural and emotional indicators of, 102, 207; caused by colonial practices, xxi, 64, 76, 85, 164, 166, 176, 200, 207; effect on Indigenous parenting, 79, 182, 204; understanding its effects in child welfare, 198, 206
Traumatic Separations and Honored Connections, 110
treaties/treaty territories, 57; Indigenous meaning of, 75; meant to destroy Indigenous identity and nationhood, 76; Treaty 1, 3, 153, 177; Treaty 5, 177; Treaty 7, 93

Treaty Elders of Saskatchewan: Our Dream is that Our Peoples Will One Day be Clearly Recognized as Nations, 89
Tremblay, Jean-François, 38
Trudeau, Prime Minister Justin, 5, 25
Truth and Reconciliation Commission of Canada (TRC), 58, 130, 138, 166, 187, 219; calling out cultural genocide, 8, 20, 59, 73; calls to action, 4, 40, 163, 168, 176, 182, 221; final report of, 151, 188; and national standards for CFS delivery, 27; recommendations of, xxiii, 97
Truth and Reconciliation Commission of Canada: Calls to Action, 24, 69, 171, 195; recommendations related to child welfare, 152
Tsuut'ina Nation, 93
two-eyed seeing (Etuaptmumk), 94

U

United Nations Convention on the Prevention and Punishment of the Crime of Genocide, 74, 77, 91, 103
United Nations Convention on the Rights of Persons with Disabilities (CRPD), 69, 117, 133
United Nations Convention on the Rights of the Child (UNCRC), 116–17, 121, 123, 133
United Nations Declaration on the Rights of Indigenous Peoples (UNDRIP), 27, 45, 117, 132–33
United Nations Declaration on the Rights of Indigenous Peoples Act, 24
University of Manitoba, 59; Faculty of Social Work, 168; Inner City Social Work Program (ICSWP), 153, 177, 187; Ongomiizwin Health Services, 177

V

Visions of the Heart: Issues Involving Indigenous Peoples in Canada, 90
Voices for Change: Aboriginal Child Welfare in Alberta, 118, 132; Data Update (2021), 132; recommendations of, 119, 127

W

Wahkohtowin Law and Governance Lodge, 32
Walking This Path Together: Anti-Racist and Anti-Oppressive Child Welfare Practice, 192–93, 195
Welcome Home Ceremony (for children formerly in care), 142
Wenjack, Chanie, 59
Wernick, Michael, 4
Why Race Still Matters, 90
Wicihitowin: Aboriginal Social Work in Canada, 212, 215
Wiijii'idiwag Ikkwewag: Restoring the Sacred Bond Birth Helper Program, 153
Williams, Robyn, 49, 64
Winnipeg Boldness Project, 185
Winter Count, 104
Winter Count: A History of the Blackfoot People, 111
Woo-Paw, Teresa, 140
Working Together: Aboriginal and Torres Strait Islander Mental Health and Wellbeing Principles and Practice, 67
Wrapping Our Ways around Them: Indigenous Communities and Child Welfare Guidebook, 45

Y

Yatdjuligin: Aboriginal and Torres Strait Islander Nursing and Midwifery Care, 68

Author Index

A

Abdill, L. R., 179, 194
Aboriginal Children in Care Working Group, 211
Absolon-Winchester, A. E., 184, 191
Absolon, K., 184, 191
Adams, I., 59, 65
Aiello, O., 192
Aitken, O., 214
Albert, J., xxiv, 3, 25, 47, 73, 93, 113, 135, 151, 175, 197
Alberta Education, 204, 212
Alberton, A. M., 183, 191
Alexander, K., 55, 65
Amaral, S., 192
Amponsah, P., 180, 188, 191
Anderson, K., 216
Anderson, S. M., 66
Angell, G. B., 191
Anisman, H., 192
Arao, B., 185, 191
Arendt, H., 8, 20, 22
Asakura, K., 179, 185, 191
Asch, M., 76, 88
Assembly of First Nations, 16, 22, 199, 212
Atter, H., 197, 212
Atwool, N., 81, 88
Auger, M., 201, 212

B

Badry, D., xxiii, 3, 25, 47, 49, 54, 66, 68, 69, 73, 93, 113, 135, 151, 175, 193, 197, 216
Baggley, C., 7, 22
Baikie, G., 202, 212
Baines, D., 194
Bala, N., 151, 170, 171
Baldwin, M. E., 66
Bamblett, M., 65
Bank, L., 111
Barker, C., 123, 129, 131
Barman, J., 199, 212
Barnett, M. A., 102, 109
Barrera, J., 198, 212
Barter, K., 171
Bartlett, C., 111
Baskin, C., 201, 210, 212
Bastien, B., 74, 75, 82, 88, 98, 111
Bastien, L., 90
Battiste, M., 75, 88
Baydala, L., 215
Bayer-Topilsky, T., 98, 110
Bear Chief, R., 66
Bejan, R., 191
Bennett, K. V., 29, 33, 34, 43
Bennett, M., 3, 25, 47, 49, 73, 77, 88, 93, 98, 99, 110, 113, 135, 137, 148, 151, 170, 175, 193, 197, 216
Berman, H., 193
Best, O., 68
Bhuyan, R., 179, 183, 191
Billingsley, D., 171
Bishop, R., 84, 88
Black, C., 65
Black, K. A., 77, 88
Black, T., 193

Blackstock, C., xxii, xxv, 3, 20, 22, 23, 29, 43, 54, 55, 57, 59, 62, 65, 96, 98, 110, 112, 127, 132, 151, 170, 171, 180, 182, 191, 192, 208, 212, 214
Blagg, H., 66, 68, 69
Bodor, R., 45, 131, 132
Bohr, Y., 200, 215
Bombay, A., 182, 192
Boylan, J., 121, 132
Breaker, K., 90
Breaker, S., 90
Brown, I., 170, 171, 192
Bruning, N. S., 187, 192
Bruyere, G., 201, 202, 212, 215
Bryce, P. H., 18, 22, 76, 88
Buhr, N., 54, 65
Buker, I., 202, 212
Burford, G., 171
Burge, P., 208, 212
Burke, S., 180, 192
Burnett, K., 16, 18, 22
Burns, G., 206, 213
Burnside, L., 62, 65

C

Cairns, A., 76, 89
Caldwell, J., 86, 89, 215
Calgary Foundation, 109, 110
Calhoun, A., 131, 132
Cameron, N., 67, 91
Campbell, Elder M. L., xxiv, 175
Canada Parliament
Standing Senate Committee on Aboriginal Peoples, 38, 43
Canadian Association for Social Work Education (CASWE), 179, 192
Canadian Association of Social Workers (CASW), 179, 183, 192
Canadian Council of Child and Youth Advocates, 131, 132
Canas, E., 193
Cardinal, H., 75, 89
Cariou, W., 86, 89
Carniol, B., 194
Carrière, J., 34, 43, 186, 192, 193, 195
Carter, M., 67
Chadwick, K., 24
Chambers, L., 16, 18, 22, 33, 43
Charmaz, K., 155, 170, 178, 192
Chau, K., 192
Chaze, F., 170
Chew, A., 54, 66
Chewka, D., 176, 192
Chisholm, R., 48, 66
Choate, P., xxiii, 3, 25, 29, 33, 43, 47, 49, 62, 66, 73, 79, 82, 85, 89, 90, 93, 100, 110, 113, 135, 151, 175, 197
Christoff, A., 209, 213
Chudley, A. E., 66
Clare, K., 153, 170
Clark, N., 64, 66, 81, 89
Clark, S., 222, 223
Clarke, E., 77, 89
Clarke, J., 180, 192
Clemens, K., 185, 191
Cloete, F., 43, 89
Clouston Carlson, J., 214
Coates, J., 170, 212
Coatsworth, J. D., 112
Conger, R. D., 109
Conley Wright, A., 121, 132
Conry, J. L., 66
Cook, J. L., 48, 66
Cook, P. A., 67
Cooper, G., 203, 213
Council of the Federation Secretariat (Ottawa), 96, 110
Council on Social Work Education (CSWE), 102, 110
Court of Appeal of Québec, 79, 89
Cox-White, T., 215
Craig, S. L., 181, 189, 193
CrazyBull, B., 43, 66, 89
Creaser, J., 206, 213
Creedy, D. K., 68
Crey, E., 33, 44, 135, 148
Cross, T., 192
Crowe, A., 176, 182, 183, 193

Crowshoe, L., 77, 89
Cunneed, C., 73, 89
Currie, V., 192

D

D'Antoine, H., 67
Daciuk, J., 171
Dalrymple, J., 121, 132
Damashek, A., 112
Dannenbaum, D., 89
Dano-Chartrand, L., xxiv, 151
Danso, R., 80, 89
Darnell, R., 90, 214
Davidson, S. F., 75, 90
Day, A., 112
De La Ronde, R., 110
de Leeuw, S., 79, 89, 180, 185, 193, 223
Degener, C. J., 103, 110
Dell, C., 213
Delver, K., 132
DeRiviere, L., 23
Desjarlais, B., 45
Deyhle, D., 203, 216
Dickason, O. P., 90
Dion, A., 127, 132
Dion, J., 56, 57, 61, 62, 66
Djuric, M., 25, 43
Doyle, M., xxiii, 47
Dudgeon, P., 67
Duran, B., 207, 213
Duran, E., 207, 213
Dussault, R., 223

E

EagleSpeaker, J., 107, 110
Earle, L., 77, 89
Eaton-Erickson, A., xxiii, 99, 113
Eaton, A. D., 193
El-Lahib, Y., xxiii, 47
Elliot, K., 193
Enosh, G., 98, 110
Erasmus, G., 223
Evans-Campbell, T., 91

F

Faille, M., 209, 213
Fairbairn, M., 186, 193
Faller, K. C., 185, 194
Fallis, J., 183, 193
Fallon, B., 171, 192, 193, 216
Family Matters, 55, 66
Farag, M., 213
Fast, E., 216
Felske-Durksen, C., 31, 43, 88
Ferrer, I., 55, 60, 68
Fieldeldey-Van Dijk, C., 208, 213
Filippelli, J., 193
Find & Connect, 57, 66
Fine, M., 214
Finlay-Jones, A., 68
First Charger, L., 194, 215
First Nations Child & Family Caring Society of Canada (Caring Society), 5, 6, 8, 9, 10, 12, 13, 14, 15, 21, 22, 39, 43, 180, 188, 190, 193
Formsma, J., 192
Fornssler, B., 213
Fortier, C., 54, 60, 66, 73, 90
Fournier, S., 33, 44, 135, 148
Freckelton, I., 52, 66
Fredericks, B., 68
Freeman, S., 110
Friedland, H., xxii, 25, 27, 31, 33, 43, 44
Fuchs, D., xxiii, 3, 25, 47, 73, 93, 113, 135, 151, 170, 171, 175, 193, 194, 197, 216
Fulcher, L., 154, 170
Fumaneri, P., 215

G

Gallhofer, S., 54, 66
Gamble, J., 68
Gardiner, T., 193
Gatwiri, K., 55, 60, 67
Gaumond, G., 183, 187, 193
Gaywish, R., 204, 213
Gehl, L., 184, 188, 193
Geia, L., 49, 67, 68
George, J., 192

Gerlach, A., 24
Gibson, P. A., 181, 183, 193
Gilbert, D. J., 49, 67
Gomez, L. E., 112
Good Striker, E., 90
Good Striker, W., 90
Gorey, K. M., 191
Goulet, S., 132
Government of Alberta, 96, 97, 110
Graff, D., xxiii, 98, 113
Graham, C., 54, 68
Graham, J. E., 90, 214
Grammond, S., 26, 44
Gray, E., 194
Gray, M., 151, 170, 212
Grech, S., 48, 67
Green, C. R., 66
Green, J., 186, 195, 213
Green, M., 89
Greenwood, M., 180, 185, 193, 222, 223
Greer, A., 207, 213
Greer, S., 54, 67
Greger, H. K., 112
Grenier, S., 191
Grietens, H. W. E., 110
Grieves, V., 205, 213

H

Hall, L., 213
Hanson, T., 45
Hapchyn, C. A., 45
Hare, J., 75, 90
Harris, B., 202, 213
Harris, E., 202, 214
Harris, S., 203, 214
Hart, M. A., 49, 67, 200, 201, 202, 204, 212, 213, 215
Hartz, D., 49, 67
Hausknecht, S., 95, 110
Hay, T., 18, 23
Hayes, B., 49, 67
Hayes, L., 48, 49, 67
Hayward, M. N., 89
Healy, K., 181, 188, 193
Hébert, Y., 212
Hedges, J., xxiv, 175, 176, 180, 193
Heinonen, T., 200, 214
Henderson, R., 89, 194, 215
Henry, R., 216
Herrick, M. A., 101, 110
Hesjedal, C., 192
Hetherington, T., 170
Hewitt, J., 198, 215
Hicks, L., 216
Hildebrandt, W., 75, 89
Hoare, C., 99, 111
Hollinsworth, D., 48, 67
Holmes, C., 90, 214
Hopkins, C., 213
Hornick, J., 170, 171
Houston, E., 193
Hughes, P., 203, 214
Hughes, T., 151, 170
Human Rights and Equal Opportunity Commission (Australia), 59, 67
Hyslop, K., 197, 214

I

Iahtail, B., xxiii, xxiv, 47, 135
Iamsees, C., 11, 16, 23
Indigenous Services Canada (ISC), 7, 23, 44, 84, 90
Innes, L. J., 202, 214
Ives, N., 202, 214
Iwama, M., 111

J

Jacobs, M. D., 55, 67
Jaffe, K., 121, 132
Jamieson, A., 194
Jensen, L. A., 107, 111
Jeyapal, D., 191
Joh-Carnella, N., 193
Johnston, P., 96, 111
Jones, E., 194

K

Kassam, N., 67

Kayed, N. S., 112
Kendi, I. X., 74, 90
Kennedy-Kish (Bell), B., 181, 182, 194
Kennedy, B., 5, 23
Kierans, K., 111
Kiesel, L. R., 179, 194
Kikulwe, D., 193, 216
Kimelman, E. C., 77, 90
Kinequon, D., 151, 170
King, J., xxii, xxv, 3
Kirlew, M., 23
Knoke, D., 112, 171
Kohler, T., 43, 89
Kohu-Morgan, H., 91
Kolahdooz, F., 77, 90
Kopp, K., 132
Kothari, B. H., 101, 111
Kourgiantakis, T., 193
Kozlowski, A., 199, 216
Krugel, L., 151, 170
Kufeldt, K., 57, 68, 151, 170, 192

L

Lafrance, J., 98, 111, 170
Landertinger, L., 198, 208, 214
Landreman, L. M., 191
LaRocque, E. D., 207, 214
LeBlanc, N., 66
Lee, E. O. J., 55, 60, 68
Lefebvre, R., 193
Lemkin, R., 74, 76, 90
Lentin, A., 74, 90
Lewis, G., 203, 214
Lightning-Earle, K., xxii, 25, 27, 44
Lilles, H., 171
Lilley, C. M., 66
Lindsay, N. M., 223
Lindstrom, D., 43, 66, 89
Lindstrom, G.–Tsapinaki, xxiii, 73, 82, 89, 90
Little Bear, L., 86, 90
Loft, M., 214
Long, D., 90
Loock, C. A., 66
Loxley, J., 6, 23, 167, 170
Lutke, J., 66
Lydersen, S., 112

M

MacArthur, C., 45
MacDougall, A., 216
MacLaurin, B., 171, 216
Makokis, L., 45, 128, 131, 132
Mallon, B. F., 66
Mandell, D., 198, 214
Marshall, A., 111
Marshall, M., 111
Martin, J., 110
Martin, K., 205, 214
Masten, A. S., 112
Mataki, T., 91
Matheson, K., 192
Mathews, B., xxii, xxv, 3
May, S. E., 68, 69
Mayer, M., 171
McBeath, B., 111
McCaskill, D., 212
McCaughey, D., 192
McCoy, H., 175, 194
McCracken, M., 190, 194
McDonald, F., 90, 214
McDowall, A., 206, 214
McFarlane, A., 66
McGrath, L., 49, 67
McKay, S., 170, 171, 194
McKenzie, B., 57, 68, 151, 170, 171, 192
McLaughlin, A. M., 184, 194
McLellan, A., 132
McLeod, S., 132
McMillan, L. J., 86, 90, 198, 208, 214
McPherson, L., 67
McQuaid, R. J., 192
McWey, L. M., 112
Meekosha, H., 48, 68
Melymick, R., 216
Menzies, P., 207, 215
Metallic, N., 27, 28, 44, 45
Midgley, J., 201, 215

Miller, J., 199, 215
Milliken, E., xxiv, 151, 154, 155, 171, 175, 185, 186, 192, 194
Milne, E., 209, 215
Milroy, H., 67
Mirraboopa, B., 205, 214
Mitchell, M. B., 101, 106, 111
Montgomery, H., 3, 25, 47, 73, 93, 113, 135, 151, 175, 193, 197, 216
Morales, S., 44
Mordoch, E., 204, 213
Morgensen, S. L., 51, 68
Mosher, J., 198, 215
Muir, N., 200, 215
Mukherjee, R. A., 67
Mundorff, K., 74, 90
Murray-García, J., 154, 171, 185, 195
Mushquash, C., 213
Mutch, R., 68, 69
Mykota, D., 213

N

Nader, F., 90
Nash, C., 110
National Aboriginal Community Controlled Health Organisation (Australia), 56, 68
National Indian Welfare Association (NIWA), 29, 31, 44
National Inquiry into Missing and Murdered Indigenous Women and Girls, 78, 91, 96, 99, 102, 111, 151, 171, 194
Native Counselling Services of Alberta, 34, 44
Navia, D., 176, 186, 188, 194, 200, 215
Nelson, H., 210, 215
Neppl, T. K., 109
Neu, D., 54, 68
Nixon, K., 183, 193
North Peigan, F., 207, 208, 216
Noyce, P., 68
Nunatsiavut Government, 79, 90

O

Obomsawin, A., 18, 23
Office of the Auditor General, 9, 24
Office of the Child and Youth Advocate Alberta (OCYA), 52, 53, 68, 95, 100, 101, 103, 111, 115, 117, 118, 119, 121, 132
Office of the Prime Minister, 5, 24
Oliver, C., 188, 194
Ontai, L. L., 109
Ontario Association of Children's Aid Societies (OACAS), 179, 194
Ortega, R. M., 185, 194

P

Pace, C., 132
PAHO Commission on Equity and Health Inequalities in the Americas, 21, 24
Pang, N., 193
Paperny, A., 168, 171
Parmenter, N., 67
Paul, L., 215
Payne, R., 34, 45
Pazderka, H., 30, 45
Penner, J., 194
Perrault, S., 207, 215
Phillips, M., 214
Piccus, W., 101, 110
Pihama, L., 81, 91
Pine, B., 209, 216
Polaschek, N. R., 154, 155, 171
Prakash, T., 23
Prete, T., 75, 91
Prokop, S. T., 23, 216. *See also* Thomas Prokop, S.
Proulx, J., 207, 215
Provost, K.–Miah'nistik'anah'soyii (Sparks in a Fire), xxiii, 93
Puzyreva, M., 167, 170

R

Raczka, P., 104, 111
Rae, J., 215

Ramsden, I., 155
Rashidi, M., 192
Rasmussen, C., 203, 215
Rayner, A., 194
Reid, N., 60, 68
Reinders, H., 112
Rich, R., 88
Richard, K., 216
Richardson, C., 193
Richardson, S. M., 101, 112
Riebschleger, J., 101, 112
Roisman, G. I., 99, 112
Rosales, T., 66
Rotumah, D., 67
Rowan, M., 213
Royal Commission on Aboriginal Peoples (RCAP), 77, 91

S

Sanders, C., 190, 194
Sangster, M., 11, 13, 16, 24
Scaramella, L. V., 109
Schalock, R. L., 100, 112
Schiffer, J., 193
Schmied, V., 67
Sharma, S., 90
Shea, B., 213
Sherman, J., 215
Sherwood, J., 54, 68
Shingler, B., 190, 194
Silver, J., 170
Silverstein, D. N., 110
Sinclair, M., 151, 169, 171, 190
Sinclair, R., 33, 45, 176, 183, 194, 195, 200, 201, 202, 205, 212, 215
Singstad, M. T., 100, 112
Sinha, V., 16, 17, 24, 86, 89, 192, 197, 199, 208, 209, 215, 216
Skinner, K., 110
Skipper, H., 91
Smith, A., 45
Smith, L. T., 91, 201, 216
Smith, S. L., 110
Soldatic, K., 48, 60, 67, 68
Solomon, M., 198, 216
Sorenson, P., 111
South West Aboriginal Land & Sea Council (Australia), 58, 68, 69
Southey, K., 91
Spearman, L., 200, 214
Starblanket, G., 90
Statistics Canada, 96, 112, 223
Steele, J., 111
Steinhauer, S., 45
Stephen, J., 180, 188, 191
Stewart, M., 68, 69
Strega, S., 186, 192, 193, 195
Strumm, B., 191
Sullivan, R., 171
Swiftwolfe, D., 178, 195
Swisher, K., 203, 216

T

Tait, C. L., 198, 216
Tatoulis, P., 43, 89
Tatz, C., 54, 69
Tauri, J. M., 73, 89
Te Nana, R., 91
Tellegen, A., 112
Temple, V. K., 66
Tervalon, M., 154, 171, 185, 195
Thibodeau, S., 207, 208, 216
Thomas Prokop, S.,170, 209, 216. *See also* Prokop, S. T.
Thomas, R., 186, 195
Thomson, G., 67
Todd, S., 191
Tortorelli, C., xxiii, 93
Toth, E., 89
Toulouse, P. R., 206, 216
Tourigny, M., 171
Tracy, E., 209, 216
Trocmé, N., 98, 112, 151, 171, 193, 208, 212, 216
Trudeau, J., 7, 24
Truth and Reconciliation Commission of Canada (TRC), 8, 18, 24, 27, 41, 45, 62, 69, 73, 74, 77, 79, 81, 91, 97,

Truth and Reconciliation Commission of Canada (TRC) *(continued)*, 112, 151, 171, 176, 182, 188, 195, 219, 221, 223
Tulich, T., 48, 66, 68, 69
Turner, A., 78, 91
Turpel-Lafond, M. E., 27, 34, 45, 222, 223
Tyler, S., 131, 132

U

Ungar, M., 212
UNICEF, 121, 123, 132
United Nations Department of Economic and Social Affairs (UN DESA), 117, 132
United Nations General Assembly, 27, 45, 56, 69, 77, 91, 117, 133
Usher, K., 67

V

van Bergen, D. D., 110
Van Bibber, M., 61, 63, 69
van Krieken, R., 98, 112
Van Kuppeveld, N., 45
Van Patton, K., 176, 195
Varghese, R., 191
Veldhuisen, A., 132
Verdugo, M. A., 112
Vives, L., 16, 17, 24
Vogl, R., 170, 171

W

Waid, J., 111, 112
Walkem, A., 27, 29, 31, 39, 42, 45
Walker, R., 67, 216
Walker, S., xxiv, 197
Wallander, J. L., 112
Warrick, G. A., 95, 112
Weasel Traveller, A., 90
Webb. S. J., 111
Wente, M., 27, 45
Wien, F., 23
Williams, R., xxiii, 47, 49, 54, 68, 69
Williams, R. J., 170, 171
Wilson, J., 95, 112
Wilson, M. G., 194
Wilson, S., 49, 69, 204, 216
Wilson, T., 190, 195
Wo, N., 210, 216
Wojciak, A. S., 101, 112
Wolfe, P., 51, 55, 69
Wong, E. H., 54, 60, 66, 73, 90
Wotherspoon, T., 209, 215
Wright, J., 171
Wright, T., 190, 195
Wylie, L., 216

X

Xiong, Z., 201, 217

Y

Yates, T. M., 101, 112
Yellow Bird, M., 170, 212
Yi, K. J., 90
Young, J., 192
Yunong, H., 201, 217

Z

Zakiya, A., 192
Zapf, M., 170, 171
Ziefflie, B., 215

www.ingramcontent.com/pod-product-compliance
Lightning Source LLC
Chambersburg PA
CBHW021854020426
42334CB00013B/329

* 9 7 8 0 8 8 9 7 7 8 9 0 0 *